Truth and Consequences

ALSO BY LAURIE SANDELL

The Impostor's Daughter: A True Memoir

TRUTH AND CONSEQUENCES

LIFE INSIDE THE

MADOFF FAMILY

LAURIE SANDELL

Little, Brown and Company

New York   Boston   London

Little, Brown and Company
Hachette Book Group
237 Park Avenue, New York, NY 10017
www.hachettebookgroup.com

First Edition: October 2011

Little, Brown and Company is a division of Hachette Book Group, Inc.
The Little, Brown name and logo are trademarks of
Hachette Book Group, Inc.

The publisher is not responsible for websites (or their content)
that are not owned by the publisher.

Certain names and identifying details of people portrayed in this
book have been changed. "Maria," "Jeremy," and "Randy"; Catherine's
college boyfriend, "Marco"; and "Jack Hearn" are all pseudonyms.

The Hachette Speakers Bureau provides a wide range of
authors for speaking events. To find out more,
go to www.hachettespeakersbureau.com or call (866) 376-6591.

All photos courtesy of the Madoff family, unless otherwise stated.

ISBN 978-0-316-19893-6
LCCN 2011939048

10 9 8 7 6 5 4 3 2 1

RRD-C

Printed in the United States of America

For my sisters,
Karyn Geringer and Sylvie Sandell

Contents

Contents

TRUTH AND CONSEQUENCES

Preface

In the summer of 2009, my first book was released, a graphic memoir called *The Impostor's Daughter*. The book was about finding out that my eccentric, charming Argentine father was in fact a pathological liar and con artist. Instead of working for the CIA, as I'd long suspected, he'd lived off stolen cash from friends and family. His college degrees were forged, his heroics in Vietnam invented. The revelations threw a grenade into the middle of our family and caused a rift that has yet to heal: My mother denied what I'd written and refused to read the manuscript; my father stopped speaking to me. Still, I knew that the consequences of remaining silent were greater than those of telling the truth. So I wrote the book in spite of my family's protests.

About a month after it came out, I was backstage after a reading when two women approached and asked if they could speak to me privately. The shorter of the two was dressed in a soft silk blouse with cigarette pants and had thick dark hair that fell in waves to the middle of her back. She looked to be in her midthirties.

"This reading really hit home," she said. "I'm so sorry for what happened to you."

"Tell her who you are," her friend urged.

"I hope you can be discreet. I'm the fiancée of Andrew Madoff." As if I didn't recognize the name, she added, "He's the son of Bernard Madoff."

I tried not to register shock; the scandal wasn't even a year old and was still making headlines on a daily basis. I now recognized the name of the woman standing in front of me: Catherine Hooper. In the press, she'd been labeled a home-wrecker. Supposedly, Andrew had left his wife of sixteen years to be with her. She said she'd heard of my book but hadn't yet read it and that she planned to give a copy to Andrew that night; she wondered if I wanted to meet for coffee later in the week. We spoke for a few more minutes and I gave her my business card. Though my father's cons were small compared with Bernie Madoff's, I could relate to the devastating effect that lies, grandiosity, and secretiveness could have on a person. I, too, believed my father was brilliant and unimpeachable, until I was in my thirties and a much-published magazine writer. I'd even had the unsettling experience of having people ask, "How do we know that *you're* not a liar, given your father's history?" So Andrew and I—and Catherine, by proxy—belonged to the same small society; we understood each other in a way that few other people could.

Still, Andrew *was* a Madoff, and that meant I needed to proceed with caution. I'd already been taken in by one sociopath—my own father—and I wasn't about to get involved with another. All I knew about Andrew was what I'd read in the press, and the majority of articles suggested he was going to be taken away in handcuffs any day. At the time, my curiosity was greater than my trepidation, so when Catherine invited me to dinner at their home, I went. Andrew looked like the photos I'd seen in *Vanity Fair*: a tall, more handsome version of his father. I found him to be humble, self-effacing, and quieter than I'd anticipated. But questions about my father tumbled out of him as if he'd been storing them up: What was my relationship like with him today? How was I handling my anger, and my grief? What had I done with the photos of him—had I torn them up? Andrew had kept only one on display, a large one that hung in the hallway near his front door. In it, Andrew stood on a dock next to a large bluefin tuna. Bernie stood in the background, smiling proudly, wearing a green velour crewneck shirt and running shorts.

During dinner, Catherine and Andrew shared highly personal details about the days and weeks following the confession. By then, they'd both read my book; I got the sense that they saw me as a comrade of sorts, though in reality I was a journalist who owed them no allegiance. Fascinated, I listened to Andrew's account of what it was like when he came home the night his father dramatically confessed to running the world's largest Ponzi scheme, and then how he handled the crush of paparazzi that appeared in the following days and the overnight alienation from his parents.

Over the next two years, I was offered a glimpse inside a world that had been stripped of a future and existed only in a tenuous present. Andrew and Catherine invited me to Thanksgiving dinner; estranged from my own father, I chose to go. They had gathered a group of friends who were also at odds with their families or lived too far away to make the trip home. But old friends of Andrew's, and even Andrew's brother, Mark, were nowhere to be found.

As Catherine and Andrew took me further into their confidence—and later introduced me to Andrew's mother, Ruth— I would come to discover that Andrew was not a sociopath; that he was, as much as he detested the word, a victim of his father like so many thousands of others. I observed, firsthand, the deep anguish he was suffering over his father's betrayal and the fallout that followed. I also learned that the Madoff family dysfunction was far worse than anything reported in the press: There had been affairs, power struggles between the siblings—even, I was shocked to find out, multiple suicide attempts. The story was Shakespearean in scope, yet only the most banal details had been made available to the public. Andrew, who'd been muzzled by his lawyers since the day of the confession, desperately wanted to tell his story. Catherine was prepared to support him, as she had all along. Ruth, whose relationship with Andrew was still precarious, just wanted her family back, telling me poignantly, "I don't miss the money—I miss nothing except my friends."

In early 2011, Catherine approached me with an idea for a book on emergency preparedness as a companion guide to her company, Black Umbrella. I offered to put her in touch with my contacts in publishing, but it quickly became clear that she was not going to be able to move on with her life and focus on her passion until she'd addressed the elephant in the room: the Madoff story. Catherine talked to various family members and together they reached the conclusion to talk about their painful past. I did not hesitate to accept the invitation to delve into their lives. After all, I'd gone through a similar—and singular—experience of betrayal. I felt uniquely qualified to cut through the emotion and self-interest that can accompany a story like this one, and get to the truth.

That said, this book is not meant to be a piece of investigative journalism. It is the human side of a tale that has, so far, been told only in terms of dollars and cents. While the world has read about the pain and suffering of scores of people at the hands of Bernie Madoff, no one has been privy to the effect his actions had upon the people who knew and loved him best.

Until this moment, Andrew Madoff; Ruth Madoff; Catherine Hooper; Ruth's sister, Joan Roman; and Mark Madoff's first wife, Susan Elkin, have told their personal story to no one. Because of the experiences we've all had with corrupt family members, I have been granted an unfettered look inside their lives. As for Bernie, I deliberately chose not to invite him to participate in this book. This is his family's story—not his. Over the course of six months, I sat down with them for dozens of hours of intimate interviews, and they held back nothing. Here is their astonishing story.

Chapter One

An Unthinkable
Turn of Events

Catherine moved through the living room, trying to find her shoes. They were black patent-leather lace-up Gucci booties, and she planned to wear them to her fiancée, Andrew's, office Christmas party that night, but everything she owned was hidden in boxes. The date was December 9, 2008. Two days earlier, she and Andrew had moved into an apartment on the Upper East Side of Manhattan, with floor-to-ceiling fishbowl windows and glossy parquet floors. Her toe caught something and she tripped; it was a stuffed bunny, left behind by her three-year-old daughter, Sophie. Picking it up, she tossed it into a wicker basket in her daughter's room. She was running late and had two hours of professional hair and makeup appointments ahead of her. Being a part of Andrew's family meant looking the part.

The night, she knew, was going to be important. The party would take place at Rosa Mexicano, and she hoped it would serve as an informal coming-out for the two of them as a newly engaged couple. She'd planned her look down to the last detail: A Derek Lam dress made up of a flimsy, sheer pink blouse tucked into a skirt with a slim black bodice, her hair blown out into soft, long waves. Her signature pearl studs were freshly polished, and her simple engagement ring gleamed. Andrew's family, she felt, was gradually coming to accept her, and her presence at the party was a step in the right direction. But she wasn't there yet. Not by a long shot.

Andrew had asked her to give it time. He wasn't even divorced from his first wife, Debbie, and his family was famously insular. His parents, Ruth and Bernie, were pleasant enough but maintained a cool distance. Not only had they not thrown the two an engagement party, but they had barely congratulated either of them. Andrew's brother, Mark, had made no secret of his feelings for Catherine, going so far as to carry out a whisper campaign against the relationship soon after she and Andrew had started dating. But the Madoffs were going to be her family now, and she was going to have to live with the lack of warmth. If she'd learned anything from her failed first marriage, it was this: Accept the man you fell in love with, not the one you hoped he might become.

The night before, Andrew's two teenage daughters, Anne and Emily, had spent their first night with Catherine and Andrew in the new apartment. Anne had stormed in from school, carrying a bag from a neighborhood bodega with canned soup, Cheetos, and Milano cookies.

"Dinner's ready," Catherine called out to the pretty fifteen-year-old as she sailed past to her room.

"Oh, really? I didn't think you were going to cook anything, so I bought my own food." The door slammed, and Catherine looked at the bubbling tray of lasagna she had made, cooling on the counter in front of her.

She sighed. She couldn't force the girls to accept her; that would have to come with time. For now, she would focus on her work for Dior.

For the past year, Catherine had worked as a brand ambassador to the storied fashion house, consulting on events, creating focus groups, and modeling jewelry and clothes at parties. It was fun, fanciful work that gave her a break from her more grueling duties as a business owner. She'd taken the beloved, ramshackle Manhattan fly-fishing shop Urban Angler and turned it into a sleek, modern Fifth Avenue destination frequented by Wall Street's most powerful executives. It was, in fact, how she and Andrew had met; an accomplished fly fisherman himself, he'd become the largest investor in the shop. While working together in the trenches to save the business, they'd fallen in love.

That morning, Catherine had dropped Sophie at preschool and stopped by Dior's offices for a wrap-up discussion about the previous night's event. She'd returned to the apartment at 3:30 PM, just as Sophie was getting home. The three-year-old came bolting out of her bedroom, blond curls bouncing around her shoulders.

"Mommy, look!" She held up a pink, glittery ball and bounced it on the living room floor, where it ricocheted off one of the boxes. Catherine kissed the top of her daughter's head and squeezed her shoulders. She'd seen her for all of five minutes; now she was running out the door again. There will be time for her, she told herself, feeling awash in guilt.

"I'll be back in a few hours, Sophie. Be good!" she called. She'd been coparenting with Sophie's father, Jon, for the past two years, but the growth in her consulting work had forced her to hire a babysitter for the first time in Sophie's life. Waving good-bye to Josie, she disappeared into the elevator that took her down to the street.

Outside, the wind snapped as she gathered her trench coat around her. Sliding into the back of a cab, she leaned against the seat and closed her eyes. She knew it might be the only moment she had to rest all day. A minute later, her iPhone buzzed with an incoming text.

"We might not be going tonight," Andrew had written. She hesitated for a moment before calling him on his mobile phone.

Catherine made a serious effort never to call him during business hours unless it was an emergency. An occasional cheeky text around lunchtime was fine, but interrupting him while he chaired a meeting at the Lymphoma Research Foundation or worked with his team to structure an energy deal would be an embarrassment. Still, if they weren't going to the party for some reason, she wanted to know before she embarked on two hours of beauty treatments while trying to get work done on her phone. Andrew picked up right away.

"Should I get my hair done or not?" she asked.

"Your hair?" He sounded distracted.

"For the party. Are we going?"

"Oh, yeah, yes, we're going. I think. I have to run."

She hung up and told the driver to continue down Park Avenue. Looking out the window, she felt a knot of dread form in her stomach. That text had to be about Mark. Andrew's older brother had grown increasingly quick to anger over the past eighteen months, and the two men had frequent blowups at the office that often resulted in canceled plans.

The cab pulled up at the corner closest to Deja Vous, a tiny salon on 56th Street that Catherine had been frequenting for fifteen years. Her stylist, Eli, kissed her cheek and led her to the shampooing station. Catherine leaned back against the molded black plastic chair and felt a gush of warm water cascade over her head. For the first time all day, she felt her shoulders start to relax. Then her iPhone buzzed again. She opened one eye and peered at the latest text from Andrew: "We're definitely not going tonight."

Blood rushed to her head and she felt her chest tighten. "I came in for nothing," she said into the air. Eli clucked sympathetically. Sitting up, her wet hair dripping onto her shoulders, Catherine punched in a quick message to Andrew: "Thanks. I could have spent those hours with Sophie." Well, nothing she could do about it now. She canceled her makeup appointment at Nars, dropped her phone into her lap, and tried to relax as Eli finished shampooing her hair. An hour later, she emerged into the crisp winter air and made her way through the throngs of people—mostly tourists—crowding the street. She took a taxi home, eager to get out of her dress.

When she walked in the door, Sophie flung herself at her legs. Catherine scooped up her daughter, breathing in the scent of her freshly washed hair. Thanking Josie, she shut the door behind her, kissed Sophie, and deposited her on the couch. Placing her hands on her hips, she surveyed the room. The apartment was as she'd left it—a mess. Where to begin? Large wardrobe boxes partially blocked a doorway; lamps, exercise equipment, and kitchen appliances were tangled in a pile by the front door. Catherine stripped off her dress and shoes, changed into utility pants and her favorite *Star Trek* T-shirt, and gathered her freshly styled hair into a ponytail. Randomly selecting a box, she slit it open and prepared to get to work.

By six o'clock, Catherine had finished unpacking the glassware and household goods and had moved on to the dishes. As she was placing them in the kitchen cabinet, she heard the elevator doors slide open. Andrew walked into the foyer and then, uncharacteristically, turned and walked straight into their bedroom. Catherine paused, holding a plate in midair. Andrew wasn't the type who liked to be crowded; when he was having a bad day, he preferred to be left alone. She turned back to the task at hand and continued stacking plates. Then she thought better of it, filled a glass with water, and took it into the bedroom.

Andrew was lying in the dark, on top of the white duvet that had been one of her contributions to their shared new home. He was still wearing his Brooks Brothers coat and shiny Alden loafers, the uniform he had worn almost every day of his twenty-year career at Bernard L. Madoff Investment Securities LLC. His eyes were closed, his hands clasped on his stomach, as though he were lying in a coffin.

All of the anger she'd felt earlier drained out of her. Placing the glass on the bedside table, she slipped out of the room. Clearly, whatever he was dealing with had nothing to do with Mark. A fight with his father, perhaps? It wasn't out of the question. He'd worked for Bernie for more than twenty years, but his father still treated him like a child most of the time. More likely, though, he'd taken a big hit in the stock market. Wall Street was imploding all around them. Bear Stearns had collapsed in March, Lehman Brothers was in bankruptcy, and the markets were in virtual paralysis as the government scrambled to prevent further financial meltdown.

At the Dior event the night before, where New York's society set had mingled with reality stars and other boldfaced names, Catherine couldn't help but notice the irony: Everyone was decked out in glittering jewels and getting photographed while talking about what horrible shape the world was in. Catherine had found herself in conversation with the CEO of Dior, Pamela Baxter, and her friend Brooke Travis, Dior's marketing director, about the topic du jour. "Andrew's trading desk is actually breaking even," she heard herself saying. "I'm proud of him for helping his guys manage the assets they're trading, considering everything that's going on." As soon as the words were out of her mouth, she felt the slightest shift in their reactions, a cooling, a knitting together of perfectly groomed eyebrows. Berating herself silently, she'd clamped her lips together and stared into her glass of Moët et Chandon. Was it really a good idea for her to be bragging about her rich, successful husband-to-be when people were losing their jobs? Especially considering where she'd come from—did she even belong in this room?

Lately, she felt, she was always putting her foot in her mouth: A recent *Vanity Fair* article had featured comments by her friend

Alexandra Lebenthal, who'd noted that many of her friends had lost half of everything they had in the 2008 financial meltdown and been forced to come to terms with how much of their social standing, marriages, and friendships had been based on their money. Now that the money was gone, did they really have a marriage anymore? Were their friends still their friends? She'd read sections of the article aloud to Andrew, who'd started to muse on his own friendships, then had abruptly stopped and said, "Don't read me any more—it's hitting too close to home."

Pausing outside the doorway, Catherine glanced back at Andrew one more time. Maybe someone had died, then...but he would have just come right out and told her.

Catherine prepared dinner for Sophie, then ran her a bath. After Sophie went to sleep—curled up like an angel in her new big-girl bed—Catherine went into her office. Huge shopping bags full of memorabilia from high school and college awaited her. Catherine started to sort through them, trying to kill time. Then she sat back and thought, I can't start this project tonight—this is a Sisyphean task. She decided to take a shower and clean off the newsprint staining her hands. The next time she looked at the clock it was 10:00 PM.

It had been four hours since Andrew had disappeared into their room, and still no sign of him. She finished applying Moroccan rose oil to her legs, slipped on a silk chemise, and tried to quell the flutter of anxiety starting to rise in her chest. Whatever it was, she now knew, it was bad. Perhaps as bad as a full-scale collapse of the firm. But wouldn't Andrew have seen such a thing coming? Surely he would have been notified ahead of his coworkers and given a few days to prepare. It could have been as simple as a bad trade. Yes, that was probably it. Or maybe his dad had made a bad trade. She didn't want to think about the alternative: a recurrence of Andrew's cancer. He'd been extremely lucky to go into remission from mantle cell lymphoma, one of the deadliest and rarest forms of the disease. Taking a deep breath, Catherine tiptoed into the bedroom with caution and braced herself for whatever she was going to face.

In the dark, she could just make out Andrew, still lying on the bed, exactly where she'd left him. His eyes remained closed; he hadn't moved from the position he'd been in hours before. She sat down on the bed next to him and resisted covering his hand with her own. Gathering her strength, she reminded herself not to make this about her own fears. It was her job to be there for him—and that was something at which she happened to excel. Whatever it was he had to tell her, she could handle it. She decided to be sympathetic but to downplay whatever it was he had to say. She cleared her throat and began. "We don't need to talk now. Unless someone has died, or whatever is bothering you is health-related, let's just talk tomorrow."

Andrew stirred in the darkness and dragged himself to a sitting position. He leaned over and turned on the light. She now saw his face: His eyes looked flat and dull.

"No, we need to talk right now. Because you need to decide whether or not you want to stay with me."

An arrow of fear pierced her heart. Whether or not she wanted to stay with him? Because, what—he was broke? There were fates far worse than moving to Brooklyn, pulling the kids out of private school, and trading vacations for extra hours at the office.

"Honey, don't be ridiculous. What happened?"

"I just turned my father in to the SEC for securities fraud." He closed his eyes and sank against the headboard. Catherine actually felt lighter, now that she knew what was going on. For years, he'd had conflicts with his father; Bernie had probably violated some minor filing rule. Andrew, being Mr. Law and Order, had turned him in.

"So he did something inappropriate...like Martha Stewart did?"

"My father told me and Mark that his business is just one big lie. It's a Ponzi scheme, to the tune of fifty billion dollars."

Catherine's mind went blank. "Do you believe him?"

"I don't know. It seems so outrageous, but I don't think he was making it up."

"Well, why wouldn't I stay with you? What are the possible repercussions of this?"

Andrew turned onto his side and held her gaze. He pointed to the large bare windows that extended the length of the apartment.

"Tomorrow, there are going to be cameras in front of our building and reporters on the roof of the buildings across the street. I am going to be deposed and interviewed, and I might have to testify against my father. My lawyers don't want me to say a word to you about any of this, but I can't do that. So you need to call a lawyer and get your own legal counsel. You may be deposed and questioned about all of this, too. And until this is in the papers, you can't say a word about this—to *anyone*."

"Did you ever suspect this?" Floored, doing everything in her power not to fall apart, she asked a question she already knew the answer to.

"Absolutely not." He sank back onto the pillow, exhausted.

Three years before, in the early stage of her business partnership with Andrew, Catherine had told him about a book called *Deep Survival,* by Laurence Gonzales. Given her upbringing—she'd been raised by a cash-strapped single mother in a small town—she had subsequently become fascinated with the topics of resilience and survival. Not only had she read dozens of other books on the subject, but she had also written a business plan for a company that built emergency plans for families in crisis. And one thing she knew about survivors from all of her reading was that survivors don't think but act. Survivors *do.* So in that moment, she didn't fall apart. She didn't hug him. She didn't cry, or scream about losing a life they might have had. She snapped into survival mode and focused on the most important immediate goal: How do we get to tomorrow?

The answer came to her almost immediately: curtains. She would put them up within twenty-four hours; everything else, she would deal with later.

Chapter Two

THE DEEP SEA CLUB

Fish are found in beautiful places, without fail. Coral reefs, pristine flats in the Florida Keys, a river in Colorado, an inlet in Alaska. Andrew learned to fish at four years old, using a child-size rod and a bucket of live shrimp for bait. He and his brother stood on a Florida dock for hours, trying to hook pinfish, snapper, and blue runners. They never tired.

For as long as Andrew can remember, the family owned a sport-fishing boat. Their first was thirty feet long, purchased when he was a baby. The next, forty-two feet, was bought by Bernie in 1970, as the securities industry was emerging from one of its most robust periods of growth. The favorite, according to Andrew, was a gorgeous, hand-built, fifty-six-foot Rybovich, a wooden fishing boat that was "a work of art." The last was the *Bull,* an eighty-eight-foot Leopard cruiser with three staterooms, docked permanently in Cap d'Antibes, France. That was the boat the world read about day after day in the tabloid press.

On a sport-fishing boat, the physical space is small. Beds are organized in bunks; bathrooms are tiny. Water is often limited, so conservation is key. Bernie taught his boys to take a "boat shower," which, when done correctly, requires less than five gallons of water: Get in, soap down, quickly turn the water off. Everything was battened down so it wouldn't move in choppy waters. Family members packed essentials only. A sport-fishing boat, says Andrew, was efficiency at its highest level, its cramped quarters a fitting metaphor for the closeness of his family.

The family was, indeed, closer than most—and as the second and last son, Andrew completed it. Born in 1966, he grew up in Roslyn, a village on the north shore of Long Island largely populated by Reform Jews. The Madoffs were similarly nonreligious: Andrew went to Hebrew school for the shortest time he could and still get bar mitzvahed. Their home, a split-level, four-bedroom ranch built into the side of a hill on a third of an acre, reflected his parents' upward mobility. They moved in when Ruth was pregnant with Andrew and stayed until the boys graduated from high school.

Andrew remembers his childhood as idyllic: riding his Schwinn Sting Ray bike through Christopher Morley Park with his best friend, Ari; playing stickball in the street with his older brother, Mark. There was no fear of predators then, nor was there the lure of computers. Kids stayed outside until their parents called their names from their front stoops. Ruth used to ring a bell that Andrew could hear from blocks away. Sports dominated his free time. Little League baseball, hockey in the Pee Wee League, fishing in the summer in Montauk, skiing in the winter.

Andrew looked up to Mark and describes their early dynamic as typical big-brother-little-brother stuff.

"We had fun," he says, "except when I wouldn't put his dishes in the dishwasher. Then he'd chase me around the house with a hockey stick and we'd go crashing into things, breaking furniture." The two spent nearly all of their time together, playing Ping-Pong in the basement, using the garage door as a backstop for hockey and baseball. The glass in the windows was thin, and they were always breaking it. Mark was mischievously funny: As a boy he used to leave notes for the cleaning lady in his mother's hand. "Dear Clara," he would write. "Please clean out Mark's drawers. Signed, Mrs. Madoff."

From the beginning, the brothers were fiercely competitive. Mark was the better athlete, Andrew the better student. Mark didn't try terribly hard in school, and it showed; typically, if Andrew had one of his brother's teachers, he or she would be shocked that he was so willing to apply himself. In high school, both were on the hockey team. Andrew became captain in his senior year but feels that was more of a testament to his leadership than his skills: "I was at best a competent hockey player, but more than that, I knew how to get the team to play together." Mark felt that Andrew "got away with" more with their parents. To even the score, if he caught his younger brother drinking or smoking pot with his friends, he would immediately report him.

"He was constantly ratting me out and I resented the hell out of him for doing it, and then pretending like he had nothing to do with it," Andrew says. He recalls a coed party he held in the basement of their Roslyn home when he was thirteen. His parents were upstairs, oblivious; the kids turned out the lights so they could make out. Mark was having none of it: He kept coming downstairs and flipping the lights back on. "That was typical of him," Andrew says, an affectionate smile creeping in. "He would try to spoil the fun as best he could."

Mark was, according to Andrew, a bit of a mama's boy from the earliest age. He was a fussy baby, and once he could talk, he could voice his displeasure. His parents' nickname for him was Archie, from his habit of arching his back, sliding out of his chair, and ending up on the floor during a tantrum. Like Bernie, who couldn't abide the feeling of elastic—Bernie in fact had special underwear made to avoid it—Mark was extremely particular about his clothing and couldn't stand certain types of fabrics touching his skin.

"Put him near wool or anything itchy and he'd start screaming and crying," Andrew says. Mark also had a nervous constitution, so much so that he used to scratch the palms of his hands until they were ragged and raw. His ex-wife and mother of his two eldest children, Susan Elkin, says that Bernie made Mark nervous—he felt he had to measure up, and never quite passed the test.

More serious problems emerged when Mark was eleven; he was diagnosed with stomach ulcers. The image Andrew has of his brother as a child, then, is of Mark constantly bending over, clutching his stomach, and moaning, "Ohh." As an adult, Mark visited a raft of specialists. First he was diagnosed with an overactive thyroid, then Hashimoto's disease—but nothing seemed to be the true culprit.

"I think one of the most satisfying moments of his life was when he was diagnosed with celiac disease at the age of thirty-nine," says Andrew. "He finally had something to point to. Once he went on a gluten-free diet, his stomach problems disappeared. But by that time, he really relished agonizing over his health. That habit didn't go away with the diagnosis."

In high school, Andrew found himself in his brother's shadow in a way he didn't like. People would always refer to Mark as "the good-looking one," something Andrew hated: "I pretended that I didn't care, but I absolutely did."

Later, when the scandal broke, Andrew found those same wounds being poked: Mark was described as the "gregarious" one, Andrew the "cerebral" one.

"At the end of the day, it was probably a lot worse for him to hear me referred to as 'the smart one' than for me to hear him referred to as 'the good-looking one,'" Andrew admits. "Because even though that never felt good, at some point I became confident enough in my appearance to know that I wasn't a complete toad."

Despite their differences, the boys were close, partly a result of how much time they spent together. By the time Andrew and Mark were fourteen and sixteen, Ruth and Bernie were leaving them alone for days at a time. Bernie had purchased a small pied-à-terre in Manhattan, where he sometimes stayed overnight when he worked late. Ruth spent nights in the city as well. Andrew learned how to make baked ziti and tacos for the nights when his mother was staying in Manhattan.

Their parents were permissive. Andrew doesn't ever remember being grounded or even scolded: "Whatever we did would have had to be pretty bad for them to get angry with us." They were proud of Andrew's grades but didn't put pressure on either son to bring home a stellar report card. Nor was Ruth a "smother mother" — her parenting style, she jokes, is best described as "benign neglect." "They were solid citizens and I trusted them," she says. "If I wasn't overbearing, it was because I respected their judgments throughout every year of their lives."

During their frequent trips to the Bahamas, from the time Andrew was ten, the boys would often take their fifteen-foot Boston Whaler to a reef they dubbed the Yellow Bar, which rests in a famously dangerous part of the Caribbean Sea known as the Tongue of the Ocean. While their mother relaxed at the resort at Chub Cay ten miles away and their father fished for billfish miles in the other direction, Andrew and Mark fished by themselves, in water that dropped from thirty feet to six thousand without warning. The boys spent days dumping chum into the water and catching everything from grouper to sharks to mahimahi. They even raised billfish that would grab the bait and tow their tiny shrieking bodies and their boat wildly across the sea before the line would break and the fish disappeared into the depths of the ocean. When storms kicked up, the boys gunned it back to Chub to beat the rain and rough seas. They had no safety gear. They had no anchor.

"My memory of it varies a little," says Ruth. "I thought they had a radio with them, and that Bernie was trolling with them in sight. Later, my daughters-in-law would joke about it when they took their kids to the dock in Montauk; they would say, 'Don't put Bernie in charge—remember the Yellow Bar!'"

Ruth did not always spend the day at the resort. She and the boys loved to search for shells at low tide. When the boys were eight and ten, Ruth, Andrew, and Mark, propelled by flippers, swam across a canal to a small cay. Once they arrived on the sandy bank, they filled their mesh bags with shells, wrestled in the scrubby grass, and soaked in the sun. But as they prepared to swim back, the tide came in. The water between the cay and the main island was fast, wide, and patrolled by sharks. The three of them struggled against the current. It was the first time in Andrew's life that he wondered if he would make it out alive. It would not be the last. "We were lucky to make it to shore," Ruth confirms. "I was scared to death."

But Andrew's memories of his childhood are mostly happy ones: "We were extremely close as a family; we did everything together. We spent a lot of time sitting around the dinner table, talking." Bernie worked long hours, commuting via Cessna seaplane to his new offices at 110 Wall Street, but carved out plenty of leisure time to spend with his family. "He was present," Andrew says. "Very loving, very supportive. He would come to hockey games, Little League games — whatever we did that was important to us, he made a point to be there."

Despite his growing responsibilities, Bernie rarely worked on weekends and took every opportunity to travel with his young family. According to Andrew, they never stayed home: "President's Day Weekend, Easter week, Thanksgiving week, Christmas week . . . whenever there was a holiday, we would go away." The family traveled to specific places at specific times of the year. In the summer they went to Montauk; in the fall, to Florida; early winter was devoted to the Bahamas and late winter to ski trips with their closest friends, the Blumenfelds — who later became victims of Bernie's Ponzi scheme, as did every one of their family friends.

One thing was not in question: The focus of Bernie's passion was always his career. "He talked about it constantly," Andrew remembers. "What he was working on, the issues in the business, what was happening in the industry. It wasn't as though he couldn't talk about other things, but what he said was interesting to us—so we didn't."

What Bernie said was interesting to everyone, it seemed. If Andrew's father was talking, the room fell silent. "Some people always have to talk over other people; my father never had that problem. It was rare for him to have any difficulties commanding the conversation. He was very charismatic when he talked about work, with a larger-than-life professional persona, but was never loud, flamboyant, or talkative. He was the kind of person who spoke quietly: People leaned in."

After spending several summers renting homes in Montauk, the Madoffs finally purchased land there in 1979, for $250,000. They spent an additional $500,000 to build a three-thousand-square-foot home on the property—the same one that, after the scandal, would sell for $9 million at an auction to benefit Bernie's victims. The house itself was modest compared with nearby properties, with simple Crate & Barrel–style furniture, nautical artwork, and a few small bedrooms. It derived its true value from the pristine beachfront property it was built on, which allowed the family to indulge in their favorite pastime.

Both boys developed a passion for fishing as a meditative experience: the calm of the water, the silvery hue of a leaping fish, the red smear of a sunset. Eventually, they would become accomplished inshore and fly fishermen and travel to remote locations as much for the beauty as for the act of catching fish.

Bernie fished for the hunt. His sport was deep-sea billfishing, which required large tackle and big boats belching diesel fumes. To catch big prey, he had to travel miles out into the ocean, where, usually, nothing happened. Bernie often dragged his reluctant family along with him. "When people think of fishing being boring, that's what they're thinking of," says Andrew. "You're rocking back and forth, inhaling fumes, waiting for something to happen. I always found deep-sea fishing very unpleasant." Ruth remembers playing with Legos with Andrew and Mark for "twelve hours at a clip. We got seasick, but we couldn't not do it, because we lived on the boat." In deep-sea fishing, the aim is to catch a marlin or another large fish, one that can be mounted on the wall with bragging rights. In Bernie's career, he caught fifteen blue marlin—a big number for Florida and the Bahamas, where marlin aren't common. His largest catch, at 14 feet and 634 pounds, set a record for years on the island of Chub Cay. When it didn't fit through the window of his offices at 110 Wall Street, Bernie mounted it in the living room in Roslyn. It stretched the full length of the room.

Ruth says they took the boys along because "the M.O. of the family was that we were always together." When they weren't on the boat with Bernie, Ruth spent hours amusing the boys: watching them run around on the docks, putting up signs to wash strangers' cars, and going clamming. "That was how we filled our days," she says.

Once the boys got older, they stayed behind when Bernie went deep-sea fishing, and that's when they went on other "incredible exploratory-type fishing trips."

As teens, Andrew and Mark worked as dock boys at the Montauk Yacht Club, then known as the Deep Sea Club. From 7:00 AM to 7:00 PM, they'd wait for the boats to come into the marina and tie them up, pump gas, deliver ice, empty garbage cans, clean the fish people had caught, throw the carcasses in a Dumpster, and clean it the next morning. "When you dumped out the cans with fish guts in them," Andrew remembers, "they were invariably loaded with maggots and flies. It was revolting, but somehow fun." They spent all day, every day, outside. "Best job on earth," Andrew insists. Once they discovered the more lucrative boat-washing business, the boys turned their attention to that. And like their father before them, who'd launched a successful business installing lawn-sprinkler systems in high school, the brothers quickly became successful entrepreneurs. Soon they had regular clients and were setting their own hours, at double the income they'd made as dock boys. In keeping with their permissive attitude, Ruth and Bernie never told the boys they had to get a job. Money, Andrew says, was a "nonissue." What they earned during the summer went a long way, and if at some point during the year they became tapped out, they could simply ask their parents for some cash. But both boys were inherently sensible about money, and both liked to work. In addition to his work on the docks, Andrew started a small ferry service to take passengers around Montauk, and Mark worked at the Athlete's Foot in Manhasset through most of high school.

Andrew doesn't remember when he knew he was going to go into the family business. It seemed almost inevitable. His father first brought his sons in as summer interns. After spending half the season on the docks, they'd spend the other half in the office. Bernard L. Madoff Inc., as it was known before it became a one-member LLC, was in the business of market making. In the world of stock trading, market makers are the wholesalers. When individuals want to buy 100 shares of Apple stock, they go to their broker (Schwab, Fidelity) to do so. When those companies receive that order to buy those shares, they send it to a market maker, where the order is executed.

BLM served discount brokerage firms such as Charles Schwab, A. G. Edwards, and Fidelity and bought and sold stocks for the firm's own account from other professionals. Andrew would watch his father buy and sell the stocks that he followed, talk about the companies, and share his opinions on whether they were likely to go up or down. Traders learn from watching other people trade and understanding how they make decisions. "For a certain personality type, it's an extremely satisfying way to make a living," says Andrew, "and I'm certainly that type of person. You have to be smart, good with numbers, and have a very good memory. But it also requires the ability to detach oneself. There's a lot of money at stake, and if you think, I just lost the value of a car, or I just made enough money to make my house payment this month, you would last about ten minutes. It needs to be treated almost like Monopoly money, or you'd lose your mind."

Andrew has been described by family members as someone who seems "cold at first—you have to warm him up." Ruth recalls a family ski trip where Mark met her in the breakfast room and said, "Susan is mad because Andrew didn't say hello to her this morning."

Ruth said, "Andrew doesn't speak to *anybody* in the morning." Later that day, she shared a chairlift with Andrew, who wore his earphones the entire way up. "That's rude; it's a twenty-minute ride to the top of the mountain," she said as the chair began its slow ascent.

"What?" Andrew said, taking out one of his earphones.

"Can't we have a conversation?"

"What do you want to talk about?" Andrew put his earphone back in.

"He totally dissed me," Ruth says, laughing.

Traders also need to be able to judge their actions objectively. When they make a good decision, it's right there in black and white, in the form of trading profits, and when they make a bad decision, it's equally obvious. "To be successful as a trader, you have to be able to say, 'I made a good decision—I made money. I made a bad decision—I lost money,' instead of constantly rationalizing and pointing fingers and blaming other things. Bernie's personality, I thought, was well suited to that and so was mine," says Andrew.

During his first summer at BLM, in 1985, when he was nineteen, Andrew worked in the market-making business—a separate entity from Bernie's asset-management division two floors below—as a clerk, taking notes, recording trades, and reconciling the day's activities at the close of the workday to figure out how much money the market makers who managed him had made. The only way to calculate profits and losses then was to keep track on a sheet of paper. At the end of the day, after data-entry clerks punched these hand-recorded numbers into the computer system and generated the market-making business's inventory and profit-and-loss statements, Andrew would reconcile each report with his own manual calculations. Invariably, there would be discrepancies, so it was part of Andrew's job to figure out why. Did the trade not get entered into the computer correctly? Was his math incorrect? The process of reconciling the trades by hand forced him to run through the series of transactions again and again.

"By doing that," he says, "I learned an incredible amount about the minutiae of the business and trading and got a strong feel for precisely how and why we were making money as market makers." The exchange-based options market had come into existence in the United States in 1973, so while Andrew was learning about it, it was a relatively young product. "I was fascinated by the concept of stock options and read books so I could teach myself as much as I could possibly learn." A stock option is a contract that gives its buyer a right—the "option"—to buy or sell that stock at a specific price for a specific period of time. A type of derivative, the value of a stock option is derived from the value of something else, a stock. But since the option is cheaper than the actual stock, it gives speculators a less expensive way to bet on rising prices and hedge against falling prices. "There's a lot of advanced math involved, and I picked it up very quickly," Andrew explains. "I loved watching how stocks traded, and how the underlying options traded in relation to the price of the stock. There were all kinds of complicated strategies that you could put together using these options, and I was fascinated by the whole thing."

In fact, he was totally smitten: "Any dreams I had of entering the family business were only cemented by my experiences over that first summer, when I learned about the market-making business and what the people who worked there, many of whom I had known for years, actually did for a living."

The only other jobs he ever held, aside from his work on the docks, were a brief stint on the floor of the New York Stock Exchange and another on the floor of the American Stock Exchange, trailing traders. Then he returned to the family fold, where Bernie taught him everything he'd come to know. Or so Andrew thought.

Chapter Three

The Book of Ruth

Seaside is a sleepy beach town on the Florida Panhandle that seems to have survived, intact, from another era. Pretty, wood-framed cottages line the wide streets. Mom-and-pop shops promote their businesses with chalkboard signs. Teens stroll up and down the boardwalk in bikinis and flip-flops, buying ice cream and tacos from food trucks. In fact, Seaside is fairly new; built in 1979 at the dawn of the New Urbanism movement, a grassroots design effort that formed in the early eighties to promote walkable neighborhoods, the town was created as an experiment in urban living. It has since drawn the interest of architects and urban planners from all over the world.

Catherine, who had majored in architecture and urban planning, had planned a visit to Seaside for the Christmas holiday in 2008. When the firm imploded and she tried to cancel the vacation, she discovered it was too late to get their money back. Andrew and his kids stayed in New York, and she took two days to go on her own, learning about some other benefits of Seaside: "It was the anti–Palm Beach. Nobody's rich. Nobody's a Madoff victim. Nobody walks around glued to a BlackBerry."

On the plane down to Florida that December, she'd allowed

herself to indulge in some magical thinking: People are going to forget about this. It will blow over. Nobody cares down here. Almost as soon as she had the thought, she overheard two strangers making small talk in the row in front of hers. "You know what I'm really fascinated by?" Catherine heard a woman say to the man next to her in a sweet Southern accent. "That Madoff case!" Scrunching down into her seat, Catherine pulled her turtleneck up over her nose.

But she was right about Seaside: That night, having a drink by herself in a local restaurant, she idly glanced at the television mounted above the bar and saw a news item about Bernie flash across the screen. The wine had already started to take effect, and the ruddy-faced, heavyset bartender had been cheerfully ribbing Catherine, his new Yankee friend.

"That's my new father-in-law," she blurted out, pointing to the screen. She was instantly embarrassed.

The bartender continued wiping a glass, slowly. "Huh. That so?"

"He just didn't care at all what was on the news," Catherine remembers. "It didn't register. That gave me the sense of hope that yes, I might run into the lady on the airplane who wanted to pick apart every detail of my family's life. But I couldn't say that was the world. I couldn't say that was the universe."

She'd found home — or at least their next vacation hideaway for years to come.

———

It is in March 2011, two years and three months into her new life as one of the most maligned women in the Western world, that Ruth Madoff first travels to Seaside to join Catherine; Andrew; his fifteen-year-old daughter, Emily; and a friend of Emily's from camp for a family vacation. Vacation for the Madoffs is now less about the luxury of relaxing and more about the luxury of escape — from the ever-prying media, the reproachful public, and most of all, the recent memory of their greatest loss yet: that of Mark, to suicide. They've rented a house a few blocks from the beach, a simple, Craftsman-style three-bedroom with basic furnishings and a small, pleasant deck on the second floor.

Tanned and wearing a white button-down shirt with a sweater thrown casually around her shoulders, Ruth is undeniably attractive, with smooth skin that hints at "work" and eyes that are the brightest blue, save for a splotch of red swimming in each, the result of a dry-eye condition. Her blond hair is cut in its signature bob but seems looser, more relaxed, and is a bit on the brassy side—as the world knows, she colors her own hair now. Slightly bent at the waist, she strides purposefully. In articles she's been described as "frail," but that's hard to see. Greeting Catherine on the boardwalk with a huge smile, she says, "How *aw* you?" with a thick Queens accent. It is Catherine who has invited Ruth to join her and Andrew on vacation, and only the second time Catherine has seen Ruth in two years. If she is going to broker peace between the man she loves and the mother he once adored, negotiations might as well begin here.

Ruth is nothing like the cool, patrician blonde in her photos. She's bawdy and funny and sharp enough to do the *New York Times* crossword, even on Saturday. She smokes five cigarettes a day, as she has for decades, and likes to tell jokes in her gravelly Lauren Bacall voice. She takes issue with her portrayal in *Vanity Fair* as a foulmouthed curmudgeon. Foulmouthed she can be, but she curses affectionately. Spotting a gorgeous woman walking along the beach, she says with a mischievous smile, "Look at how good she looks in that bikini...that bitch."

Ruth's interests are simple: She likes to take long walks. She spends her nights reading fiction she borrows from the library in Boca Raton or watching movies on her computer with Netflix's Instant Play, anything to distract her from the haunting thoughts of her dead son. She lives for her grandchildren, all six of them, though she's been denied access to Mark and Stephanie's children since her husband's fall from grace.

Repercussions from the scandal ripple through her life daily; Ruth was asked not to attend her granddaughter Anne's high school graduation, for fear that her presence would distract from Anne's big day. Anne had graduated at the top of her class at Dalton and had given the commencement speech before heading to Harvard in the fall. Ruth considered sneaking into the back of the assembly in a wig before electing to come up to New York a few days after the big event.

Fear rules her life: fear of being written about, yelled at, or even physically assaulted. She's terrified of the press. Of airports. Of running into a victim. Forced to live on a meager income, she lives in a state of financial terror. She's terrified of chipping a tooth, because she can't afford to go to a dentist. Though she was originally allowed to keep $2.5 million by the Southern District of New York, she has only a fraction of that left. But Ruth has one fear that outweighs them all: being recognized. Once, at an airport, a security guard looked at her driver's license and asked, "Are you related?"

"Unfortunately, yes."

"How come you're not flying first class?"

Ruth shakes her head. "The public impression is that I'm still rich, which couldn't be farther from the truth."

The day after she arrived in Seaside, she drove Emily and her friend to a little outlet mall on the outskirts of town. The girls wanted to go into J. Crew, and when they approached the counter to purchase a tank top, a salesclerk turned to Ruth and said, "Are you Mrs. Madoff?" Ruth shrank in horror, but the woman leaned in sympathetically and whispered, "I'm sorry for your loss."

Ruth used the encounter as an excuse to say to Andrew, "You see? I can't leave the house. I can't go anywhere." Andrew argued that it meant that public opinion was changing—at the very least, there were *some* people on the planet who didn't want to see her broken and destitute, or worse.

At the rented house, Ruth spends most of her time cooking: In 1996, she co-authored a cookbook called *Great Chefs of America Cook Kosher: Over 175 Recipes from America's Greatest Restaurants,* which is still available on Amazon. (Ruth is not an Orthodox Jew but loves traditional cooking.) Had she been given the opportunity to develop her own identity, rather than getting married at the age of eighteen, she might have become a foodie, someone who delighted at the discovery of hole-in-the-wall ethnic finds. But Ruth always deferred to Bernie, who had no interest in venturing away from local restaurants, where he was known by the staff and could count on being treated well.

Ruth is a wine drinker, a habit that has, perhaps understandably, escalated since her husband's confession and her son's death. In the early evening, she pours herself a glass and by dinnertime has entered what she has called her "rosé coma." For a woman who has, since the scandal, wanted nothing more than to escape reality, she is now in the worst possible situation: thrust into the discomfort of the present moment again and again. She might be in the middle of telling a funny story, and something—a word or a phrase—will trigger a memory, and her face will crumple. She'll dissolve into tears, weeping over her lost family.

The alcohol has another effect on her: She keeps forgetting things. It's not that she is trying to cover anything up—it becomes clear from spending time with her that she is eager to help and wants to recover her memories—but the combination of trauma, age, and glasses of wine makes her function a bit like a dying battery: She'll talk something through and have a crisp understanding, and then, a few hours later, it's gone.

"What did I think about that again, Andy?" she frequently asks her son. One afternoon in Seaside, she comes down the stairs and thrusts a copy of a book into Andrew's hand. "Look what I found!" she says, her eyes twinkling. It is Nora Ephron's essay collection *I Remember Nothing.*

One of the most difficult things for Ruth to deal with, says Andrew, has been the searing hatred of the public, since his mother was always so well liked. It was one of her defining qualities, at the very core of her identity. Bernie was the person who grabbed people's initial interest, but Ruth was the reason their friends stuck around.

Ruth drove to Seaside in a Honda Civic from her sister's home in Boca Raton. The trip took seven hours, and she did it without stopping. It's hard to picture this tiny, seventy-year-old woman cramped in a car, driving seven long hours by herself. But she will cross great divides to see her family. Every moment she has with them is precious.

One of the few times the corners of her mouth relax is when Emily comes bounding into the room, wearing shorts and a bikini top, and plants a quick kiss on her grandmother's cheek. "Hi, Grandma, what are you up to?" she asks. Ruth's happiness then is palpable: She offers her granddaughter the wide, white smile she conferred upon her family when they were whole. It stretches across her face, shining with love and delight. "Cooking for you, my love."

As Ruth takes a stroll along the boardwalk early that evening, she cannot pass a child without stopping in her tracks and offering a smile. To one little boy's parents she says, boldly, "What a beautiful child you have." All her fear of being recognized melts away in the pure presence of a child.

But in no time, reality intrudes again. She pops into a little jewelry store to look for a birthday gift for Emily. Ruth reaches into a wicker basket full of stretchy necklaces and scoops up a handful of the brightly colored beads. Then she drops them, abruptly, as if burned, when she sees the tiny price tag affixed to the clasp.

"Thirty dollars!" she exclaims. She picks up a ring, a bracelet, examines them, puts them back on the shelf. Her jaw works as she seems to reconsider; then she returns to the wicker basket. "They're really pretty...," she muses, turning one of the necklaces over in her hand. Appearing to have made a decision, she strides with it to the cashier.

"Can you wrap it?" she asks. Suddenly her eyes fill with panic. "But what about my granddaughter's friend? I can't get a necklace for my granddaughter and not get one for her, too. Maybe I'll ask my son to give it to Emily when they're back in New York..." The salesclerk assures her that the girls will understand, even if she wants to present the necklace to her granddaughter herself.

Ruth shakes her head. "No, no, I couldn't do that. It wouldn't be right. I'll ask Andy to give it to her later." Carefully counting out thirty dollars plus tax, she slips the necklace, nestled in pink tissue paper, into her purse. She heads outside, into the balmy night.

On Ruth's first morning in Seaside, she and Catherine go to a yoga class. Will people recognize her? They seem not to. Ruth gamely rolls out a mat and moves into every position the teacher names—Down Dog, Cobra, even Standing Split—only occasionally sinking into Child's Pose to rest. The other students can hardly keep up with her; the strength in her arms is astonishing. As always, though, she takes every opportunity to put herself down: "I look like an idiot," she says. "I'm terrible at yoga." Then she adds the refrain that serves as a tagline at the end of nearly every sentence she will utter: "Oh, God."

The world needn't spend its time flogging Ruth Madoff. Her internal dialogue does it for them, on a continual loop: "I'm an idiot. I'm so stupid. That's just dumb." Later that afternoon, Ruth is sitting on the second-floor deck of the house, eating carrot sticks. Ruth has wanted to get some sun but doesn't fail to point out the "crepiness" of her skin. "Terrible," she says, flicking the loose flesh under her arm. "Oh, God."

Bernie started criticizing Ruth almost as soon as they were married. Fastidiously neat even then, he pointed out every gaffe, every error, of his teenage bride. She couldn't do anything right. "I didn't know how to clean up," Ruth recalls. "I used to have a teenager's room, with what I wore three days ago under a pile of what I'd tried on for the day." Well, naturally, given the fact that she *was* a teenager, not much older than her giggling granddaughter, who is goofing around with her friend downstairs.

Bernie would often snap at Ruth dismissively. When a teenage Andrew tried to defend her, Ruth would shake her head mournfully and say, "I don't know what I'm going to do when you're gone." Over time, she came to understand her husband's expectations and tried to meet them as best she could. Ruth was in charge of decorating their homes — she worked with her best friend, Susan Blumenfeld, on all domestic projects — no small task, once the Madoffs started acquiring boats and multiple residences. But Bernie was not content to defer to his wife's judgment, often checking and double-checking the work she had ordered to make sure it was to his satisfaction. Ruth's friends used to joke, "Here comes Bernie — get out your clipboard!" Ruth puts it more grimly: "I always felt like I was going to be fired."

She didn't complain enough about how he treated her, she says, and admits that it was probably her undoing. But it wasn't as if she was afraid of him; he was "open and comfortable and relaxed in ten million ways. So it's hard for me to tell."

The two met in 1954, when Ruth was thirteen and Bernie was sixteen, during a party in a friend's finished basement set up to look like a nightclub, with tables and a jukebox. She spotted the tanned, blond lifeguard across the room and was instantly smitten. "I flipped out," she says. Bernie also liked what he saw, a bubbly, ponytailed blonde wearing the style of the day: a crewneck sweater revealing a crisp white Peter Pan collar and cuffs, a red pleated skirt that fell just below the knee, and white Capezio shoes. He asked her to dance, and they spent the rest of the party flirting and talking. That night, he walked her home with the girl he'd brought, dropping his date off first. At Ruth's door, he asked her to the movies—a group date, of course, as was the norm.

From that moment on they were inseparable. All summer long, Ruth hung out by Bernie's lifeguard chair in her ruffled, pink-and-white-checked one-piece bathing suit. They went to the movies, frequented a "dumpy hamburger joint," and annoyed her parents by watching TV for hours in her family's tiny living room. Occasionally, they'd spot each other on the Long Island Railroad on their way to school and wave. Their only sexual contact occurred when they managed to steal into her parents' finished basement and neck. But again, as was the norm for the day, that was as far as it went.

"In those days, the only solution was to get married," Ruth says, "which was one of the reasons people did it so young."

So marry they did, on November 25, 1959, at Laurelton Jewish Center, in Queens, when Ruth was just eighteen and Bernie twenty-one. Ruth's parents offered to give the young couple $10,000 instead of a party, to start their young lives. Ruth and Bernie wanted to take the offer; Bernie's parents insisted they have a wedding. So Ruth borrowed a dress from a friend who'd just gotten married, a white gown with a heart-shaped neckline and a full skirt, and married the man who would both make and ruin her life. The only hiccup was a fight Ruth had over flowers with her father, who barked, "Why are you ordering those? They die the next day." A quick honeymoon at the Concord Hotel, in the Catskills, followed, with mammoth portions of kosher food and a Saturday-night show with a singer. By Monday, Ruth and Bernie were back at school, at Queens College and Hofstra, respectively.

It's not unusual for a teenage girl to fall fast and hard for her first love, but Ruth, perhaps, had a greater motivation to latch on to Bernie.

Born on May 18, 1941, in Crown Heights, Brooklyn, Ruth Alpern spent her earliest years at 240 Sullivan Place, a two-family house in a largely Orthodox neighborhood. "All you had to do was step out the door and there was someone you could play with," Ruth recalls. With little traffic, kids played stickball and marbles in the street and ran after rumbling trolley cars. Ruth remembers a milkman arriving via horse and wagon in 1947, during a snowstorm; the horse died in the middle of Sullivan Place and lay in the street for days, frozen solid. The whole family shared a bathroom, and in those early years, she and Joan were close. But once Joan went off to college, the two drifted apart and never shared that closeness again. That is, until the scandal broke and Joan became one of the only people willing to take Ruth in, even though it was Ruth's husband who had decimated Joan and her husband's finances, forcing them out of retirement and back to work as cabdrivers in their mid- and late seventies.

But that wouldn't happen for decades, of course, and Ruth remembers a mostly happy childhood. The family wasn't religious but belonged to a local temple on Eastern Parkway, where Ruth went to Hebrew school. Ruth's father, Saul Alpern, was an accountant: "very straight, very serious." Her mother, Sara, was also serious, because she'd had a terrible childhood. She'd grown up in Russia in a "hovel" and was ashamed of her mother, Ruth's grandmother, who'd been abandoned by her husband and was forced to make a living by washing lice out of children's hair. Sara's mother used her to try to lure her husband back to Russia—it never worked. Several times they saved up enough money to make their way to the United States, only to be rejected by Sara's father and sent back overseas.

Sara flouted convention in more ways than one: She didn't marry until she was in her late thirties; went to New York University and got a degree in social work; then got a job. She was also in group therapy, which was quite revolutionary for the early 1950s. Ruth's father was more conventional, though he also married late in life. Ruth adored her father, who was older than any of her friends' parents, but when she turned twelve—and likely started to develop—he abruptly pulled away from her, refusing any further affection. He'd done the same thing to Joan. Only one year later she met Bernie, and it was in that frame of mind—rejected by her father, left alone in the house due to her sister's departure for college—that she fell in love.

In the beginning, marriage was harder for Ruth than she'd anticipated. She was stressed about studying and trying to make her picky new husband happy. With her mother as a role model, she enrolled at Queens College with a major in psychology. But her ambition didn't extend much beyond graduation; she was a mediocre student. Bernie had spent six months at the University of Alabama but then, missing Ruth, returned home and enrolled at Hofstra. Ruth was trying to graduate early so she could get a job and put Bernie through law school. That plan fell by the wayside when Bernie dropped out after one year to start his own brokerage firm.

Bernie's father, Ralph, wholly disapproved of his son's decision to leave law school and start the firm. "He was wild with anger," Ruth recalls. "He was a product of the Depression and felt very strongly that [Bernie] should have a specific degree that would lead to a job." Ralph had already seen his family through a series of financial hardships: In 1951, the company he'd started, Dodger Sporting Goods Corporation, was forced to file for bankruptcy when it was unable to fulfill its biggest order, for the Joe Palooka punching bag. Costs for the steel required to make the toy were astronomical then, thanks to the Korean War. He later launched a one-man brokerage firm called Gibraltar Securities; that failed, too.

Bernie was determined to be a bigger success than his father, but he wanted to do it his way. So on January 19, 1960, with $5,000 he'd saved from his lawn sprinkler business, he opened the doors of Bernard L. Madoff Investment Securities, at the age of twenty-one.

Ruth pitched in a few days a week when support was needed, doing "anything that needed to be done." If the air conditioner went on the fritz, Ruth called the repairman. She answered phones and made copies. When things were slow, she sat in the front room of the office, playing solitaire. In 1963, Ruth left the firm and did not work there again until 1980, when she set up the bill-payment system and handled payroll until a bookkeeper was hired. She also used the offices as a place to work on her cookbook and master's degree, and to manage her homes, foundations (she sat on the boards of Queen's College and the Gift of Life), and personal finances. She especially loved going to the office to see her sons, who often had new photos of their children on their desktop computers. Occasionally she would go to lunch with a trader, though, she says, most ate at their desks. "I liked going there," she says.

In 1964, when Ruth was pregnant with Mark, the young couple moved to a two-bedroom apartment in Great Neck, Long Island, with a terrace over the garage. They moved again a mere two years later, when she was pregnant with Andrew, to a house they purchased for $35,000 and would occupy for more than twenty years, in Roslyn. The living room was decorated with a coffee table, two club chairs, and plaid couches; the overall effect was "that of a doctor's office," Ruth says. Their furniture was Early American pine, much of it built by a craftsman from Great Neck. He made chairs and tables that resembled other things: a chair in the shape of an apple, for example. "Looking back, it was horrendous," Ruth says, laughing. "But I loved it at the time."

Now a young mother, Ruth again found herself struggling. "Those were not good days," she says. She found the suburbs monotonous and lonely and had trouble managing two small children, one of whom was colicky, and a house. "Nobody ever told me raising young children was difficult, and in those early years, you were not allowed to say such a thing."

In Roslyn, there was no place to go in the dead of winter; "Mark would wake up at six-thirty, then Andy would start, and I would think, I'm never going to make it through the day." With two children under the age of three and a husband working long hours, Ruth was simply overwhelmed.

Then, as often happens, life got easier; things worked themselves out. The boys grew older and started school full-time; Ruth started to make friends in her community; and Bernie's business began to flourish. He moved his offices to a bigger space, at 110 Wall Street. Occasionally, Ruth would book a sitter for the kids and she and Bernie would go out for a "big time" in the city, eating at a restaurant in Chinatown and seeing a movie. This is the time Ruth remembers as the happiest of their lives: They were an upwardly mobile, tight-knit family of four. The boys adored their parents. Bernie's business was growing, and there were no bickering daughters-in-law yet or demanding clients. No sign of what was to come.

Chapter Four

TROUBLE IN PARADISE

Mark Madoff entered the University of Michigan at Ann Arbor with a plan: He would major in economics and join his father's firm directly upon graduation, bypassing business school. In the first week of his freshman year, he met the woman who would become his first wife: Susan Freeman. A pretty blonde from a good Jewish family in tony Rye Brook, New York, Susan had been asked by her parents to look up a nice young man who was the son of mutual friends. She'd already come across his picture while flipping through the high school yearbook of a friend from Roslyn. "That's the guy I'm supposed to meet," she'd mused, taking note of his good looks.

When she met him in person she was even more impressed—in fact, she was instantly, irrevocably smitten. Mark Madoff looked like a movie star, with an athletic build, longish blond hair, and a strong jaw. After he mumbled a hello and ambled down the hallway of their dorm, Susan turned to her mother and said, "I'm going to marry him someday." She just knew, she says.

If Mark felt the same way, Susan says, he wasn't able to show it. Never comfortable in his own skin, he would stare at the floor when introduced to someone. Once Susan and Mark started dating, her mother tried to give him some friendly advice: "Mark, if you're going to succeed in business, you're going to have to learn to look people in the eye."

Despite his shyness, Mark possessed a sophistication and a worldliness that far surpassed that of his young friends. By the age of eighteen, he'd spent a significant amount of time in Europe, eaten in a wide variety of five-star restaurants, and slept on sheets that boasted a very high thread count. "Mark taught us everything," Susan recalls. "He knew about fashion, food, wine. He taught us about Girbaud jeans."

The two dated throughout college with a few small breakups in between. They were, says Susan, "copacetic." Both liked to be in bed by 11:00 PM. Neither liked to party. Susan had grown up with a father who had a terrible temper; Mark, by contrast, was "incredibly calm." He was, she says, very much a peacemaker: "When he did get angry, you knew he'd been pushed to the limit."

"Our relationship was a little bit explosive in those days," she remembers. "I had this crazy temper: I was always yelling at him, fighting and throwing things. Mark was a very sensitive and vulnerable guy, and I think because he knew that about himself, he kept his emotions at bay in romantic relationships. I was always trying to rile him up because I wanted an interaction. Andy thought I was horrible; he wanted Mark to break up with me."

"I had never met anyone as volatile as Susan," Andrew says. "In my house, we would say that everything was out in the open — but it really wasn't. With Susan, it actually was. She would yell or throw a hairbrush at him. And I couldn't understand why he would let himself be treated like that."

Mark's nervous constitution followed him to college, the stomach problems that had plagued him as a child returning in force. Susan's reactions to his ailment evolved from sympathy to annoyance as his doubling over became a constant occurrence. Mark tried to control the uncontrollable by becoming, Susan says, "incredibly routinized." In his closet, his shirts were lined up from blue to pink. His dorm room was spotless. At one point, when nothing was helping his stomach, Mark visited a naturopath named Dr. Peter D'Adamo, who would later write *Eat Right 4 Your Type,* a diet plan based on blood type. On the doctor's advice, Mark stopped eating carbohydrates. He didn't veer from the diet, falter, or cheat even once: If he and Susan stopped by a deli for a sandwich, he would order nothing but meat. When Dr. D'Adamo told him he needed to start exercising, Mark got up every day at 5:30 AM and ran. He did it for a year.

Susan says that Mark felt he couldn't measure up to his father. Though he was grateful to have been born into a family where he reaped the benefits of his father's successes, he knew that no matter what he did, he would only ever be Bernie Madoff's son. He desperately wanted to please him.

If Mark respected his father, he absolutely adored his mother. "What college kid talks to his mother every single day?" Susan asks. Susan, who was also close to her parents, fell into an easy intimacy with Ruth and Bernie, spending every summer weekend with them in Montauk. She was allowed to sleep in Mark's room, and Andrew's high school girlfriend was also allowed to stay over. Ruth used to joke, "I feel like I'm running a brothel!"

In 1984, Andrew headed to college at the Wharton School of the University of Pennsylvania, an undergraduate business program. He majored in finance and, like his brother, planned to join his father's business right after graduation. Ruth, suffering from a serious case of empty nest syndrome, was eager to move to Manhattan. During Andrew's senior year in high school, she and Bernie started to look for an apartment in earnest. Their broker showed them a beautiful duplex on the top floors of a quiet building on 64th Street, and as so often happens with Manhattan real estate, they reached beyond their original budget of $1.2 million to buy it for $1.6 million. Had they been able to hold on to the property, they would have turned a nice profit despite the burst of the real-estate bubble: In 2010, it sold at auction for $7 million.

Ruth calls the home that later became her husband's first prison cell an "upside-down" apartment: The bedroom, study, sitting room, and his and hers bathrooms were downstairs, and the living room, dining room, and kitchen, upstairs. After a renovation, Ruth and Bernie hired celebrated decorator Angelo Donghia to design the interior; he gave it a formal "English country" feel, with heavy armoires, trays with crystal decanters, and a poufy velvet sofa that would reveal a huge dent whenever someone who'd been sitting on it stood up. Andrew remembers his father constantly puffing up the cushions. The jewel of the apartment was a four-thousand-square-foot wraparound terrace that Ruth and Bernie never set foot on. "There was no overhang, so it got too dirty," Ruth recalls. "You'd clean it one day, and the next it'd be covered in soot."

To get a clear picture of what life as a Madoff was like, it is necessary to put the family's wealth into perspective. In the world of successful multibillion-dollar hedge fund managers with multimillion-dollar art collections, stables of Thoroughbreds, and garages housing dozens of luxury cars, they lived a wealthy but grounded life.

Catherine notes, "They weren't crazy rich; in my experience, they were 'medium rich.' Of course they had plenty of money, more than I would ever have, but Ruth drove a ten-year-old Mercedes station wagon and bought T-shirts at the Gap."

Indeed, before the 1990s, when they began flying private, the Madoffs often flew coach. Though they owned several properties, most were unremarkable by the standards of the Forbes 400. Their 1,300-square-foot one-bedroom pied-à-terre in France was considered downright humble by Bernie's wealthy clientele.

When Bernie's client and friend Norman Levy wanted to build a 150-foot yacht, Bernie consulted on the construction. The final result was "absolutely beautiful," recalls Andrew, but when Norman died and left Bernie in charge of his estate, Bernie didn't attempt to buy the boat.

"He wouldn't even talk about it," Andrew recalls. "I thought it was because he was so attached to Norman that he couldn't bear to look at the boat. Now I wonder if there was a certain level of opulence above which he could not live, or it was going to raise alarm bells. But I never thought, *Aha,* he's a criminal."

Ruth herself didn't realize quite how wealthy she'd become — not only because Bernie didn't share with her the full scope of his holdings (or with anyone, as the world is now all too aware), but because everyone around her was affluent. Many of Bernie's clientele enjoyed the same financial comforts as the Madoffs had, including their closest friends.

What Ruth and Bernie really lived was a normal upper-class Jewish life. Not a part of high society, they spent most of their leisure time going to dinners and movies with friends. Every now and then they would be invited to a formal dinner in Europe, which Ruth would dutifully attend, though she admits she "wasn't crazy about making small talk" with people she didn't know. Always lurking beneath the surface were their modest roots: Ruth remembers a luncheon in London where a waiter leaned in with a platter of crab and Bernie reached for the porcelain crab ornament instead of the edible crustacean. "The English people at the table didn't laugh," Ruth recalls. "But Bernie and his tablemate were roaring."

By the time Andrew went to work for his father, in 1988 — Mark had started at the firm two years earlier — Bernie had moved his business a final time, to the now-infamous offices that occupied the seventeenth through nineteenth floors of the Lipstick Building, at 885 Third Avenue. Around that time, the family started to travel to Palm Beach, flying down on a Thursday to a small apartment, then returning to New York on Sunday.

It was always Bernie who pushed their life to the next level. He wanted to join the Palm Beach Country Club—something Andrew realizes, in hindsight, was a mercenary effort on Bernie's part to ingratiate himself with affluent people he hoped to lure into his scheme. "He actively recruited investors from these pools," Andrew says, noting, "he couldn't have done that eating at Alabama Jack's with my mother."

For her part, Ruth didn't want to join, protesting that there was a perfectly nice golf course at the Breakers. She was trying to avoid the Palm Beach social scene, she says: "I didn't want to spend two out of three nights in Palm Beach at black-tie events. You'd play golf with these people, see them at lunch and at a party that night; then you'd go to another party with the same people the next night. Or someone would call and say, 'I'm having a dinner party on April fourteenth.' You'd say, 'Oh, too bad, we're not going to be in Florida that weekend.' They'd say, 'That's OK, I'm having another one next Friday.' They'd have three in a row to make sure everyone was covered! I wasn't going to do it. Bernie would say, 'Just lie.'"

Mark and Andrew were bored in Palm Beach. The fishing wasn't great, and what they wanted to do in the winter was ski. "Who wants to go on vacation with their parents, anyway, unless it's to save money?" Ruth says. As always, Bernie eventually got his way: In 1990, they joined the club.

Andrew moved into a one-bedroom bachelor pad bought for him by his parents in the fall of 1988, in his brother and sister-in-law's building on East 49th Street, Sterling Plaza, in Manhattan. It was a building developed by Mets co-owner Fred Wilpon, which was in keeping with the Madoff penchant for doing business with friends and family. Mark Madoff had married Susan Freeman on a clear day in September 1989, at Fresh Meadow Country Club in Long Island. It was a lovely but not lavish wedding. Andrew had recently started dating Susan's assistant, Debbie West, whom he'd met on a blind date arranged by Susan. Andrew had taken Debbie to dinner at a restaurant on the Upper East Side, and they'd "talked and talked and talked." Andrew, who wasn't a chatty type, found that she put him at ease. He was drawn to her sparkling intellect and independence. She'd lived in Italy and graduated from college in three years. And she was the polar opposite of the women he'd been dating, carefree party girls who were hardly wife material. A year later, they were engaged. They married at the Union League Club, in New York City, on January 18, 1992.

Both sets of grandparents were in the waiting room when their first grandchild was born: a boy, named Daniel, to Mark and Susan, on April 24, 1992. Ruth calls the night of his birth "the most extraordinary experience I ever had in my life." When she and Bernie got the call that Susan was in labor, they were in Florida. At two in the morning, they rushed back to New York on a private plane. Everything that was difficult about being a mother evaporated in the presence of her new grandson: "All those silly jokes that everyone tells about having your first grandchild; they're true. I remember reading an article where someone talked about clipping a baby seat to an eighteenth-century dining room table, when before, he wouldn't even let his kids eat there. It was hilarious; I could totally relate." Bernie doted on his first grandson, too.

By then, Bernie was engaged in an affair with Sheryl Weinstein, then president of Hadassah, a Jewish women's volunteer organization, who later wrote an embarrassing tell-all called *Madoff's Other Secret*. They'd met a year earlier. But Ruth was oblivious to this fact, as was everyone around her. She was utterly focused on the baby and impressed with Mark's parenting skills, calling him "the most devoted father you've ever seen." Unlike the men of her generation, who waited outside, chomping on cigars, while their children were born, Mark was not only in the delivery room but later would race home from work at 6:30 PM to change dirty diapers, give Daniel a bath, and walk his fussy son around the apartment for hours. When Andrew and Debbie's first daughter, Anne, was born a year later, he displayed the same slavish devotion. Two more grandchildren followed: a daughter for Mark, named Kate, born in 1995, and a daughter for Andrew, Emily, who arrived in 1996. The brothers' lives revolved around their children.

With both sons settled and no major domestic projects on the horizon, Ruth returned to school to get a master's degree in nutrition at NYU. Her goal was to set up a private practice once she graduated. But by then, she and Bernie were frequently traveling to Europe for business and pleasure, and she couldn't commit to a job. "The timing was off," she says. It became one of her biggest regrets.

When she was in school, she recalls, she was happy. She liked having a place to go and classes that took up part of her day. Lack of structure was "always a huge problem" for her. She had a sewing machine; she knitted; she decorated and did crafty things. But none of that was her passion; she was just killing time. "If I'd had a separate life, and hadn't been so dependent on a man, I would have been stronger, I think..." Isolated within the deceptive embrace of her husband, Ruth allowed her extended family to drift away. In deference to Bernie's wishes, they didn't socialize with her sister, Joan, aside from the occasional family gathering. The same went for his sister, Sondra, who lived a mere hour's drive away. "He never wanted to do anything he didn't want to do—and for the most part, he didn't ever want to see family," Ruth admits. "He felt his time was precious; he was somewhat selfish on that score." Was he troubled by the prospect of seeing a close family member he knew he was fleecing? Perhaps. More likely, he was insisting on a narcissistic need to have things his way. Always his way.

The Madoffs acquired more luxuries. He bought his suits at Kilgour, French & Stanbury and his shirts and underwear at Charvet. Because his weight fluctuated, he had to have his clothing taken in and let out, no small enterprise, since it was custom-made in London. He stored two steamer trunks at the Lanesborough Hotel in London and the Plaza Athénée in Paris so that polished shoes and cleaned and pressed suits and shirts were available when he arrived. In 1994, Bernie and Ruth purchased a house on the shores of the Intracoastal Waterway in Palm Beach for $3.8 million to make room for their children and grandchildren. It boasted terra-cotta floors; a large, wraparound double veranda; and an eighty-foot dock, where Bernie parked the Rybovich that he had bought in the 1970s. (The home later sold for $5.65 million, considerably less than its $8.5 million asking price.) Before they decorated, they rented vinyl La-Z-Boy recliners complete with drink holders, and "it was one of the best times we ever had in Palm Beach," says Ruth.

As Bernie's lifestyle grew more extravagant, his ruthless perfectionism gathered strength. He complained about the mess made by the grandchildren: sticky fingerprints, wet towels, crumbs on the floor.

"You're crazy! Leave them alone," Ruth would plead, fearful her sons were going to stop coming to visit. The adults weren't immune to his quirks, either: "Don't touch that!" Bernie would shout if someone curiously fingered a vase. Mark would snap, "Goddamn it, Dad, you want me and Susan to come here, but you make life miserable for us." It got worse as he got older, Ruth says: "He ruined our time."

Ruth found it easier to comply with Bernie's rules, saying, "What was the difference? It wasn't any big deal. I just made sure to keep my closet door closed." Andrew and Mark would try to laugh, or ignore their father. Then Bernie would have to lie down, he was so upset.

At work, he was no less fastidious. The walls of the office were oval, due to the unique shape of the Lipstick Building, and vertical blinds hung around the entire perimeter of the rooms. If someone pulled up a blind, often one of them would go crooked. Or they might not be at the exact same angle after someone had turned them to open them and the cleaning person turned them back that night. So Bernie would spend a certain amount of time each day crawling along the ledge at the edge of the windows, lining up the blinds. "People got used to seeing him doing that," Andrew recalls. "Nobody, of course, was capable of doing it to the degree of precision he required."

Then, of course, there was the underwear that Bernie had custom-made due to his aversion to elastic; it had buttons up the side. He gave Andrew a few pairs to try out. "This is ridiculous," Andrew said. "You can't wear this underwear. It doesn't have elastic. It doesn't stay up."

The brothers rolled their eyes at their father's quirks but tried not to give him too much grief: After all, they were the beneficiaries of his significant largesse. Neither one had a trust fund, so any money they made came from their salaries. But Bernie's generosity was legendary. As Susan remembers it, Mark would say, "OK, Dad, we found a house, it cost this much money." And just as it did with the bicycles and ice cream cones of their childhood, the money for the house would appear.

Susan and Mark bought a charming house in the backcountry of Greenwich, Connecticut, with Ruth and Bernie's help. The elder Madoffs would send them tickets to come visit them in Florida. Once or twice they flew the young couple to Italy on a private plane; another summer they sent them to France. Or Mark and

Susan might go to Aspen, with or without Ruth and Bernie, all expenses paid.

There were blips, little annoyances. Mark would complain to Andrew that Ruth and Bernie wouldn't babysit their kids when they went away, that Susan's parents were always stepping in. But he wouldn't say a word to his father. A first-born and a pleaser, he "revered" his father, according to Susan. He would not question him. "And he would not, I don't think, have said that his father was a bully. Clearly, he knew his father picked on people. But Mark would just say, 'Oh, my dad's crazy.'" He would seldom get mad at his father. And Bernie adored his sons. He might grumble at the beginning, says Susan, but ultimately he would give them anything they wanted.

Andrew and Debbie bought a summer home in Old Greenwich; every weekend they would show up on Mark and Susan's doorstep with their infant daughter, Anne. She and Daniel were best friends from the time they could walk and talk. In those years, says Susan, the young couples were extremely happy. They spent time in Montauk together, traveled together, were all best friends.

But when the kids got a little older, problems started to arise. The brothers had completely opposing parenting styles. Andrew and Debbie were super hands-on, very protective. Susan and Mark were more relaxed. It was mainly a problem in Montauk, says Susan, when the couples were all together in a small beach house with no rugs or upholstery to absorb sound. "You could hear a pin drop from one end of that house to the other," Andrew says.

Every day, Anne went down for a nap from 12:00 PM to 3:00 PM. Daniel had no regular naptime; his parents put him down when he was tired. During Anne's naptime, Andrew and Debbie would spend the whole time shushing Susan, who was "walking around and slamming doors," says Andrew. Another ongoing issue was snacks: Daniel was allowed to have four cookies; Anne could have only two. Neither set of parents would compromise and give the kids three.

Each brother had reservations about—and, at times, out-and-out dislike for—the other's spouse. Mark and Susan had a volatile, tempestuous relationship. They would get into huge screaming fights in front of the family, leaving Andrew stunned. "In the early years of our marriage, I was impulsive and excitable, very emotional," Susan recalls. "I remember Bernie saying to me, 'That's part of your charm.'" If she expressed dismay with Andrew, Mark would say, "I don't want you getting into a fight with my family, OK? I work next to them every day." Mark, for his part, thought Debbie was too controlling.

Soon, the tension transferred from the brothers to the wives, and Debbie and Susan stopped speaking. Grateful to have the attention off their own relationship, Mark and Andrew allowed their wives to fight the battle secretly brewing between the two brothers. The family continued to vacation together, but one of the couples might stay at a hotel, Andrew remembers. He and Mark continued to work next to each other every day, "compartmentalizing, as is the Madoff skill. We just sectioned off our personal lives from our relationship with each other, never discussing what was happening with our wives. There was no pressure to see each other socially, since we saw each other every day at work."

Was anyone in therapy? "No, definitely not," says Andrew. "As a family, we would have insisted, 'It's all out there.' And there was a lot of stuff that was out in the open and talked about. But the deeper, more serious issues festered beneath the surface."

Ruth stayed out of it. "Sometimes it got sticky with the wives," she recalls. "But you can't take a side, so I never did." Her refrain became "I don't want to get involved."

"The Madoff way of doing things was incompatible with marriage," admits Andrew. "There were no boundaries—everyone was in everyone else's business. And there was a sense that Mark and I were married to the job, the firm, each other. The wives always felt like, where do we fit in here?" Andrew and Mark pretended that nothing was wrong, working side by side without ever discussing their problems. As was the norm for the Madoff family, they all insisted they were happy. All conflict was quietly ignored.

Chapter Five

WORK/LIFE

On August 1, 1988, after a month spent backpacking around Europe, Andrew officially reentered the family business in the market-making division, no longer as an intern but as a full-time staffer. Bernie had already transitioned from working with his brother, Peter, in market making to running his asset-management business full-time, two floors down from where Andrew sat. It was an auspicious time for Bernie to change roles: In the 1970s he had orchestrated an industry-wide innovation, the creation of a centralized clearance and settlement system through the Depository Trust & Clearing Corporation. In the early 1980s, he developed the controversial practice of payment for order flow—paying brokerages a few pennies per share for steering orders to him. Originally decried as bribery, payment for order flow not only received a congressional seal of approval but also became an industry standard practice. It was now time for him to make a mark in new territory. In Bernie's absence, Peter would go on to create a system that automated the buying and selling of stocks for firms that catered to retail investors. These "automatic execution" systems brought prominence to the name of Bernard L. Madoff Inc. Although Bernie was not directly responsible for them, he was the one invited to attend conferences and make guest appearances on TV.

Mark had started at BLM two years earlier, as a trading assistant. Coming into a family business as the boss's son certainly had its advantages, but it also came with drawbacks. Bernard L. Madoff Investment Securities had no mechanism by which employees could ever have equity in the business — which is almost unheard of on Wall Street. Most firms were partnerships where employees could eventually become partners, or public companies in which they could receive stock options. A handful of firms were sole proprietorships or LLCs, like BLM, but they had all been snapped up by bigger firms as the industry consolidated. Andrew's coworkers would never own a piece of the family pie, and they resented the fact that he might, by simple virtue of his last name. The only way to prove himself, he knew, was to become a successful trader.

Trading is an intense occupation, requiring an enormous amount of focus. It involves a lot of information processing and the ability to make important decisions quickly and easily. Right out of the chute, Mark was good at trading but never really liked it. A worrier, he agonized over every decision he made. Andrew was the opposite. Unafraid of big risks and positions, he traded aggressively. He was consistently successful on the desk, making millions of dollars for the firm by employing arbitrage strategies in companies like Intel, Iomega, Pepsi, and Johnson & Johnson. There were only a few notable blowups, such as the time he famously — and disastrously — shorted Bell Atlantic in the 1990s and threw up in the garbage can under his desk. Within three years, he was promoted to full trader and got his own "pad," or list of stocks he was responsible for. With about a dozen traders on the desk, competition for the best stocks was fierce. Andrew, of course, knew he had an unfair advantage as the boss's son: "There was an enormous amount of pressure on both Mark and myself that we'd better trade profitably." Andrew rose to the challenge, trading more profitably on a per-stock, per-share basis than any other employee at the firm. But as he honed his skills, he came up against a problem that threatened to cut him off at the knees.

All trading firms have a culture, born from an inverse relationship between profitability and compliance. Blue-blood, traditional, regional brokerage firms such as A. G. Edwards in St. Louis, Olde Financial Corporation in Detroit, Alex. Brown in Baltimore, and Fidelity in Boston — firms that had been around a long time and had reputations of being run by good, honest people — leaned toward the conservative, taking the minimum profits from the trades that they executed. At the other end of the spectrum were the penny-stock firms on Long Island and in Boca Raton, as well as some of the biggest names on Wall Street: Goldman Sachs, Morgan Stanley, Merrill Lynch. The legal limit for the markup a firm was allowed to make on a trade with a customer was 5 percent of a trade's value. But 5 percent — or $5 on a $100 trade — would be a massive profit, and firms often didn't go that far. A firm might make a trade with a client and take more money than was appropriate. Yet the temptation to go further than they should was often too much to resist. In the midnineties, a scandal arose around this very issue: Big firms like Merrill Lynch, Smith Barney, and Lehman Brothers were accused of colluding to fix prices on the NASDAQ to cheat their clients. All settled with the Securities and Exchange Commission, signing a consent order that didn't admit to their guilt but agreed to new restrictions, such as having their phone conversations taped. It changed the entire industry.

BLM was one of the few firms that didn't get caught up in the scandal, because Bernie and Peter had designed its trading systems to favor efficiency and speed over profitability. The outer limit for a profit on a trade with its clients was 12.5 cents per share, and it was often far less than that. That, says Andrew, was very good for the firm's reputation but a real challenge in terms of making the business profitable. Still, Andrew loved the respect he received when he visited other firms around the country: Yes, you're a New York firm, they would tell him, but you're not like other New York firms. BLM's sterling reputation allowed it to pick and choose its customers.

Andrew always understood that there were two businesses and that they were separate. On the nineteenth floor, where he worked, Peter was the ultimate boss of the market-making and proprietary-trading businesses. One floor below were the systems and operations people who supported their business. And on the seventeenth floor was Bernie's asset-management business—the scene of his infamous fraud. There were separate personnel, separate floors, separate computer systems, and almost no interaction between the businesses at all, with the exception of the office Christmas party and the company weekend in Montauk.

While Bernie was free to run his asset-management division as he pleased, with little or no government oversight, the market-making division, by contrast, was closely monitored. All brokerage firms were given a score by an auditing firm called Transaction Auditing Group, based on its execution quality—meaning its level of compliance. Those scores were intensely, competitively monitored. Out of dozens of firms, BLM ranked number one, year after year. "Any time we weren't number one it was a crisis," Andrew says. As trading systems changed and adjusted, firms cropped up that were willing to push the limits of regulatory compliance, giving them the ability to grow more, build bigger systems, and market more aggressively. That frustrated the brothers to no end. At a certain point, their limitations on profitability were "ludicrous," says Andrew. "Every time we made a highly profitable trade, our father or uncle would say something was wrong and we needed to modify the system. If we weren't making any money at the end of the day, what was the difference if we were number one in the TAG ranking?" He remembers arguing, "It shouldn't be our goal to be the least profitable firm on Wall Street."

With the benefit of hindsight, Andrew now realizes that his father's entire fraud hinged on the firm's sterling reputation. He could never afford to have anything less than "pristine perfection" in the quality of the business he was running, so that when regulators came in to examine the trades, they never found anything untoward. And they never did. But the price to pay was a dramatically reduced level of profitability.

If the other traders on the BLM desk found fault with the system, they didn't complain with their feet; people worked there for decades. They made a "good, not a great living," says Andrew. "By Wall Street standards, they were not the best paid." In the 1990s, a BLM trader could follow the drill, keep his head down, and make a couple of hundred thousand dollars a year. It was a low-stress job that came with fantastic job security. When the tech bubble burst in 2000, the firm carried a bunch of traders rather than letting them go. And as technology became more integral to the trading process, making their jobs obsolete, BLM held on to its traders longer than anyone else.

Few traders made over $1 million a year, with the exception of Andrew and Mark, who, at the height of their salaries, each took home $3 million. Considering the positions they eventually held — head of equities and sales, respectively — that still wasn't excessive by Wall Street standards. They could have made millions more in the same positions at a larger firm, but at this stage in their careers, they hoped to one day inherit the business. And Andrew wasn't at all unhappy with his salary. "Three million dollars a year is a ton of money," he says.

Bernie was not abusive, Andrew says, but he could be mean. He would say things like "You're welcome" before Andrew had a chance to say "Thank you," and "In case you forgot, it's my name on the door." He had a strong personality and a way of seeing his point of view as the absolute truth. If someone didn't agree with him, they were "deluding themselves." It was one of Bernie's favorite phrases.

Andrew was the person who disagreed with him most often. "Pick a topic; I was the one who was going to be in his face about it," he says. The two almost always agreed on big trades—and if Andrew was trading on a scale that required Bernie's permission, he "wasn't so quick" to argue. Bernie was boss. But if he was making a strategic decision—changing the way one of their systems worked, for example—they would butt heads. As the eighties had turned into the nineties and then the 2000s, the computer systems grew more extensive and the technical elements had gotten away from Bernie. His brother Peter was the one who had built all of the firm's trading systems, but after his bout with bladder cancer in the late nineties, much of his responsibility for overseeing the firm's technology platform had been ceded to Andrew. Andrew was the expert in that arena, but if he didn't agree with Bernie's conclusions, he was "deluding" himself.

Less irksome to Andrew, but still annoying, was his father's refusal to change the name of the firm from Bernard L. Madoff Investment Securities to Madoff Securities. He wanted his father to acknowledge the growing role he and Mark had taken on in the intervening decade, not to mention his uncle's key contribution. It was Peter's role in the market-making business that had cemented Bernie's name on Wall Street. Stubbornly, Bernie insisted it had to be "my name on the door." They'd argued about it numerous times. A golden opportunity to change the name arose in 2000, when Bernie reorganized the firm from a sole proprietorship to an LLC. Letterhead stationery, business cards, pads, legal documents— all had to be changed to reflect the firm's new status. Andrew and Mark once again asked their father to change the name of the firm. He refused; they fought and finally gave up. Andrew now realizes that it was, perhaps, a misguided attempt on Bernie's part to protect his family by labeling the firm as exclusively his, but in the absence of that knowledge, Andrew simply saw it as a slight.

★   ★   ★

In 1997, Andrew decided to expand the firm's market-making operation to include the trading of NASDAQ-listed securities. Before that, the firm had specialized in the "third market" trading of NYSE-listed securities. This expansion required significant changes to the firm's trading systems and was an enormous undertaking. By 2000, after some ten years on the desk, Andrew was managing the entire trading desk. His favorite trades involved arbitrage, anything having to do with complicated math, multiple securities, options, convertible bonds, and warrants and rights. For a long time, he was able to do all the numbers in his head; once that was no longer practical, he built spreadsheets and models that set the stage for the trading systems he would later have built for the entire desk. Andrew found he had talent for maintaining his composure during huge market dislocations, like the one that occurred after 9/11. If a trader got into trouble or burst into tears and walked off the desk, Andrew would immediately sit down and pick up where the trader had left off. He continued to trade until 2002, when he became head of equities. From time to time during Andrew's early years with the company, Bernie would ask Andrew if he was happy and insist, "You don't have to stay in the business if you don't want to." Later, those words would become enormously important when Andrew called his father's bluff and tried to leave. But early on, there was no pressure for him to stay at the firm. When Andrew asks himself if his father manipulated him into going into the business, the answer, he says, is no. Staying there later on was another matter.

For the duration of their careers, Mark and Andrew sat side by side on the trading floor. As a team, they worked together well. Aware of each other's strengths, they divided up their responsibilities accordingly. Andrew built the trading systems; Mark built the sales team. But as their careers as traders developed, it was now

Mark who found himself in his brother's shadow. Once the brothers were in a professional setting, the labels that had so plagued Andrew in high school—he was "the smart one," Mark "the good-looking one"—were no longer subjective. They were quantifiably measurable, determined by who was the better trader. And that had to do with who made the most money. Undeniably, that was Andrew.

As a result, Mark gravitated toward being a manager and a customer guy. Oftentimes, women ran the retail order flow desk at BLM's client firms. They loved the handsome young salesman who visited them and would send him all their business. As manager, though, he had a horrible temper and a very short fuse. The systems Andrew had built to manage and analyze risk were complicated; Mark didn't always understand the math that supported the model. Whereas Andrew wanted the people who worked for him to be as smart as possible, Mark felt threatened when challenged by a trader. "He would bully them in a way that was embarrassing," Andrew recalls. "He would just get so angry, screaming at them, insulting them, even threatening them. Once he started shrieking, there was no stopping him—you just had to let him go. People would watch him fall apart and roll their eyes."

Andrew tried to win arguments intellectually, telling the person who was challenging him, "This is why you're wrong." Mark would say only, "You're an idiot, because I said so." It wasn't so different from the way he saw his father humiliate and bully the people who didn't share his worldview. But lacking the name on the door and the clout that came with it, Mark was far less convincing with this approach.

The division between BLM's two businesses—or perceived lack thereof—lies at the heart of the vitriol, accusations, aspersions, and doubt cast on Andrew and Mark, because few can understand how they could have worked so closely with their father for so many years without an inkling that a massive fraud was unfolding two floors below them. There were, in fact, a number of factors in play.

According to Andrew, the sudden and early loss of Bernie's parents left him reeling, and, ultimately, terrified about his own mortality. Ralph Madoff succumbed to a heart attack in 1972, at the age of sixty-two. Two years later, Sylvia Madoff died during an asthma attack; she was also sixty-two. Conversations about Bernie's health were verboten. He refused to get yearly physicals and, when he was sick, had to be dragged to the doctor. Sometime around 1999, he was diagnosed with a minor blood disorder. That was as far as it went; he refused to pursue it. "How many times could I say to him, 'You have to take better care of yourself; you need to go to a doctor'?" Andrew asks. "He would say, 'I'm not doing it.' And at the end of the day, that was his choice." Bernie's refusal to so much as address his mortality led to the "granddaddy of all problems" for Andrew and Mark: the lack of a succession plan.

When the two young men started at the firm, each fresh out of college, with no business-school degree or significant outside work experience, it was only natural that they would take their father at his word when he explained the way the business worked. Certainly, they knew he ran an asset-management company on the seventeenth floor. But with an entire business to learn about on the nineteenth floor—and they were aspiring traders, not financial planners—they didn't have an interest in asset management. As they grew older and became more involved in the business, they started to ask questions. What were the actual logistics of running the firm as a whole? The elements of the overall, day-to-day operations as they encompassed all business divisions? Most important, what was going to happen when Bernie passed away?

"Peter will run the business," he would tell them. There was a formula for a split: Peter would get half, Ruth the other half, and when their mother died, they'd get her piece. "But there are elements of the day-to-day operations we're not familiar with," Andrew would protest. "Everyone is going to walk in here saying, Now what? And I'm not going to sit here at forty years old and look like a knucklehead."

Ironically, Bernie often worried about the firm's vulnerability to the loss of certain key executives, saying, "What if so-and-so gets hit by a bus?" And in 1997, the firm's bookkeeper, Sylvia Hendel, indeed was killed by a bus. But Bernie still refused to address his own mortality.

Mark would push his father, too: Susan, his ex-wife, remembers more than one dinner-table conversation where Mark said to Bernie, "Dad, the trading room can't make money forever. You've got to let us in on the arbitrage side of the business." Bernie would "get angry very quickly," Susan recalls. "He'd say, 'Listen to me. I gave you guys the trading operation. It's yours to make what you want of it. This is my business, and it's gonna die when I do.'" She remembers that conversation as "an incredible point of frustration that came up again and again." Although Catherine was romantically involved with Andrew for only a few years before Bernie's arrest, she witnessed the same kind of scenes.

Mark would try another tactic with Bernie: "We need to know everything if we're supposed to step into your shoes. You could be in a plane crash, get hit by a bus, or have a heart attack—it could happen." At that, Bernie would start to get emotional. Parents dying before their time was a topic that was too close to home for him. The brothers, hyperaware of Bernie's sensitivity about his parents' death, would back down.

But not for long. "When are you going to teach me how to do this?" Andrew would ask. "Don't you think I can do it? Haven't I proven myself?"

It was a constant source of embarrassment, he says, when clients would inquire about their accounts with the asset-management business. "How are we doing this month?" someone might ask as he passed through the trading room on their way to the office Bernie still maintained upstairs. Or Andrew would meet a new person at an industry event, and they would say, "Oh, you're related to Bernie Madoff? What's happening with my account?" Or a call would come into the trading room: "Hi, this is Irving Schwartz, I'm missing a dividend check..."

"I have no idea," Andrew was forced to respond. "Ask my dad. Let me transfer you downstairs."

Later, Andrew would find himself shouting at Bernie: "You're going to teach me what you know or I'm leaving the business! This is unacceptable; I won't live like this!" Then Bernie would offer answers for "certain elements," promising, for instance, that one piece would be handled by Frank DiPascali, his lieutenant. "But I'm not giving you details about that," Bernie would say; "you'll get them when you need them." Andrew, growing apoplectic, would reply, "So what happens if Frank decides to screw you? I don't even know how much money you're worth. Is it a billion dollars, two billion, three? I don't have a clue. What if Frank lies? What if there's really three and he says there's two? And takes a billion dollars and disappears into the sunset?"

"Calm down, it's all written down and in a safe-deposit box," Bernie would insist. "When the time comes, you'll speak to our attorneys; they'll handle it."

"So what about the investment part of the business?" Andrew wanted to know. Bernie had an answer for that, too: "We'll wind it down and people will get their money back." The warning note in Bernie's voice made clear he was finished talking. There the conversation would end.

In an attempt to verify whether Bernie was giving his clients the same story, Mark once approached his friend Jeff Wilpon, son of Fred Wilpon, and asked: "Has Bernie ever told you what will happen to your accounts when he dies?"

"Your father told us that you guys don't want to take over the investment business, so our money comes back to us when he dies," he said. Astonishingly, the story that Bernie had told his sons—that he would dissolve the asset-management business and return his clients' money to them—checked out. To this day, Andrew still doesn't know what the growth trajectory of his father's business looked like. When did it surpass $5 billion? Ten? Fifty? He has no clue.

Andrew, of course, had his own account at the firm, yielding the same steady dividends that Bernie's other clients received. He looked at the statements when they arrived and understood the trading strategy employed in the account. He understood the options positions, which looked, he says, "completely plausible." As for the steadiness of the returns, well, as far as he could tell, his father was a genius. After all, some of the most sophisticated investors on Wall Street believed it to be true. So did the people who elected Bernie Madoff president of NASDAQ, as well as the organizations that had showered him with awards. Why wouldn't his own son, who'd learned most of what he knew about trading from Bernie and Peter, who'd worked at the firm since high school, believe him? Andrew takes issue with the idea that he and Mark were "two dumb rubes, too naive to know what was going on. We had a very keen sense of what was going on in our division and, in spite of that, managed not to know that there was a crime being committed in the asset-management division two floors below us, just like hundreds of highly sophisticated investors who got swept up in this did not see it coming," he says.

In 2001, Andrew and Mark had a heart-to-heart about how to protect their careers, given Bernie's lack of a succession plan. "We're going to inherit a huge sum of money, even though we don't know how much it is," Andrew said. "It could be on the scale of a billion dollars or more. We need to manage that money the way a hedge fund would." The firm's proprietary-trading desk at that point was relatively small, managing a few hundred million dollars. If Andrew and Mark wanted to do things right, they needed to scale things up considerably in terms of technology, trading systems, and personnel. They told Bernie of their plans, and he gave them his blessing. So Andrew built portfolio-analysis systems and risk-management tools and put all of the pieces into place—everything required to run a multibillion-dollar hedge fund.

The lack of a succession plan is a common problem in family-run businesses: Only one-third survive the transition to a second generation. Andrew took some comfort in knowing he and Mark weren't alone. But a series of major events was about to rock Andrew's world, forcing him to admit that even if Mark could continue to accept Bernie's terms for staying at the firm, he could not.

Slowly, he would start to take steps to separate himself from the family business he'd hoped to someday take over.

Chapter Six

A PAINFUL AFFAIR

As Bernie's business continued to flourish and he upgraded his lifestyle, his sons followed suit. Susan and Mark moved from a "comfortably small-size house" in Greenwich to a much bigger one on several acres, also in Greenwich, and immediately did a big renovation. That, Susan feels, put enormous pressure on Mark to prove to his father that he was worthy of the gifts he'd been given.

Mark was conflicted. On the one hand, he was proud to show off the beautiful home Susan had taken such care to decorate—she remembers Bernie coming over and being "impressed"—and on the other, he didn't want people to think he'd been born with a silver spoon in his mouth. He'd been given many opportunities by his generous father, he knew, but he'd also worked hard for them.

And Mark was content running the administrative desk at BLM. In the earliest years of his career, he'd toyed with the idea of becoming a photographer; Susan and Mark had had a darkroom installed in their first apartment. When he would come home after a particularly stressful day at work, Susan would say, "Let's move to

Aspen. You could become a photographer there. Or a ski instructor. What's stopping us?" "Because this is where the action is," Mark would always respond. "This is where my family is. I want to be close to my father." Family was extremely important to Mark, and though he saw his father every weekday at the office, he continued to call home every weekend.

Yet despite his charmed life, a dark cloud lurked over Mark. Like Ruth, he was motivated by fear. "Maybe we should have a third baby," Susan remarked one day. It was an offhand comment, made to shake her husband out of the complacency that had settled into their eleven-year marriage. "I'm not gonna mess with fate," he immediately responded. "We have two healthy children already."

The two drifted apart. Mark, unable to access his emotions, buried himself in his work. Never having been given a chance to sow her oats and feeling emotionally disconnected from her husband, Susan looked elsewhere for comfort.

"We had grown apart," she says, "and I was having a midlife crisis. But that's not a reason to go outside the marriage. I didn't know what the repercussions would be."

Susan "unraveled," she says, thinking, Oh God, if I'm doing this, I must not love Mark. This marriage must be over. And so that's what she told her husband when she admitted what she'd done.

Mark was destroyed. He adored his wife. He didn't want the marriage to end. As he always had for major life decisions, he went to his father for advice.

"I've done things I'm not proud of," Bernie offered mysteriously. "Marriages go through ups and downs."

It was, Susan says, the first time Mark ever saw a flaw in his father.

Willing to forgive his wife for her indiscretion, Mark begged her to work on the marriage. Susan told him she wasn't sure what she wanted; she needed time to think. For a man who was, underneath his gruff exterior, desperately sensitive, her indecision was agonizing. He simply could not deal with the pain and anxiety of not knowing. Up went the armor again.

"If you don't know what you want, I'm filing for divorce," he told her. "I'm not going to sit around waiting for you to figure this out." She suggested they try therapy. During the third session, Mark asked the therapist, "What's your prognosis for us?"

"If I had to make a prediction right now, I don't think you're going to stay together," he said.

"That gives me my answer," Mark said. That was their last therapy session.

Nine months later, practically to the day, Susan Freeman and Mark Madoff were sitting in a courtroom, signing divorce papers. "He was a trader," says Susan; "he wanted it off his desk." Susan was sobbing so hysterically that the judge turned to Mark and said, "Mr. Madoff, I don't know that we should go through with this today. I'm not sure your wife is in the right frame of mind to sign these papers."

"What's done is done," he said, bending over the papers to sign. Mark instructed his parents not to speak to his soon-to-be ex-wife. Susan, who'd been married since her early twenties, didn't know what to do next. She slogged through her days in a fog of denial, relief, and depression.

A year later, the clouds parted and she asked herself, What have I done? She begged Mark to give her another chance. He was furious. "You don't get to destroy our family and try to come back to me!" he shouted. She retreated, licking her wounds. A few months passed, and she begged their friends to talk to him on her behalf, saying, "I know I made a mistake." He rebuffed her. Every few months she would try again. His answer was always "I appreciate the fact that you feel remorse. I know you're sorry. But no." She spent hours writing numerous letters to him that she never sent.

Andrew watched his brother harden after his divorce. He saw how much he missed his children. But he didn't see what was happening in his own home, to his own marriage. By the time Debbie and Andrew's daughters were out of diapers, Debbie had started to rebel against the Madoff way of doing things. Frustrated by the family's lack of boundaries — the time they spent together at work, the shared vacations, the numerous family functions — she subtly started pulling away. She would show up to an event late, dressed in inappropriately casual clothes, or sometimes she wouldn't show up at all. She spent more and more time with her horse, at a rented barn in Pine Plains, New York. Andrew found ways to convince himself that her eccentricities were endearing. But they didn't escape the notice of his family.

In January 2000, Debbie and Andrew had traveled to St. Moritz, Switzerland, for the Interbourse, an annual ski junket sponsored by international stock exchanges and held in a different fabulous location each year, including Cortina d'Ampezzo, Italy; Davos, Switzerland; and Aspen. All the major stock exchanges in the world brought their best skiers along to compete on a world-class slalom course; some hired Olympic skiers as traders, just so they could race in the event. Andrew was representing the Cincinnati Stock Exchange. As the best skier in his group, he was the obvious choice to compete, but with no real training as a racer, he fumbled his way down the heavily iced slopes.

That night, on a high from racing, exhausted but happy, he attended a banquet organized for the skiers. Busy mingling with other executives, all trying to outdo one another with inflated tales of bravery, he failed to notice the man in the corner chatting up his wife.

They returned home. Debbie started losing weight and taking

more care with her appearance. Her clothing, which had tended toward loose T-shirts and jeans with sneakers, grew more feminine. For the first time in eight years of marriage, she got a Brazilian wax. "All the classic signs, if you were paying attention," says Andrew. "But I wasn't." Focused on his kids, work, brother, and parents—everyone but his wife—Andrew didn't see his marriage deteriorating right before his eyes.

Two years later, Andrew was at work when his cousin Shana, Peter's daughter, called him into her office. Sitting behind her desk, she looked grim and asked him to sit down. "I have something I need to tell you, and I don't know how to say it, so I'm just going to come out with it," she said. He stared at her blankly.

"Debbie has a boyfriend."

"Debi Taratunio?" he asked, referring to one of their sales staff. "So what?"

Shana knitted her brows and repeated, "No, *Debbie*. Your wife."

Andrew's mind couldn't process what she was saying. It didn't even occur to him that she could have been talking about his wife. "I don't understand what you mean," he insisted. Shana patiently explained what she'd learned. Her boyfriend had been having dinner with a few guys. One of them had mentioned to him that Andrew's wife, Debbie, had a boyfriend. Apparently, they'd been together for two years. Andrew sat rigidly in the chair across from Shana, stunned.

"I'm absolutely positive," Shana added.

Numb, Andrew made his way back upstairs to his office. He picked up the phone and dialed his home in Old Greenwich, where he and Debbie were living for the summer. No answer. Mumbling an excuse to his secretary, Andrew left work, walked to the garage, and picked up his car. Robotically, he made the trip he'd made so many times before. He found himself at the dock, by his boat. He climbed on board, shell-shocked. Sitting on the deck, his legs gathered up to his chest, he waited, not knowing what to do.

His phone rang.

Andrew leapt up and answered it. "I know you have a boy-friend!" he shouted. "Is it true?" There was dead silence on the other end of the line. He experienced, then, a degree of shock unlike anything he'd felt in his life. He snapped the phone shut, drove to the house, and started packing his bags. When he finished, he put them in the car and drove back to the city. Debbie called again later that night. "It's true," she said, crying.

"Then we're finished," Andrew informed her. "I'm not com-ing back."

"We need to talk about this," she pleaded.

"I don't want to hear anything you have to say."

Debbie drove into the city to talk to Andrew. He doesn't remember what was said, just that it was one of the most gut-wrenching experiences of his life. The shock and betrayal were debilitating. He couldn't think. Couldn't speak. He was out of his mind with rage. Never before had he experienced emotions like these, under any circumstances.

Bit by bit, Debbie revealed everything that had happened. She and her boyfriend had met in St. Moritz; it started out innocently. E-mails back and forth. They eventually grew flirtatious. Within a couple of months they'd met and had sex. She'd been seeing him ever since, intermittently. She was going to end it.

Unlike Mark, who wanted to know nothing about his wife's indiscretion, Andrew wanted to know everything. No detail was too sordid or painful to leave out. Where did she see him? What was it like? What did they do? He'd been so in the dark, he would settle for nothing less than a brilliant spotlight on her deception.

If you ever want there to be any hope of reconciliation, Andrew told her, you'll do that for me. So Debbie shared every horrible detail with him. Slowly, he came to realize that every one of their friends had known about the affair. Maria, whom they'd met through their kids. Her husband, Jeremy. Their friend Randy. The parents of kids whom they saw every weekend at the pool, waving to him. They all knew.

Even his brother's ex-wife, Susan, knew. "How could you do this to me?" he screamed at her.

"I hated that Debbie was doing this," she said, trying to placate him. "I told her to stop, but she couldn't. I was in an impossible situation. I felt loyal to her. If it was between the two of you, I had to choose her."

To Maria and Jeremy, he listed the events they'd attended together, when they'd been smiling, laughing, looking him in the eye, and letting him pick up the dinner check. "All this time you knew," he spat.

"Your anger is misguided," they said. "You should be mad at her. What were we supposed to do?"

"I'm plenty mad at her," Andrew raged, "but you have to bear your share of the responsibility."

The fury and shock were bad, but they were nothing compared with the humiliation he felt. It was staggering. Soul-crushing.

It had been exactly one year since Mark's divorce.

Andrew stayed in the city for a week, telling the kids he was on a business trip. He spent the time thinking, allowing his anger to cool, trying to gain perspective. For years, he'd been emotionally dead. He'd gotten into a marriage he'd thought he'd wanted and, when it wasn't fulfilling, pushed his feelings down and buried himself in his work. While he had chosen Debbie for her intellect and independence, she resented the role she had settled into: that of a stay-at-home mom dependent on her husband.

Andrew had urged her to go back to work or school, or to take up charity work — anything to ease her malaise. When she wasn't interested, he grew numb to her complaints. Learning of her betrayal, he says, "woke up every emotion I ever had."

As Mark had before him, he approached his parents for advice. They told him that if he wanted to leave Debbie, they would support him, but if he wanted to forgive her, they would support that, too. Andrew asked Bernie point-blank: Did you ever cheat on Mom? Again, Bernie responded cryptically, talking around the question. You shouldn't judge people, he said. You need to give them the benefit of the doubt. Andrew left the conversation assuming his father had cheated and that his parents had worked it out. He wasn't going to worry about it. It was his father's problem. And his mother's.

Having spent the last year watching his brother struggle, Andrew didn't want to go through the same thing. He felt Mark should have tried to work out his marriage, if only for the sake of the kids. Andrew had had a week to think about the ten years he'd spent with his wife. They had lots of good memories. Two beautiful daughters. Enough that worked. He decided he was at least going to try.

Couples counseling, which had been a total failure for Mark, was a "transformative" experience for Andrew. At thirty-six he "self-reflected" in a way he never had. Now he was examining everything, in a thousand different ways, which was a revelatory experience. Previously unwilling to look at himself, he saw his own failings in stark relief. He evolved from feeling rage at Debbie to blaming himself for the affair. But even after years of couples therapy, it was clear that she still felt entitled to the indiscretion. "I never felt she was sorry for having the affair; she was only sorry she got caught," Andrew says. But at the end of the day, the children came first. Andrew and Debbie would attempt to stay together, at least until the kids were out of the house.

In June 2002, the family took a previously planned vacation to a dude ranch in Idaho. For five days, they fished, rode horses, took walks under wide-open skies. Andrew took it all in, with a heightened awareness of the fragility and beauty of life. Emotionally alive for the first time in a decade, he felt his feelings wash over him in waves. Again and again, he cried. The feeling was incredible.

Chapter Seven

"You Will Have Everything You Want in Life, but Not in the Way That You Expect It"

Andrew was relaxing under the competent hands of his weekly masseuse, Brenda, who had set up a table in his study. It was December 2002.

Seven months had passed since he learned of Debbie's affair. Their reconciliation had been tenuous at best: The accusations, anger, and tears that marked the revelation of the affair had turned into petty bickering or, more often, silence. And Andrew had changed. He was more vigilant about what was happening in his home and less self-absorbed. Keenly aware of the unhappy marriages all around him. He worked out four days a week and lost fifteen pounds.

By then, Bernie's Ponzi scheme was flush with cash. He and Ruth had purchased a tiny townhouse in the south of France and had started to spend their summers there, playing golf, yachting, and lunching at the nearby Hôtel du Cap. Andrew had stopped trading and was running the equities desk full-time. He continued to work on the infrastructure he'd built to manage his prospective inheritance. But he had also begun to put feelers out for alternatives, investing modest amounts in small businesses he believed in. He'd bought a 10 percent stake in a fishing lodge in Alaska and contributed to a fly-fishing club that worked like a time-share, booking its members for weeklong fishing trips at exclusive resorts around the world. Whenever he had downtime from his responsibilities at BLM, he kept an eye out for his next investment.

For years, Andrew had been buying his fly-fishing equipment at a shop called Urban Angler. The only fly-tackle dealer in Manhattan, the store had moved from its ramshackle third-floor location on 25th Street to a sleek Fifth Avenue site but was still run like a mom-and-pop outfit; fishing enthusiasts would come in, lean against the counter, and talk to the owners for hours. Quietly, it catered to some of the most powerful names on Wall Street and in entertainment; Paul Volcker, Hank Paulson, Jimmy Buffett, Sam Shepard, Edward Norton, and the sculptor Joel Shapiro were all customers. Perfect, Andrew thought, I'm going to buy Urban Angler. He set up a lunch with one of its owners, Jon Fisher, and invited Mark along. Jon mentioned he would bring along his girlfriend and business partner, a woman named Catherine Hooper.

On the appointed day, Andrew and Mark swung by the store to meet Jon. They walked in, the bell on the door tinkling, and a dark-haired woman wearing a belted A-line dress emerged from the back. She's cute, Andrew thought. Not sure how I missed her.

The four went across the street to Eleven Madison Park, an upscale restaurant with a soaring art·deco dining room. The restaurant was closed, but the chef was a fly fisherman, so the group was granted access to the main dining room. Mark, who was there mainly for moral support, ceded the floor to his brother, who "tried to impress Jon and Catherine with my financial acumen and knowledge of fishing." Both listened patiently.

"We appreciate your interest," Jon said when Andrew had finished his sales pitch. "But we just reorganized the business and brought in partners. We can certainly keep you in the loop, but right now, we don't have a need for capital."

Catherine found Andrew arrogant and was put off by his assertion that he had "a pretty good handle on how to run companies." He might know everything there was to know about Wall Street, but he knew nothing about running a small business, as far as she was concerned.

"Are you sure you don't want to reconsider?" Andrew asked. "Because I think you guys could use some help from a professional."

Catherine crossed her arms. "Give me an example of how I could use your help."

Andrew shrugged his arms out of his jacket and leaned forward in his shirt and tie, clasping his hands on the table. "I came in recently, wanting to buy four RIO tri-tip lines. You only had one in stock. So I ordered them from a fly shop in California and they came a week later. It's not good business for you to lose a sale like that. Those lines are a hundred dollars each."

Catherine also leaned forward. "Well, let me explain. Those lines are terrible. We sell about four a year, mostly to people who've just gotten started and don't know what they're doing yet. None of my serious clients would buy that line; instead, they'd buy four spare spools and four new fly lines. So instead of getting a four-hundred-dollar sale, I'd get a four-thousand-dollar sale. And *that's* why I don't stock those lines."

She sat back and thought, I hate this person. I hate everything he represents, with his Wall Street attitude. How dare he talk to me that way?

"You only sell four tri-tip lines a year? I'm scared; I want to run," Mark joked.

The foursome wrapped up their lunch and shook hands;

Catherine said they would be in touch, though she had no intention of seeing the brothers again.

Brenda, who was working out a knot in Andrew's right shoulder, suddenly stopped what she was doing. There, she said. Feel that?

Andrew reached up to his shoulder, and his masseuse guided his fingers to an area to the right of his collarbone. There he found a grainy, one-centimeter ball just beneath the surface of the skin; it was hard and noticeable, but painless. Huh, he thought. He didn't panic. He'd already had a few precancerous moles removed and was due for his next screening the following month. Making a mental note to call a doctor ASAP, he tried to relax as Brenda worked out some kinks in his back.

Andrew visited a doctor recommended by a friend immediately following the massage. The doctor examined him and said the nodule was unusual but not necessarily alarming. He and his partner both agreed to keep an eye on it, to see if it changed.

A month later, Andrew arrived at his dermatologist's office for his periodic skin-cancer screening. As soon as the doctor felt the bump, his eyes widened in alarm: "You've got to get this biopsied right away." Andrew immediately booked an appointment with a surgeon for a fine-needle aspiration, and within days, he was lying on an examining table, grimacing, as the doctor jabbed a needle around in his shoulder. Next the doctor injected the sample onto a slide and handed it to a pathologist, who slid it under a microscope.

"This isn't good," the pathologist said, his eye pressed against the glass.

Andrew fell in love with her. She was the first person who'd conveyed an overwhelming confidence in her diagnosis and treatment. She was cold, yes, but in a way that he found comforting. Appointments were scheduled. He left her office feeling lighter than he had in weeks.

Cyclophosphamide. Adriamycin. Vincristine. Prednisone. Andrew had developed a whole new vocabulary. On April 15, 2003, he began chemotherapy at Memorial Sloan-Kettering Cancer Center. Every two weeks thereafter, he made his way to the center for five hours of treatment. Debbie sat with him during the sessions and gave him daily injections of Neupogen when required. After the second round, his hair started to fall out, and he allowed his two daughters to shave his head, an activity they greatly enjoyed and one that also helped them manage their fears. He was otherwise lucky, never experiencing a moment of nausea. The highly skilled doctors and nurses were wonderful, perpetually heartened by his progress, which always seemed to go "the good way." He experienced a shorter recovery time, better response, and fewer side effects than most.

The worst part of the process came when chemotherapy ended and localized radiation treatments began. Andrew was instructed to lie down on a cold steel table. Four dots were tattooed across his collarbone and a rough plastic mask was form-fitted across his face. The mask was then bolted to the table underneath him. Unlike the procedure for a dental X-ray, in which a technician throws a lead blanket over the patient's chest and lap and casually walks out of the room, Andrew found himself alone in a formidable steel-encased room with a three-foot-thick steel-and-lead door that would slowly swing shut before they blasted him. The claustrophobia, panic, and terror he felt were overwhelming. Mark took his job of older brother very seriously during this time, always offering to accompany Andrew to appointments and protecting him from overly curious colleagues at the office. But Mark came to only one radiation appointment, finding the mask and the vault too terrifying to face.

Through it all, Andrew continued to go in to work. This was his "take charge" moment, his chance to prove to his father that he could handle anything. Whenever he grew tired from the treatments, he would nap on his office couch. At BLM, Bernie was boss. When it came to cancer, Andrew was boss. For the first time in his life, he was making all the decisions.

Andrew's cancer battle changed him in another measurable way. Though his family had given generously to a number of charitable causes, Andrew had never been an activist. He might attend the occasional fund-raiser for the Special Olympics or go to a charity ball. Now he found himself wanting to get much more deeply involved. He'd donated $5,000 to the New York City chapter of the Leukemia & Lymphoma Society when his young cousin had been diagnosed. After Roger had gotten his diagnosis, Andrew had reached out to the head of the organization, letting her know that his family might want to fund some large projects. This time, the Madoffs gave $6 million to the charity, making them the single largest donors in the history of the Leukemia & Lymphoma Society. Andrew was appointed to the board of their research foundation and invited to visit hospitals, labs, and research centers. He was greatly inspired by the cancer researchers and came to learn that nearly all of them had lost a parent, sibling, or spouse to cancer, subsequently dedicating their lives to eradicating the disease. The work, Andrew found, was fascinating and fulfilling; he loved it and wanted to learn more.

Soon, he became aware of another organization, called the Lymphoma Research Foundation. Its scientific advisory board included every top doctor in the field from around the world. Mantle cell lymphoma, Andrew knew, was woefully under-researched, too rare to attract funding, since it represented a mere 6 percent of all lymphomas. So Andrew approached the president of LRF, Suzanne Bliss, asking what he could do. She suggested he sponsor a conference to talk about mantle cell lymphoma; people who were doing research on the disease could submit proposals for funding. Andrew jumped at the opportunity, though he declined an invitation to attend the conference itself. He couldn't bear to hear one researcher after another start his or her presentation with the inevitable doomsday prediction: Everyone dies.

The researchers at the conference came up with a list of proposals for grants and submitted several dozen of them to the LRF for review. After a rigorous vetting process, the LRF's advisory board approved nine of them, totaling $11 million. Andrew approached his father and showed him the list of proposals, asking him to pick any that seemed worthy of funding.

"Fund them all," Bernie said.

Was he motivated by charity, his desire to people-please, or simply a need to play savior? Andrew says it was the last: "He was paralyzed with helplessness over my diagnosis and my refusal to let either of my parents play a role in my medical decisions. Finally, there was something he could actually do."

Used to having their work with mantle cell lymphoma largely ignored, the researchers were floored. Andrew was immediately appointed to the board of LRF, where he took an active role sifting through grant proposals with the help of a hired scientific consultant.

The following year, word got out and the conference doubled in size. New grants were proposed; Bernie funded them all again. Andrew soaked up as much knowledge as possible, attending scientific advisory board meetings, meeting with researchers, and reading as much as he could. Over the next few years, the Madoffs funded millions more in grants, the profile of the LRF skyrocketed, and the Mantle Cell Lymphoma Consortium became recognized as one of the most important lymphoma conferences in the world. Privy to debates most people never got to see, Andrew gained incredible insight into the process of cancer research. A passion was born.

The combination of cancer, the lack of a succession plan at BLM, and the fact that his marriage was running on "autopilot" completely extinguished any desire that Andrew had once had to take over his father's firm. He started spending less and less time in the office, focusing his energies on the LRF and a few new business endeavors instead. He and Debbie decided to move, so he gave Debbie the project of finding a new apartment for them, but she was back to spending four days a week with her horse in Pine Plains, so Andrew took it on himself, eventually choosing a $7 million apartment at 10 Gracie Square, one of Manhattan's most desirable addresses. The five-thousand-square-foot duplex boasted spectacular views, multiple fireplaces, and graceful balconies; when Andrew finished working with the designer, it was featured on the cover of *Elle Decor*. And yet the beautiful new apartment did nothing to fill the void he felt inside. On weekends, drifting along and fishing alone on his boat became an escape from his emotionally unfulfilling marriage.

Mark, too, had moved on. During one of his early morning workouts at Equinox gym, he'd met an attractive, energetic blonde named Stephanie Mikesell, and the two had gotten engaged. Susan made one last-ditch plea: "Are you sure you want to spend your life with this girl? Give me the chance to make it up to you so we can rebuild our lives together."

"I'm marrying Stephanie, Susan," Mark said, cutting her off.

Mark blamed his family for Susan's affair: They were too enmeshed and spent too much time together, making couple building impossible. Determined to do things differently, once he married Stephanie he kept his family at arm's length. Ruth and Bernie were told they could no longer speak to Susan.

In 2006, Andrew got a call from Jon at Urban Angler. He'd been approached by a company in the United Kingdom called Sportfish, which had an interest in the store. Jon didn't really want to sell to them but thought he should see what his options were. The year before, Urban Angler had looked into launching an online store and, as a result, needed a cash infusion. By then, Jon and Catherine had a five-month-old baby, and Catherine was considering leaving the business to form a family-preparedness consulting firm called the Contingency Group. Jon said he might want to move out of the city, buy a house, and sell his equity in the store. Andrew reviewed the financial statements and realized that the store didn't need a buyer—it merely needed an influx of cash. An investment in Urban Angler seemed like the perfect way to combine his love for business and fishing without having to move to Montana. It would also be part of his escape plan from BLM. So he made an offer, which Jon accepted, on the terms that he could play an active role in the company management.

But Andrew and Jon butted heads from the start. Jon had launched the business with his father in 1989, and Jon preferred to do things the way they'd always been done. Andrew pointed out that as times had changed, the store had started to founder; it needed a greater Internet presence, advertising, more space. Jon would go home and rail about Andrew to Catherine, who was on maternity leave with their daughter, Sophie, and writing a business plan of her own.

"He's making me crazy," Jon would complain. "He's terrible." Catherine would cluck sympathetically as she breast-fed their newborn, remembering the cocky trader she'd met at lunch. "The guy's a jerk," she agreed. "Making a deal with him was a mistake."

When Sophie turned one and stopped nursing full-time, Catherine returned to work at the store. Jon, who was at the end of his rope with Andrew, said, "I'm not dealing with this guy anymore. You deal with him."

I'm going to set this guy straight, she thought; I know how to be direct with him.

Andrew and Catherine met for breakfast at Brasserie, a modern French restaurant in Midtown. They sat down and exchanged niceties.

"Jon and I have had our differences, and I understand you're going to be my key contact at the company now," Andrew said. "That's fine with me, but I want to make sure we're not circumventing him. Is he OK with this?"

Catherine was pleasantly surprised that Andrew was so sensitive to professional dynamics.

"He prefers it, so if that's OK with you, we can get started."

They covered the agenda she had laid out for the discussion in record time. She had come in expecting to do battle, but she had met someone who didn't consider himself an opponent. As talk turned to their respective business strategies, Catherine found that all of the things Andrew wanted to do to grow the company were things she'd wanted to do for years. He hoped to revamp its struggling mail-order division. Streamline the layout. Open a second location, in New Orleans. Yes, she said, me too! Huddled over their coffee and eggs, they chatted excitedly, refining their dreams. As breakfast drew to a close, Andrew noticed a dog-eared book on Bach in her tote, about the Goldberg Variations.

"Are you reading that? I'm not a big fan of Bach, but I really love Brahms," he said, revealing that he'd been playing piano since he was young and that his piano teacher of fifteen years was a close friend. That, says Catherine, "humanized him." By the time they said their good-byes, she no longer saw an arrogant banker but a person she looked forward to working with.

By January 2007, Andrew was spending two days a week at Urban Angler, going through the books, learning how they did inventory and how the point-of-sale system worked. He loved getting behind the counter and dealing with customers, figuring out how to update their systems, even digging through boxes of merchandise.

For nineteen years, he had been working at a high level of intensity at BLM, where his days were increasingly plagued with family conflicts. The proprietary-trading desk he'd built was operating smoothly, and the manager he had brought on board to run it hardly needed his oversight. More and more, he was asking himself if he really wanted to spend the rest of his professional life tethered to a trading desk.

Bernie started to grumble that Andrew was "abandoning" his brother. Mark, he said, had told him as much. Stung by the accusation, Andrew approached his brother and told him what their father had claimed.

"I never told him that," Mark responded. "You want to leave? Leave. Do whatever you want."

Andrew pushed the envelope further, gathering his father and brother in a conference room for a confrontation. Bernie was forced to admit that Mark hadn't actually said those things.

"Then you need to stop hammering me with guilt!" Andrew cried. He was a man in his forties, in the process of building a dynamic new life, and yet his father could still cow him into submission with just a few words. With nothing resolved, he returned to his desk.

A trader at the firm introduced Andrew to the idea of buying oil and gas assets directly, instead of just investing in stocks. Andrew saw the possibility of forming an entirely new company: Madoff Energy. Combining his work at LRF, Urban Angler, and a new energy company that he would own himself promised a fun, engaging, and lucrative future.

But by summertime, Urban Angler's sales were falling and Andrew's investment was starting to look bad. He and Catherine began to have weekly strategy sessions about the store at Mangia, a coffee shop in Gramercy. "It was very professional," Andrew recalls.

"Yes, I enjoyed spending an hour with a beautiful woman, but she was also smart and knowledgeable and I wanted to hear her ideas. Unlike my job at BLM, which was always fraught with tension and politics, working with Catherine was thrillingly productive. I was excellent at spotting problems, and she had a knack for creating clever solutions almost instantly." Ready to take on a larger role in the company—partly driven by a crush on Catherine that he hadn't yet admitted to himself—he negotiated to buy Jon out. When the deal was done, Andrew went from having a 20 percent stake in the company to a 46 percent stake, making him the largest investor. Now he and Catherine were free to put their plans into action.

In September, Andrew traveled with the Urban Angler team to Denver for the International Fly Tackle Dealer Show. There they would meet all the fishing-supply manufacturers, see their new products, and place their orders for the upcoming year. Urban Angler held a special place in the industry; Andrew loved being at the convention as its representative and largest investor. One of their last meetings was with a company called Abel, which manufactured fishing reels. Don Swanson, the firm's president, whom Catherine had known for more than a decade, greeted them warmly. Rumors were swirling about the fate of Abel, but Don wasn't answering anyone's questions.

"Come on, Don. You've known me for years. You can tell me what's going on," Catherine said.

"All I can tell you is that the company changed hands, but the underlying financing turned out to be a mess. Now the bank is planning to auction off the company in the UK."

"What does a company like this cost?" Andrew asked.

"We're hoping to get it for under a million dollars," he said.

"Seriously?" he asked, aware that Abel was one of the best-known brands in the fly-fishing world. "Do you think you can get it for that price?"

Don nodded. "Sure. But at this point, we don't know where that money will come from."

"You do now. I will back you."

In the end, the company sold for more than Don's estimate, plus additional working capital. The deal required some complex due diligence: reviewing financials, ordering environmental studies, evaluating the liabilities to creditors, and settling a lawsuit against the company's founder. Catherine, Mark, Andrew, and a college friend of Mark's put up the capital, but it was Catherine and Andrew who managed the deal. During that tumultuous ten-week process, their weekly discussions grew more intense. The two started spending an enormous amount of time together, learning how the business ran, how the factory worked, and how it was going to fit into their plans for Urban Angler.

Andrew tried to ignore the obvious attraction between them, pushing it down as he had so many other things.

In September, Andrew and Catherine traveled to Los Angeles to visit Abel's offices. As usual, they flew separately to accommodate their schedules. Catherine had booked them into one of a hotelier friend's favorite Los Angeles hotels, the Sunset Marquis.

When Andrew arrived, Catherine was sitting by the pool with a childhood friend who lived in LA, a fashion photographer. Catherine had her hair in pin curls and wore a stylish black bathing suit and a silk wrap. Her legs were stretched out in front of her, her ankles crossed, her open-toed sandals revealing a glossy magenta pedicure.

She waved Andrew over, saying, "There's a screwup with the rooms; the hotel is overbooked. Is it OK with you if we share one of the two-bedroom apartments?"

"I knew in that moment I was head-over-heels in love," he recalls. "I was just gone. There was no chance I was going to survive this encounter intact. There was nothing I wanted more than her." He felt the sort of dizzy excitement he'd felt in college, when he'd managed to score a date with the elusive Diana Burns, or the time he'd rushed to the dorm room of a blond Swedish girl at 2:00 o'clock in the morning, professing his love. Yet here he was, forty-one years old and the father of two, having these feelings.

After the first rush of endorphins, Andrew's next feeling was one of "complete panic." He was, of course, still married. Oh, my God, he thought, what am I going to do? Am I really going to walk away from my marriage? What if this feeling fades?

Though he didn't know it, he needn't have worried. Catherine didn't feel the way he did—not yet, anyway. When Andrew had walked into the pool area at the Sunset Marquis, sporting a "terrible buzz cut" and wearing "giant balloon khakis with a million pleats and a shirt four sizes too big," Catherine's first thought was, He is so geeky.

It wasn't that she hadn't noticed the attraction—she had. But she was practiced at rebuffing the attention of the bankers and businessmen who frequented Urban Angler. And she didn't have to ask herself the questions that Andrew was grappling with; after all, he wasn't an option for her. He was married. He'd had a particularly virulent form of cancer and could still die. He had two preteen daughters, and she had a two-year-old. The last thing she needed in her life right now was a man—particularly this one.

That streak of independence came from her roots. Catherine Heather Hendren was born on August 1, 1972, in Columbus, Ohio, to parents in their early twenties. By the time she was two, her mother had decided to leave her father. As Catherine's sole caretaker, she paid the bills with waitressing and working in retail, even doing light construction work in the summer months. By the time Catherine was in third grade, her mother owned an independent bookstore. From early on, Catherine learned that the answers to everything she needed to know could be found inside books.

In the early 1980s, her mother remarried and sold her business. The family moved to Glens Falls, New York, a town so all-

remake its legend. With no clue about how to structure a deal or how to raise money, she turned to the solution of her childhood: reading everything she could get her hands on, this time about the retail business. She took a class in retail accounting and the mathematics of merchandise buying, opened a business bank account, and approached her husband for the start-up capital.

At first, Susan loved the idea. But as they solidified the deal in writing, she changed her mind. Her son, David, who was only a few years older than Catherine, had plans to take over the store himself. After months of preparations and talks, the deal was dead—along with Catherine's plans for her future. "There was a lot of sitting on the sofa at two AM, sobbing," Catherine recalls.

In March 2000, while in line at the grocery store, she picked up a copy of the now-defunct *Sports Illustrated for Women*. In it was an article by a young, unknown writer named Elizabeth Gilbert (later the author of *Eat, Pray, Love*) about the sport of fly-fishing. Gilbert had traveled to a remote location in Venezuela and written a beautiful piece about finding her soul through fishing. I want to have that experience, Catherine thought.

A few days after reading the piece, she called the store in New York that had booked the trip: Urban Angler. Within a matter of days, Catherine was on a plane to Caracas.

The trip was eye-opening: In Caracas, her driver flew through red lights at night, explaining that it was safer to drive though them than to stop. On her morning flight from Caracas to Los Roques, a group of sun-bleached islands in Venezuela's part of the Caribbean Sea, other passengers talked on their mobile phones and smoked. It was not Glens Falls, or Philadelphia. It wasn't even the first world.

On the main island, Gran Roque, Gilbert's guide, Felipe, greeted her. He barely gave her time to set down her bags before leading her to the flats, where shimmering, translucent bonefish swam. Although they were nearly invisible, scaring just one of them resulted in an eruption of the entire flat. How did I not see all those fish? Catherine would ask herself with wonder as hundreds instantly changed direction at her feet.

For miles, Catherine and Felipe walked in silence along the edges of mangroves, hunting and walking in a meditative flow. "I think we said three words to each other," Catherine recalls. The two cast lines over and over until she learned how to feel the fish and land them. "I still couldn't cast worth a damn," she recalls, "but I had this joyous feeling of having accomplished something."

For four days, she walked on the flats with Felipe, casting lines, marveling at the beauty around her, and "feeling" the fish.

On the last day, as her plane lifted from the runway, she took one final look at the shimmering water below. Though she knew it was impossible, she had the distinct sensation that she could see the fish, flickering and glinting just beneath the waves. This cannot be the last time that I do this, she thought. I want to do this forever.

Weeks later, Catherine and Tom spent the weekend in New York, and she paid a visit to Urban Angler. Felipe had told her, "You have to talk to this guy, Jon. He knows everything." Catherine climbed the narrow stairwell to the third floor and opened the door to the next stage of her life. Model boats were hanging from the ceiling; people were tying flies; Tom Brokaw was browsing in the aisles. In that moment, her purpose became crystal clear: It didn't work out to buy Sophy Curson, because I'm supposed to buy this business, she thought.

Without even realizing she was doing it, she started to build two separate worlds. Every few days she would travel to New York City to visit Urban Angler and talk to Jon about the possibility of buying into the business. Then she'd travel back to Philadelphia and spend half the week with Tom. She bought gear for trout and bonefishing, returned to Los Roques, and explored new destinations, such as the Seychelles' Outer Islands.

It took her a very long time, she says, to accept the fact that she was not going to be able to have her fairy-tale life in the suburbs and also run a business in New York that would be the absolute focus of her life. A year after their visit to Urban Angler, she and Tom parted ways yet remained close friends.

Catherine and Jon started working together and romantic feelings developed. Marriage held no appeal for Catherine, but the two fell into an easy intimacy, and six years into their relationship, when she was thirty-two, she learned she was pregnant. "I just thought, this might not be the world's best relationship or perfect set of circumstances, and I have plenty I want to do with my life that I will have to put on hold, but this is my baby."

It was too bad, she thought, that the father of her child was not her soul mate, but she'd given up on that idea. She didn't yet know what a soul mate was.

Chapter Eight

CATHERINE AND
ANDREW IN LOVE

By October of 2007, the deal to buy Abel had been solidified and Andrew had turned over management of the equities desk to his brother. He spent as little time as possible in the office, focusing instead on his work at Urban Angler, Abel, and the ambitious venture he'd started six months earlier: Madoff Energy.

In March, a trader at BLM who dealt in energy stocks had presented Andrew with a number of opportunities to invest directly in energy properties. Oil was starting its first major ascent to $100 a barrel and the economics in those projects were "absurdly good." Eventually, Andrew was offered an opportunity to invest in a natural gas well in East Texas. In exchange for providing short-term financing for the middleman negotiating the deal, Andrew would receive a piece of the well. He put up several million dollars and financed eight different wells, eventually becoming part owner of all of them.

The company had the potential to generate enormous amounts of money for Andrew, Mark, and their cousin Shana, all of whom had invested. But it also served a much more important function for Andrew: It was a way for him to establish credibility in a business that was completely disconnected from BLM. And given what was happening on Wall Street at the time, he needed that validation. The mortgage crisis was well on its way to toppling some of Wall Street's biggest banks and insurance companies. Though the proprietary trading business at BLM was doing well, it was still subject to the fluctuations of the markets. The entire office was feeling the heat, and Andrew found himself unloading to Catherine during their weekly meetings at Mangia.

"So why do you even keep your toe in the door?" she asked. "You're forty-two years old and running your own business. Get your own office space. Every time you bring this up, all you talk about is family disputes and office politics. That's horrible, negative energy, and you're sitting right in the middle of it." But the last thing Andrew felt he could do was abandon his father and brother—especially with the markets in such a state of flux.

His life, he knew, was about to experience major upheaval. He was falling in love with Catherine. But he agonized over whether to leave his marriage. *Maybe things aren't so bad*, he kept telling himself. *We share two beautiful daughters.* And he hadn't yet shared his feelings with Catherine—what if she didn't return them? Day after day, he weighed the pros and cons in his head, oscillating wildly.

In early November, Catherine flew to Edinburgh to meet with the managing owner of Sportfish, Colin Rutherford. For years, the dashing businessman had made entreaties to Urban Angler, trying to coax Catherine to come and work for him. Rutherford wanted to turn the company into a business like Orvis, selling fishing gear, luggage, and apparel. It was a dream job, everything Catherine wanted Urban Angler to be. On the plane to Edinburgh she read Sylvia Jukes Morris's *Rage for Fame: The Ascent of Clare Boothe Luce*. Catherine underlined a sentence taken from Clare Boothe Luce's journal: "I'm not living my life for anybody but myself from now on."

When she and Andrew had stayed at the Sunset Marquis, she had noticed the way he'd looked at her by the pool. The second night there, they'd had a working dinner at a steakhouse on Sunset. Walking back to the hotel, as they were crossing a side street, Andrew had guided her to a safer place, away from the traffic. The small gesture had caught her off guard and given rise to a powerful feeling that Andrew would always protect her. Catherine, who was, she says, "always the aggressor" in her relationships, relished the unfamiliar sensation. That night, as they sat on the couch in the living room of the large apartment, watching *Battlestar Galactica* on her computer and each putting off going to bed, she'd had the feeling that she was on a roller coaster, going up, up, up, toward the peak. Something was coming—something inevitable—and she felt powerless to stop it.

That last morning, on their way to the airport in a Hertz van, Catherine couldn't stop smelling her own "overpowering" perfume. Convinced her body chemistry was reacting to the feelings she was having, she faced an uncomfortable truth. She not only needed to end things with Jon—and to get out of their shared business—but she probably also needed to get away from Andrew. Catherine found herself writing in her journal about all the reasons she couldn't ever allow herself to fall in love with Andrew. He was married—not happily, she knew, but married nonetheless. He had cancer; it was a bad idea to fall in love with somebody who might die young. They would have to break up their children's homes—and of course their hearts. Then there was the fact of his staggering wealth: Was he really going to go through an ugly, protracted multimillion-dollar divorce just so they could explore their relationship? And... and... This cannot be happening, she told herself. There's no way I can surrender to these feelings that are stirring, because then they might grow.

Married, cancer, kids, she kept repeating to herself.

★　　★　　★

"The hell you will!" Andrew found himself shouting on the phone to Catherine. He was in his study; Debbie was in the living room next door. He didn't care. He couldn't control the wild feelings of anger rising up through his chest. His face was red. He raked his fingers through his hair, paced in front of his desk.

"You are not moving to London to work for Colin Rutherford!"

It hadn't occurred to Andrew that Catherine could disappear. He'd thought the decision was his to make. He was the one who was married, after all. The second the prospect of losing her was dangled in front of him, every ounce of doubt he was having vanished. The question was no longer *maybe*. He was ending his marriage.

That Sunday, as he was sitting on his docked boat on an overcast afternoon, he finally worked up the courage to call. She answered breathlessly. He didn't hesitate to say the words. "I love you." She didn't say it back; she just listened.

They avoided seeing each other in the ensuing days and kept their phone calls professional. She needed to be on her own for a while and not jump into a new relationship. Still, she couldn't deny that her feelings were changing.

The following Saturday, as Andrew watched a movie with Emily, his phone buzzed with an incoming e-mail. It was from Catherine. Andrew's heart pounded as he opened it. She'd taken a photograph of some graffiti scrawled above the sign for Waterloo Street. "I love you," it read.

It was all the confirmation he needed.

The following weeks were a blur of gut-wrenching conversations with Debbie, who wasn't entirely surprised; she couldn't miss how much time he'd been spending with Catherine. After days of anger and tears, the two broke the news to their kids and Andrew moved into a temporary rental on 84th Street and First Avenue. He spent his first few nights with high school friends and often cried, missing his girls.

Within a matter of weeks, the initial shock wore off and he started to appreciate his new life. He cooked the same meals he'd cooked as a bachelor, remembering how much he'd enjoyed them. He got to help his daughters decorate their new rooms. He grew comfortable with the idea that he hadn't left his marriage for Catherine—he'd left because his marriage was over. Hopefully, things would work out with Catherine, but if they didn't, that was OK: He would move forward on his own, creating a new life for himself. He felt, he says, like "the happiest man alive."

Catherine moved into a loft in Long Island City, Queens. It was a month after that, in February of 2008, that Catherine and Andrew shared their first kiss and consummated their relationship at the Waldorf Astoria Hotel. On Valentine's Day, Andrew visited Catherine's apartment for the first time. One of the brand-new building's first tenants, she hadn't yet furnished the large, raw space. A pair of roller skates in Andrew's size were leaning against the front door, along with a note: "Don't ring the bell until you put these on." Bristling with anticipation, he laced up the skates, rang the doorbell, and waited. Catherine opened the door, wearing a cheerleading uniform and skates of her own. Miley Cyrus was blasting from her stereo system. She smiled at him and took off, expecting to throw him off balance. Andrew once again surprised her, demonstrating his "mad skating skills," the result of years of playing hockey. For an hour, they zipped around the room, embracing, kissing, laughing, skating backward, and performing tricks. After years spent in unfulfilling relationships, both felt like they were experiencing first love all over again.

And those first few months were dreamlike: Catherine traveled to a health retreat called the Ashram in Calabasas, California, for a previously planned trip, then met Andrew in Los Angeles for a weekend at the Chateau Marmont Hotel. They had too much champagne at the Bar Marmont, where Catherine crawled across a banquette, climbed into Andrew's lap, and started "attacking and kissing" him, people watching and clapping. Later, in New York, they picnicked in Central Park with Sophie, visited museums, introduced each other to their favorite hole-in-the-wall restaurants. All the things a new couple does in the first flush of love.

Andrew, in particular, felt his world crack wide open. Suddenly he was dating the most glamorous woman he'd ever met: She wore dresses, big hats, boas, and gloves. Everywhere they went, says Andrew, heads turned, jaws dropped, and he found himself saying, "I'm with her." Even more exciting than the element of drama her sartorial choices provided were her honesty and self-awareness, her openness and ability to talk about feelings. She didn't have his wealth, but she managed to live a luxurious life anyway, staying in magnificent homes around the world, thanks to the friendships she'd made. Andrew, used to traveling in circles where unhappy marriages were the norm, suddenly found himself surrounded by "happy single people, happy married people, happy divorced people, happy old people, happy young people." Normally, he would have been very dismissive of that "Wavy Gravy stuff," but once he became a part of it, he wanted her to teach him everything she knew. For him, their union was "an awakening in every sense of the word."

Catherine, too, felt as though she were being taken on a safari into a different world. She found Andrew "dignified and honorable, decent and kind, a little more rules-y and proper than I was, but I needed that. He inspired me to be a better person, and when I was with him, I felt like my best self." Had it not been for the storm clouds gathering within Andrew's family, he would have called the first months of 2008 the happiest of his life.

By March, Andrew was spending most of his time out of the office, but he still saw his brother almost every day. He'd confided in Mark about his feelings for Catherine as early as December, after the three had taken a trip to California to visit Abel. "He wasn't so supportive, and it wasn't clear to me why," Andrew says. "I just knew that I was in love and wanted my brother's support and I wasn't getting it. That was very painful to me."

Once Andrew started dating Catherine openly, Mark made his suspicions more clear: Who is this girl? How well do you really know her? You're not even divorced, yet; isn't it a little soon to be getting into a new relationship? She's a single mom; you must look like a pretty good meal ticket to her.

Mark wasn't the only person in the Madoff family distrustful of Catherine's motives. Andrew's parents, uncle Peter, and cousin Shana all expressed concerns.

She's not Jewish. *Where'd* she grow up? She never married the father of her child?

"The family was like a club—either you were in or you were out, and there was a natural suspicion about any outsider," Andrew says. "I knew my family was 'concerned.' But their concern was this amorphous, disembodied cloud of doubt that couldn't be pinned down to any root cause. And I was vulnerable to it because I felt obligated to check in with these people I loved and respected. I didn't want them to feel like I was going through life in a reckless fashion, or was going to get hurt because I didn't heed their warnings. So my instinct was to listen to them, and that ended up being a mistake."

Catherine, at first, was oblivious to the family dynamics. The first time she met Bernie, she had gone to Andrew's office for a conference call with Abel. As she sat in the conference room taking notes, she spotted Bernie through the glass, standing next to Mark at the trading desk. When Bernie caught her eye, he smiled flirtatiously and fluttered his fingers at her. She found his flirting "charmingly inappropriate," more cute than creepy, and dismissed it.

"He seems nice," she said to Andrew.

"Wait until you get to know him a little better."

In March of 2008, two months after they'd started dating, she would accompany Andrew to her first family function: Mark's forty-fourth birthday party, at Lure Fishbar in SoHo. By then, she'd caught whispers of family discord: There had been "tremendous back-and-forth" about whether she should be allowed at the party. You're barely out of the house, Andrew's parents had argued; should you even be dating? Mark's wife Stephanie had lobbied for her presence, perhaps looking for an ally in the impenetrable Madoff clan.

Anxiously, Catherine got dressed, choosing a royal blue tunic with an obi-style sash. Before she left the apartment, she calmed her nerves with a few sips of champagne.

The party was in full swing when they arrived: Fifteen close friends and family members mingled about the room, eating the gluten-free cake that had been made especially for Mark. Adam Stracher, the family doctor, was there, as was Devin Okay, the family dentist: When it came to the Madoffs, one medical professional served the entire extended family. Ruth and Bernie were there. Andrew pointed out a few traders from BLM and a couple who were friends of Mark and Stephanie's. Seeing so many old friends, Andrew moved about the room, leaving Catherine to fend for herself. Friends of Mark and Stephanie cornered Catherine first.

"I introduced Mark and Stephanie at the gym," said the woman, shouting over the music. "I told her, give him a shot. He's great-looking and rich—what could go wrong, right?" She laughed, revealing a mouthful of canapé.

"My first thought was, I am not in Kansas anymore," Catherine recalls. "They struck me as very frank about money and status. But I loved Andrew, so I knew this would be part of the package."

Catherine exchanged her first words with Bernie that night, when he pulled her aside. "Hi, I need to talk to you," he started, but he was drowned out by the music. Thinking the conversation had lagged—and spotting Ruth, whom she hadn't yet spoken to—Catherine had hurried away.

Nervously, Catherine made her way over to Ruth, who had been avoiding eye contact with her ever since she'd walked into the room. It was the first time she had met Andrew's mother, and she desperately wanted to make a good first impression on the tiny, perfectly coiffed blonde. Ruth broke into a wide smile when Catherine approached.

"Look at you, you're so pretty, and you're wearing such beautiful shoes!" she cried. "I can't wear high heels anymore because my feet are messed up. But if I could, I'd wear shoes just like that."

Catherine felt her shoulders start to relax. The two chatted warmly for a few more minutes but then were separated by the crowd. Later that evening, Catherine found herself next to Ruth again and said the words she'd been practicing in her head all night.

"I know it's not easy for anyone that Andrew and I are dating. But I want you to know that I really care about him and don't intend to hurt him in any way."

Ruth smiled warmly and squeezed Catherine's arm. "I'm so happy to hear that."

Then Andrew rushed over.

"Hey, you just walked away from my dad in the middle of a sentence."

"Oh, really? I hadn't realized," Catherine said. She apologized.

"Go talk to him," Andrew urged.

Catherine returned to where Bernie was standing. He immediately picked up where he'd left off.

"I want you to know that he's not from money, despite what you see," he said. As Catherine listened in stunned silence, he continued, "I know you think he's a rich guy, but we're from nothing. My father was broke. We're humble people."

Recovering, Catherine said, "Well, that's perfect because my mom and stepdad are a couple of hippies who live on a farm. And I wasn't raised to care about that." To her relief, Andrew appeared and introduced her to some new arrivals.

In retrospect, she wonders if Bernie was trying to warn her: If you're here for the money—think again.

Chapter Nine

FAMILY TIES

Catherine had received high grades at Mark's birthday party, and Andrew was relieved. He'd gotten pats on the back from friends; even his parents had offered a tentative nod of approval. And one thing Andrew desperately craved was family unity. During his marriage to Debbie, his brother and wife had pitched epic battles against each other. After Mark married Stephanie, there had been tension between his new wife and Debbie, culminating in a shouting match at a family event. There were days when Andrew felt like the referee in a boxing ring.

With Catherine, he hoped all that would change. She and Stephanie were close in age, with daughters the same age. If the two got along, Andrew's private life would be far more peaceful.

With Andrew's hopes weighing on her shoulders, Catherine rode the elevator to Mark and Stephanie's fourth-floor loft in the elegant New Museum Building in SoHo. Stephanie had suggested she stop by for an informal get-together before Catherine was set to drive out of town to a friend's house for the weekend. The visit would have to be quick, but Catherine was looking forward to getting to know Stephanie in person, rather than hearing about her from a distance.

"She's sensitive," Andrew had warned. "Just make sure you don't say anything that could be taken the wrong way."

Catherine told Andrew not to worry. She knew that Stephanie, the daughter of Pinks London, an attractive Upper East Side blonde, and stepdaughter of Marty London, a well-known litigator, had worked as an administrative assistant to designer Narciso Rodriguez before she'd married Mark. If the conversation flagged, they could always talk about their shared experiences in the fashion industry.

The doors of the elevator slid open, revealing an imposing metal door that looked like a bank vault. Stephanie pulled it open as the elevator came to a stop. She was dressed casually in jeans, a striped T-shirt, and black Converse low-top sneakers. With her fine blond hair clipped into a chin-length bob, she was a dead ringer for the Ruth that Catherine knew from the childhood pictures on Andrew's mantel.

"Welcome, Catherine, come on in."

They hugged.

"You look great. Did you cut your hair?"

"I *just* cut it. Chopped it all off. Look what else I just did."

Stephanie pulled up her sleeve to reveal a black star tattoo on her inner arm.

"Is that real?" Catherine asked.

"Totally!"

"You must have thought about it for a long time."

"No, I was just walking by the tattoo place, and thought, Why not?"

So Stephanie was not the shrinking violet Andrew had made her out to be, Catherine decided. She was a risk taker. She invited Catherine to follow her into the apartment.

And what an apartment it was. With its soaring ceilings and enormous windows, industrial lamps harvested from old film sets, and Navajo rugs, the Ralph Lauren–influenced loft was on par with anything splashed across the pages of *Architectural Digest*. Every piece of furniture suited the grand scale: Giant coffee-colored leather sofas could comfortably seat a basketball team; a rough-hewn Indonesian dining table ran the length of the window bays; a lap pool–size gas fireplace dominated the room.

"I'll show you around," Stephanie said. She led Catherine into the kitchen, where stainless-steel appliances gleamed in the late-afternoon light. A graceful Biedermeier chest served as an extra pantry, and a collection of antique rolling pins, displayed on museum mounts, rested along the tops of the custom cabinetry. A nanny fed Audrey at the massive kitchen island.

"This place is beautiful. You have incredible design sensibilities."

Stephanie shrugged as if to say, This old place? She led Catherine toward the home office, where hundreds of pictures of Mark, Stephanie, and Audrey smiled down from plexiglass blocks. As they passed through the back bedrooms, Stephanie pointed out the custom draperies, shutters, and cabinetry.

"Susan Blumenfeld worked with you on this, right?" Catherine asked as she admired the fineness of the woodworking. Susan was Ruth's best friend, and a successful real-estate developer and commercial interior designer. She was the only person detail oriented enough to satisfy Bernie's need for absolute perfection.

"Who told you that?" Stephanie asked.

Oh, no, Catherine thought. What did I say? It's been ten minutes and I've already stepped in it.

"Andrew did—I mean, I think."

"The design of these shutters came from my old apartment. I picked everything out myself."

"It's...it's obvious that this design is really personal."

"Do you want some coffee?" Stephanie asked, at once flashing back to the pretty, smiling woman who had answered the door.

Back in the kitchen, Stephanie pulled mugs from the cabinet.

"So, have you met Andy's kids?"

"Of course. We've been friends a long time, so I met them before we got together. But I haven't met them in the context of being his girlfriend, no."

"Are you worried about it?"

"No. It will happen one day, when the time is right."

"Don't let Andy do to you what Mark did to me," Stephanie confided as they sipped coffee.

Catherine felt her stomach do a little flip.

"Mark didn't want to tell his kids about our relationship," Stephanie continued. "When they came to our apartment on the weekends, he would say I was just a friend. He made me sleep in the guest room."

"But now you're married, which is great."

"It's not over now. He's always off to some family function. Is every single one important?"

Catherine sighed. "To be honest, Stephanie, Andrew's the same way. There is no way, no matter how close we become, that I will ever be as important to him as his daughters. I knew that going in. I accept that."

Stephanie thought for a moment. "I guess I can't."

Catherine nodded. It *was* hard to accept. They were all living with families patched together like quilts. Hurt feelings and confused loyalties were inevitable.

"You have a great relationship with Mark's kids now, though, right? That's what is important."

Stephanie frowned. "Kate's bat mitzvah is coming up in a couple of months. I'm not comfortable going, but he's insisting, no matter how much I can't stand to be in the same room with Susan. Or Debbie."

Catherine took a deep breath and placed her coffee cup on the table. "It's not easy," she agreed. If she and Andrew wound up together forever, she would probably face some of the same challenges.

As Catherine rode the elevator back down to the street, she cursed herself for the gaffe she had made. It had seemed innocuous enough, but perhaps Stephanie *was* sensitive. She's Andrew's sister-in-law and Mark's wife; that's all I need to know, Catherine told herself. At the same time, she wondered just how many times she could put her foot in her mouth before she became the person with whom Stephanie couldn't stand to be in the same room.

There were bigger things going on in the world to worry about than family dynamics—both for Catherine and Andrew. On March 16, 2008, Bear Stearns had collapsed, shaking Wall Street to its core. Two days earlier, the Federal Reserve had extended an emergency line of credit to the storied brokerage firm, intervening for the first time in its history. As a result, the Dow had plummeted nearly 200 points. In the ensuing weeks, the atmosphere at BLM was one of guarded panic.

Given the turmoil on Wall Street, Andrew felt increasingly confident about his decision to step away from the trading desk. Both he and Catherine had sold their equity in Urban Angler that January and were immersed in new professional projects. Catherine had landed a consulting gig at Christian Dior, and Andrew accompanied her to company events when she needed to make an appearance. When Andrew wasn't traveling with Catherine or spending time with his children, he was visiting Abel vendors around the country and attending to his administrative duties as the newly elected chairman of the Lymphoma Research Foundation.

"Where are you? When are you coming back?"

"We were looking for you. We didn't know where you were."

Mark and Peter, but especially Bernie, acted as though Andrew had never left. They called often, asking "all kinds of questions that could have been answered without me." He thought eventually they would give up. As the weeks turned into months, they still hadn't. It was time, Andrew decided, to leave BLM altogether.

He approached his father in the glass-walled office he kept on the nineteenth floor, where Bernie sat behind his desk, sifting through papers.

"Hi. What's up?"

"You know I've been spending a lot of time on Madoff Energy."

"Yes, I'm happy you've found something you enjoy doing so much. That's important."

"I need to get in there, take a more active role in the business."

"Uh-huh."

"It's taking an increasing amount of my time and attention. I need to hire more people."

"What are you saying?"

"I'd like to take office space somewhere else."

Bernie hit the roof.

"You can't do this. You're abandoning your brother. This is unacceptable."

"Hear me out. There are a million things I'm interested in."

"Have I ever tried to stop you?" Bernie raged.

"The business is capital intensive, and I'd need money to get it started. You could invest if you wanted. It could be hugely lucrative and diversify the family assets."

"It's bad enough that you've been spending time in a fly shop. The market's very tumultuous. Your brother is suffering."

"I know, but..."

"Everything you need is here in the office! We have lawyers, support staff, supplies, computers."

"I know that. And I'm grateful. But I'm ready to strike out on my own."

"After everything I've done for you!"

It was a different version of the conversation he'd had with his father dozens of times about the succession plan, bringing with it the same feelings of guilt, confusion, and shame. As always, Andrew's mind started to look for ways to rationalize Bernie's seemingly irrational edict. All businesses had issues, including politics that had to be navigated at the senior levels. His father was right to point out the tremendous infrastructure already in place at 885 Third Avenue. Setting up Madoff Energy within the confines of the Lipstick Building obviated the need to hire the dozen support staff Andrew would require to run the business at the scale he envisioned.

Andrew didn't want to be some whiny rich kid who bolted at the first sign of trouble. Nor had he ever lost sight of the many advantages he'd enjoyed by being a Madoff. Bernie *had* brought Andrew into the business. Paid for apartments, vacations, and cars. Given him emotional support through Debbie's infidelity and his subsequent cancer treatments. Funded every cancer research proposal Andrew had put in front of him. And this was how he repaid him?

Andrew knew when he was defeated. Just as he had so many times before, he threw up his hands and left his father's office.

It never occurred to Andrew to question why his father was so adamant about keeping him close to the business. The truth, as we now know, was that Bernie needed the presence of both his sons in the trading room to perpetuate his scheme without raising red flags.

"In hindsight, it's obvious that the fact that we were there provided cover," says Andrew. "He used us as a shield. He would parade clients through the legitimate trading operation, then sit down with them in a conference room for an hour. I have no idea what his preamble was. He may have lied to them about the role we played in the firm, but I don't know, because he never actually put us in front of investors. He knows we would have told them what we actually did, which had nothing to do with his asset-management business. The fact that they could physically see us in the trading room, working, might have lent to the air of legitimacy. Maybe the people at the firm who were in on it would have panicked if they'd seen us jumping ship."

Andrew stayed put.

In May, Catherine asked Andrew if he thought she should invite Ruth to have coffee sometime before Mother's Day weekend. While they would be away for the weekend itself, they were planning to come back in time for Sunday night dinner, and Catherine thought it might be a nice, informal way for her and Ruth to get acquainted.

"Do you think it's the right time, since we've only been dating for a few months?"

"Absolutely," Andrew said. "She would love to get to know you better."

The next time Andrew spoke to his brother, he told him about his upcoming weekend. Debbie wanted to take the girls away for the weekend, and Sophie would be with her father, so Andrew and Catherine were planning to visit their mutual friend Jeffrey Cardenas, an accomplished saltwater angler, in Key West. They would spend each day deep in the Marquesas, fishing for giant tarpon with tiny flies. He mentioned offhand that Catherine would be calling their mother to invite her to coffee.

"You gave her permission to do that?" Mark asked, sounding incredulous. "It's way too soon. She can't be contacting Mom."

Mark, four (right), and Andrew, two, at Lloyd Neck, Long Island, in 1968.

Mark (standing) and Andrew on the flying bridge of the *Bull* in Montauk, 1972.

Chub Cay in 1970. Mark (in boat) and Andrew with their Boston Whaler.

In the cockpit of the *Bull,* Montauk, 1974. Bernie would later replace the *Bull* with a fifty-six-foot Rybovich sport-fishing boat that he would own until his arrest.

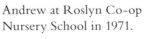
Andrew at Roslyn Co-op
Nursery School in 1971.

Andrew, Ruth, and Mark at
Mark's bar mitzvah, in 1977.

Andrew and Mark at
the bar mitzvah.

Andrew lands one of his first
fish in Montauk, 1974.

Fishing on the *Bull* in Montauk, 1972.

The Madoffs celebrate Andrew's twelfth birthday at Chub Cay, 1978.

Ruth in 1969, the center of her sons' lives.

A happy moment that Andrew would later write about for his school paper: catching a 315-pound bluefin tuna off Montauk. Bernie and his longtime captain look on with pride.

The American Jewish Congress honored Bernie in 1986. Bernie's numerous accolades would both impress and intimidate his sons.

The Madoffs on a family ski vacation in Aspen on Valentine's Day 1984.

Mark, Ruth, and Andrew at a cousin's wedding in 1985.

Andrew graduating from the Wharton School of the University of Pennsylvania, in 1988.

Bernie and Mark in the pool at the Montauk house in the late 1980s.

Mark, Bernie, and Andrew don tuxedos for Mark's wedding to Susan Freeman, in 1989.

Mark at Ruth and Bernie's 64th Street apartment in 1991. It was in this apartment that Bernie would later confess to his crimes.

The "boys" at a firm cocktail party in 2006, a year before Andrew would step away from the business.

Ruth with Andrew, fourteen (left), and Mark, sixteen, on the way home from hockey practice, 1980.

Ruth and Bernie on the beach at the Breakers in 2003.

At the 1986 American Jewish Congress event honoring Bernie. As always, Ruth is by his side.

Ruth and Bernie at a securities industry convention in Boca Raton.

A Montauk weekend in the early 1990s.

"She asked if it was OK with me, and I said yes," Andrew protested.

"No, no, no, no. You need to control your woman."

Andrew laughed off the comment, but when he got off the phone, he asked Catherine to hold off on calling Ruth. "If it's going to be that irksome to Mark when he's so upset over the markets, it's probably better to wait," he said.

Catherine said nothing, continuing to pack their shared suitcase.

As Andrew and Catherine flew down the highway from Miami to Key West in a rented convertible, Andrew reassured her that the right time would come. "Mark said I needed to control you," he added.

Catherine squeezed her eyes and pinched the bridge of her nose, feeling a headache start to develop. "Doesn't that sound crazy to you?"

Andrew sighed. "That's my brother. That's Mark all the way."

This relationship isn't going to work out, she thought. He's in love with his brother.

As Catherine and Andrew settled into their room in the little guesthouse they'd booked, Andrew found a group e-mail Stephanie had sent, announcing that she had scheduled Mother's Day dinner at a bistro named Raoul's. Sadly, the restaurant was able to accommodate them only an hour before Andrew and Catherine's flight was due to land in New York.

"It's too bad we'll miss it," Catherine said as she unpacked their fly rods.

"We're going to that dinner," Andrew insisted angrily. He canceled their return flights and chartered a small private plane that would bring them back in time for the party.

Two days of fishing in the Keys with Cardenas provided a magical, welcome respite from the tension brewing at home. Each morning, they set out before dawn, buying Cuban coffees from the back of a Laundromat near the docks. After a twenty-mile run in the boat through pounding chop, they explored the Marquesas, a protected atoll with gorgeous white-sand beaches. Every few hours they would leave the tackle behind on the boat and stroll along the water's edge, holding hands. Then they took the plane back to New York, still wearing their fishing clothes.

When they walked into Raoul's, they found the restaurant empty, save for the table occupied by the Madoff party: Bernie; Ruth; Mark; Stephanie; her stepfather, Marty London; and Stephanie's mother, brother, and his wife. The waiter brought extra chairs for them. Stephanie reached into her bag and said, "I have presents for everybody. Here you go." She handed a small wrapped gift to every woman at the table except Catherine—maybe it was possible she hadn't realized they were coming, Catherine thought, but then she noticed that Stephanie wouldn't make eye contact.

Ruth quickly said, "I have presents for everybody, too. Catherine, this one's for you." As Catherine unwrapped three wooden bangles, she felt Stephanie's eyes on her. Oblivious to the tension that was unfolding, Marty London asked Bernie how he thought history might remember former U.S. secretary of the treasury Bob Rubin.

"I think he's more focused on his family and his policy ideas than on what the *Wall Street Journal* has to say tomorrow," Catherine interjected. "He said as much to me last summer in Montana."

Marty turned to Catherine with interest. "You know him?"

"He was one of my partners in Urban Angler."

"You wouldn't believe the connections she has," Bernie interrupted. "She knows all these Wall Street guys from fishing. She used to have this dinner where all these luminaries would come;

she would be the only woman invited. And she introduced them to Andy." His face registered pride.

Catherine glanced fearfully at Mark. She immediately regretted mentioning Bob Rubin. The move sounded like name-dropping and had brought her too much attention from Bernie. Mark was glaring at Andrew. Was he not *controlling her* well enough? she wondered.

Catherine shifted the conversation to fastidiousness, a topic she knew would interest Bernie. "I like everything to be clean, but I need the insides of my drawers to be organized, too; all the cutlery needs to be lined up," she said. She turned to Bernie. "What type of organizer are you?"

"Oh, I'm not like that," he said. Then he offered a remark that would be meaningful only in hindsight: "I don't care what's inside the drawers; I just care about what people see."

Dinner finally came to an end. Ruth and Bernie gave Catherine a warm hug, and she and Andrew slipped into a taxi.

"That wasn't so bad, but I thought my brother's head was going to fly off when we walked in," Andrew mused as they smoothly maneuvered through traffic.

"Your mother was nice to me. I won't forget that." She fingered the wooden bangles in her purse as the cab wove through traffic.

Of course Andrew's phone was ringing again, only thirty minutes after he'd left the office. He was now late for a board meeting at the Lymphoma Research Foundation. Glancing quickly at his phone, he saw that his brother was calling. Frowning, he held his Black-Berry up to his ear. Now what?

"Where the hell are you? You need to get back here!" Mark was shouting at the top of his lungs. He was apoplectic, out of his mind.

"What happened? What's going on? Is everything all right?"

"If you want to maintain your relationship as my brother, you need to get back to this office right this minute!" he screamed. With all the rages Andrew had witnessed, he'd never heard his brother like this.

"I can't. I'm running to a board meeting. I'm the chairman, I can't miss it. Tell me what happened. Why are you screaming at me?"

Mark hung up. Andrew looked at his phone, blinking. That morning, he'd stopped by the office to check in with Mark. He'd shown him pictures of the tarpon he and Catherine had caught, as well as a video of Catherine hooking a giant tarpon, losing it, then hooking another one as she pulled the line in. Mark, he remembered, had remained curiously silent during that conversation. He put his phone into his jacket pocket and continued on to his meeting.

The minute Andrew stepped onto the trading floor, Mark charged at him, hustling him into a little conference room behind their desk.

"Do you want to know what your girlfriend said to me? She said I'm a bad parent! How dare she judge me as a parent!" His face was bright red, the veins in his neck thick, ropy cords.

"Take it easy," Andrew said. Through the glass, he could see traders craning their necks. Andrew feared his brother was going to have a heart attack and die, right there in front of him. "What are you talking about? You talked to Catherine?"

"She said all these horrible things about Daniel and Kate!"

"What? I can't imagine...let me at least call her, OK? Let me see what she has to say."

"She's an awful witch and you need to leave her immediately!" he screamed and stormed out of the conference room.

Andrew sat at the table, breathing heavily. He dialed Catherine at her apartment.

"Did something happen with my brother?" he asked.

"He called me. Why?"

"Because he's hysterical. He's screaming at me, saying you said all this stuff."

Catherine sighed. "He told me to stop seeing you, Andrew. He said I was ruining your life, destroying your relationship with your kids, and driving your career into the ground. I told him that I understood he felt that way, and that you and I had both heard him and would make our own choices. Then I told him it was time to mind his own business."

Andrew grimaced, knowing precisely how angry that last comment would make Mark.

"Did you say anything about Daniel and Kate?"

"Who? Oh, no. Of course not. But I did say that you didn't get involved in his life or comment on his relationships with his kids, so why would he do that to you? I don't understand why he is so upset. When we got off the phone, he was fine. He certainly wasn't hysterical."

Andrew returned to his brother's desk.

"I talked to Catherine. She said she didn't say anything about Daniel and Kate."

"Are you calling me a liar?" he screamed, half standing up in his chair.

"No, but..."

"So you're going to pick your *girlfriend* over your own brother!"

Andrew didn't know what to think or believe. Nothing had ever happened, personally or professionally, that had sent Mark into this kind of rage. Rattled, he sat down beside his brother and tried to finish out the workday next to Mark as they had done after past arguments.

That night, Catherine and Andrew met at Vol de Nuit, a Belgian beer lounge in the West Village. Andrew looked across the table at the woman he loved, not knowing what to think. "Are you sure you didn't say anything about Mark as a father that…maybe got misconstrued?"

Catherine drew a deep breath. "Andrew, I don't know what to say. You know me. You know my friends. Do you really think I would call up your brother and lecture him on his parenting? About kids I've never met?"

She had a point, Andrew thought. He'd watched her finesse sticky business negotiations, awkward cocktail parties, even play-dates gone awry. She was not the type to provoke; in fact, she was a peacemaker. Mark, on the other hand, was more temperamental every day. For the twenty years they had worked side by side, Andrew had seen Mark spill his coffee nearly every morning. It was a running joke, one for which Andrew kept extra napkins. These days it was more likely to throw him into a rage, shouting at traders who had "made him spill."

"Well, my brother is my brother," Andrew said carefully. "But if he's this upset, I have to ask the question."

Furious, Catherine put down her drink. "If you don't know who I really am, no one does."

"Would it be OK…can we eat and talk about this later?"

They ate in silence, Andrew trying to reconstruct the events of the past few days.

In the weeks after the fight, says Andrew, people began to reach out to him to offer sympathy for the terrible, manipulative treatment he was supposedly getting from Catherine. He heard about it from Bernie, who had heard about it from Mark. He heard about it from Peter and his wife, Marion, who had heard about it from Shana—who had heard about it from Mark. Mark, in turn, had talked to his kids, his ex-wife, Susan, the traders in the office, and his friends, many of whom had never met Catherine. And Andrew felt powerless to stop it. Every time he mentioned some plans he had with Catherine, the person he was talking to would stare at his or her shoes and say, "Oh, yeah, Catherine. I've heard about her."

There had to be more to the story, Andrew thought. He found himself questioning Catherine's role in the drama. Then his mind would flip to his brother's involvement. He turned the questions over in his head, looking at Catherine, looking at his brother, not knowing whom to believe. He approached his mother.

"I can't get involved," said Ruth. "Work this out among yourselves."

Catherine tried her best to ignore the toxic atmosphere surrounding her new relationship, but the smear campaign did make her wonder. Was she a home-wrecker? Was she destroying Andrew's relationship with his kids? Was she, in fact, motivated by money? She asked herself those questions as she sat in church, before she fell asleep at night, and while she read self-help books about sibling dynamics on the subway. But every time she caught sight of Andrew rounding the corner to meet her, her fears evaporated.

In June, Catherine and Andrew booked a fishing trip to New Orleans. An Austin-based businessman Catherine knew from the Ashram had given her an open invitation to use his house in NOLA any time she visited that city, so she wrote him an e-mail to see if the offer stood. A day later, his keys and alarm codes had arrived via FedEx.

"You're kidding," Andrew said, as he turned the envelope over in his hand. "He's just letting us stay there? My parents would never let us stay at their house like that."

"What do you mean? You couldn't stay in your parents' house?"

"Without them there? No *way*. My father would never allow it."

The two flew to Louisiana, rented a car, and pulled up in front of a graceful, three-story town house on Royal Street. While

Catherine looked for a parking spot, Andrew carried their bags up to the house. He opened the door to find a magnificent French Quarter home with gilded ceilings, a stone courtyard on the interior, and a four-poster bed in the master bedroom. In the kitchen, a bottle of bourbon and two glasses awaited, along with a welcome note from the hosts. When Catherine arrived, Andrew answered the door, both glasses in hand.

"You won't believe this place!" he exclaimed.

Really, it was Andrew who couldn't believe they were staying in this resplendent home simply because Catherine had befriended a generous Texan. He had lived a life of luxury and privilege, but every perk he enjoyed had been bought and paid for. He would stay in hotels that were "beautiful but expensive as hell" (a week of skiing with his family could run him upwards of $20,000), which always gave Andrew a twinge of discomfort. There was a difference between hiring staff to attend to his needs, where everyone was fawning over him because he'd paid them, and having someone open up their home to him, simply because they liked him. Getting treated well because he was a friend—not because of how much he could spend—was a completely novel experience for Andrew, and he loved it.

Later that night, Catherine and Andrew met up with Catherine's friend Sean Cummings, a hotelier and real-estate investor, at his unrivaled home in the Quarter. In front of the giant chandelier that spilled from ceiling to floor in the entry hall, Sean embraced Andrew, poured him a glass of wine, and invited him to take a look around the rest of his three-story mansion. When they went out that night, they all piled into Sean's girlfriend Gina's Ford Pinto. They drove to Bacchanal, a wine bar in the Ninth Ward, arms and legs sticking out of the tiny car. Sean introduced them to local celebrities, new entrepreneurs, and strangers he'd just met. At the end of the night, with Sean and Gina long gone, Andrew had started to fret. "How are we going to get back to the French Quarter?" he said. "Taxis don't come out here. We're going to be mugged if we try to walk back."

Catherine looked around, then grabbed a guy who was exiting the bar. "Hey, are you going to the Quarter? Can you give us a ride?" she asked.

As she and Andrew sat in the back of his car, sandwiched between two of the stranger's friends—who turned out to be in the energy business and with whom Andrew traded cards—Andrew shook his head.

"You go places, stay with friends, meet strangers, get into their cars, and the universe is a safe and friendly place to be," he said. "My parents go to the same four restaurants, socialize with the same four people, and visit the same four vacation spots. They are constantly terrified that someone is going to rip them off or give them bad service in a restaurant. I don't understand you. I don't understand your world."

Then, almost without warning, they would be thrown back into his world. Catherine returned from New Orleans to find in her mailbox a letter from an old friend, sounding desperate and sad. A financial manager had invested terribly on her behalf and she'd lost half her money. Just starting to feel secure enough in her relationship with Andrew to mention his father's asset-management business, Catherine called him at work.

"I want to ask you a question and please be absolutely honest with me. I have a friend who doesn't trust her financial manager, and I'd love to recommend that she call your dad. Would that be OK?"

Andrew paused for a moment. "Let's have this conversation once, because I never want to have it again," he said. Catherine felt her heart sink.

"Over the years, hundreds of people have approached me and

said, 'Can you get me into your dad's fund?' It's not a matter of how much money she has, whether she's a friend, or how much she needs it. My dad just doesn't take new money. Period. No begging or pleading on my part will have any sway. In fact, if I said to my dad, 'Would you take on my friend?' he'd be even more likely to say no just to spite me. So I would love to be able to say, 'Tell your friend to call my dad, because he's a solid investment manager.' But he won't take her on as a client and it'll be embarrassing to me. It's been embarrassing to me for years that he treats me this way. So I'm really sorry, but please don't ever ask me again." Catherine got off the phone feeling shaken and embarrassed herself.

And yet despite the many obstacles in their way, the turmoil in the markets, and the drama in Andrew's family, they were still two people falling in love, and Catherine wanted to capture that moment. So she surprised Andrew by arranging to have their picture taken on the roof of the Cosmopolitan Club by her friend Emily Wilson, a portrait photographer. For an hour the two posed on a bench, laughing at Emily's instructions to "tell Catherine a secret" or "say the dirtiest thing you can think of." Andrew would lean over, whisper "pig pen" in her ear, and then the two would crack up, as Emily captured the shot.

Later, when she posed them by a ledge, Andrew leaned over, put his arm around Catherine, and pointed to a spot in the distance. "See that building right there?" he said. "That's my parents' apartment."

Emily snapped the shutter as Catherine followed his gaze to a "large, beautiful wraparound balcony, nicely planted with dozens of trees."

"It's lovely," she said, turning to kiss him. Snap went the shutter again.

Days later, Andrew came into the office to look over the contact sheets the photographer had sent of the shoot. As he scrolled through the photos, Mark peered over his shoulder. "That's sick.

That's just gross. Those look like wedding photos. Do you not see how creepy that is? You need to get out."

The more Andrew's family—Mark in particular—attacked Catherine, the more Andrew withdrew from their confidence. "I decided that if I had to choose between having a relationship with Catherine and having a relationship with my brother, I was going to pick Catherine," says Andrew. His decision would create a rift between the brothers that would never be repaired.

Chapter Ten

THE CALM BEFORE
THE STORM

The moment had finally arrived, and Catherine stood in front of her open closet, carefully considering her options. Ruth and Bernie had invited her and Andrew to spend the Fourth of July weekend with them on their yacht in France. To Catherine, the invitation was an undeniable nod of acceptance—a sign, at least, that the winds were shifting in her favor—and it was crucial that she make the best possible impression. She'd learned how to put together outfits by watching old films, like *The Band Wagon,* from 1953, starring Fred Astaire and Cyd Charisse, and all the Stanley Donen classics. Later, at Dior, she'd learned about the difference between cotton and silk faille, about Happiness Pink and Prince of Wales check. But where she was going now, to the Côte d'Azur in the South of France, would require a more advanced set of skills.

In Glens Falls, New York, people wore L. L. Bean all year and ChapStick when they dressed up. Andrew's family can never know I wore Duck Boots, Catherine thought—that would never pass muster with them. She laid out on the bed a white shift dress, large pearls, and a Dior clutch. That was better. She thought about her college boyfriend, Marco, and his glamorous, exquisitely beautiful

Italian mother. When they met, Marco's mother had been warm, but she had looked at Catherine's clothes from Limited Express as if they were gum stuck to the bottom of her Tod's loafer. But this was no longer a college boyfriend she was just dating; this was Andrew, a man whose parents' approval meant the world to him. This was her Bryn Mawr experience writ large, her chance to choose the track that challenged her the most—but this time, the stakes had never been higher.

The first months of 2008 had been a wildly turbulent time for Catherine and Andrew. They'd spent half of it falling in love, gazing at each other with wonder, unable to believe their luck; the other half defending themselves against accusations. And the drama showed no sign of abating: As recently as a week earlier, Catherine had responded to a perfunctory e-mail from Mark. After she'd responded, their only communication since Mother's Day, a furious Stephanie had called Ruth in France, upset she hadn't been cc'd. Ruth had called Andrew, asking, "What's a 'cc'?" She didn't know, she said, but from what she could gather, Catherine had done something awful.

"This is crazy," Catherine said to Andrew, when he hung up the phone. "Mark didn't include Stephanie on that e-mail. Why would I randomly elect to cc her when he hadn't chosen to?"

He shrugged apologetically and tried to change the subject.

"Are there books about e-mail etiquette? I think I need to buy one. No. You know what I need to do? I need to officially stop caring about any of this! I need to focus on our trip and pack."

The instant Catherine dragged her beat-up Patagonia suitcases out of her closet, she knew she could not take them to France. They were a symbol of the person she'd been before, when her biggest ambition had been to travel the world, fish in remote locations, and perhaps one day write a novel. That person still lived within her, but someone new had emerged, with grander dreams. Now she would go through life with an equal, both enjoying fulfilling careers. They would throw outrageous dinner parties, raise their children with love, laughter, and silliness, and push each other to great heights of achievement. She would not get absorbed in the minutiae of life. And she would not carry these battered Patagonia suitcases forever.

That night, strolling through Central Park on their way back to Andrew's apartment after dinner, she'd rushed to confess to some feelings she'd been having.

"You don't know what it's like to date you. There's so much pressure for everything to be perfect. And even when it's perfect, it's not perfect."

"What do you mean?" Andrew asked as they rounded the corner to his apartment. "I don't get it."

"We're going on this fancy trip and I have old Patagonia suitcases. Your parents are going to judge me."

She had bought their airline tickets for the trip herself, wanting to make a contribution. New luggage, too?

Andrew stopped and put his hands on her shoulders. "Go buy any suitcases you want."

"But I don't..." Catherine struggled to complete the sentence.

"Stop," he said, as though reading her mind. "Let me do this for you."

The next day she went to Longchamp on Madison Avenue and picked out a cosmetics case and a small duffel. Andrew called just as the salesperson was showing her the buttery orange-leather exterior, expensive bifocals perched on her nose.

"I found a few suitcases I like," Catherine said, fingering the soft fabric.

"Where are they?"

"At Longchamp on Madison."

"I'm sending Errol over to pick them up. They'll be at your apartment in two hours."

Seven outfits were spread out on her bed, two for each day of the trip and another for traveling. Unlike her new luggage, the beautiful clothes were something she had earned and saved for, or were part of her generous clothing allowance from Dior. Each had been coordinated with jewelry, shoes, and a bag. She'd paired capri pants with a Mexican lace blouse and sandals. A sequined top with white jeans and Dior Jazz platform pumps. A palm-leaf skirt with a blue silk twin set and denim heels. After photographing each ensemble for easy reference, she'd hung them on hangers, then draped them in plastic that could be rolled and zipped into the duffel. The jewelry, shoes, and clutches were separated into packing cubes.

Days earlier, Andrew had mentioned that they were headed to Club Cinquante-Cinq, in Saint-Tropez.

"Do you know what that is?" he'd asked.

"Of course," she'd lied.

When she finally figured out what he was saying—Club 55, or *cinquante-cinq*—she'd looked up YouTube videos of people vacationing at the famed resort. She scrutinized what they were wearing, how they ate, where they were standing, and what their body language was. She tried to absorb everything there was to know, so she'd know what to do when she arrived.

Dior had lent her thousands of dollars in jewelry, and gifted her a pair of ballet flats, in the softest white calfskin, to wear on the boat. Andrew had warned her about his father's near-maniacal protection of its pristine, polished wood floors, so she hadn't even bothered to remove the shoes from their tissue-paper wrapping.

The day before they were due to leave, Catherine headed to Spa Castle, a Korean bath in Queens, where $30 would buy her a relaxing afternoon in the heated jade saunas. She needed it. Jorge, the livery cab driver whom she often hired to take Sophie to school and make runs to the airport, drove her around to the front of the building. She took a deep breath and prepared to soak her cares away.

Just as she stepped out of the car, Andrew called.

"I know it's a day early, but how would you feel about leaving right now? I don't have anything going on in the office tomorrow."

Catherine pounded on the window of the car before Jorge could pull away. "Let's do it," she said.

"Can you meet me at JFK in ninety minutes?"

She told Jorge to "drive like thunder" back to her apartment, her pulse racing. She ran upstairs. Jorge appeared in the doorway.

"What can I do to help?"

"Can you go into my bathroom and sweep all of my toiletries into this bag?"

The two moved wildly about the apartment, gathering tooth-brushes, books, and papers she needed for work. Within minutes Jorge was barreling toward the airport, where Andrew awaited.

"I love it about you that you're willing to just go," he said, lifting her carry-on from her shoulder and hoisting it onto his. After they collected their boarding passes and got on the plane, they settled into their seats. Andrew as a rule flew coach. He was never able to sleep on planes anyway, and he felt the larger business-class seats were wasted on him. As the plane started to taxi, Catherine's anxiety skyrocketed. They'd never been on a long international flight together before. What if my breath gets bad? What if I fall asleep with my mouth open? she worried.

Stop it, she chided herself. Would Uma Thurman worry about that? No. So don't you worry about it either. Do what a beautiful, glamorous woman does on an airplane: Read your book.

When they landed in France, they passed a driver holding a

sign that read TRUMP. Minutes later, Ivana Trump breezed past them, wearing a suit and pumps, and disappeared into the crowd. Catherine attempted to feel as fresh and perfectly coiffed. At the same time, Ivana Trump looked terribly unhappy. Could she have it both ways?

"Your parents went to Monaco, sir, so you might have to wait a bit," the driver called to Andrew, as he jogged around the car to open Catherine's door. They had pulled up in front of the dock where Bernie moored his boat. Catherine gazed at the gleaming white yachts, packed into the marina like sardines. She glanced at her brand-new luggage, her handsome boyfriend, the palm trees caressed by the warm Mediterranean breeze. *You will have everything you want in life, but not in the way that you expect it.* Yes, she thought, all her dreams were coming true—dreams she didn't even know had been hers.

It wasn't long before Andrew spotted Bernie's boat gliding up to the marina. The $7 million yacht was even more impressive than Catherine had imagined: Eighty-eight feet long, it looked like a giant Italian speedboat, with a large open deck, cushions for lounging, and the name of the boat, *Bull,* printed in large, block letters on the back. Inside, Andrew had told her, were three gorgeous staterooms, each with its own private bath. They would be staying in the master suite—a privilege his parents had never before extended—while Ruth and Bernie slept at their town house nearby. In addition to the captain, a male and female mate would attend to their every need.

Ruth and Bernie stood at the back of the boat, waving and smiling, as Captain Bruno skillfully guided it into a space between two other yachts. The distance on either side was "no wider than a piece of paper."

"My father is going to lose his mind if there's a single scratch on that boat," Andrew mused as they watched it inch into port. When it came to a halt and a mate lowered a ramp onto the deck, Andrew and Ruth released a collective sigh.

Reaching into her carry-on bag, Catherine took out her new Dior flats. She slipped them on and prepared to step onto the boat.

"What are those?" Bernie barked.

Catherine froze.

"No shoes on the boat!" He stood at the top of the ramp, glowering.

"But they've never touched—"

"Shoes go here," he said, roughly gesturing to a large wicker basket filled with slip-ons and flip-flops.

Catherine felt a knot rise into her throat. I'm not even on the boat yet, and I've already messed up, she thought.

Andrew shot her a warm, forgiving look. "Don't worry about that," he said softly. "I'm so happy you're here. We're going to have an amazing time."

"Why don't you take a few minutes to freshen up?" Ruth asked as Catherine recovered, stepping barefoot onto the boat.

"Right this way," the female mate said, as the other hoisted their bags over his shoulder. They followed her down a narrow staircase with a polished banister and into the master suite. The entry was a gleaming wood study, tailored to crisp perfection by Susan Blumenfeld. On the deck sat a large humidor, decorated with inlaid re-creations of cave paintings from Lascaux. Creamy engraved stationery with the yacht's name and flag rested next to a fountain pen. In a separate bedroom, a king bed dominated the tiny space, and closets lined the walls. Catherine tiptoed around the luxurious suite, trying not to leave fingerprints. She watched as crew members laid white linen mats on the carpet and placed their suitcases on top.

Then Bernie appeared, eager to show them around.

"This is how you use the shower," he said, gingerly opening the frameless glass door. "In order to avoid getting any spray of water into the room, you'll want to lay a towel across the bottom, like this, *then* close the door..."

"Yeah, Dad, we're going to trash the place the minute you leave," Andrew joked.

"And close the lid on the toilet before you flush, or it'll be a shit shower."

Catherine stifled a nervous laugh. Even she, wearer of the dreaded shoes, could probably avoid *that*. Still, a part of her understood his fastidious rules. Perhaps if she were wealthy and privileged and everyone were bending over backwards for her, she thought, she'd be that way, too. Thank you for telling me the right way to behave, she silently prayed, because I'm in love with your son. And if you are the roadblock, then I will try to please you.

When Bernie left, she stepped into the bathroom and brushed her hair. Then she took a paper towel and ran it around the sink, gathering up the strays. Andrew appeared in the mirror behind her, smiling.

"You're so thoughtful in how you do everything," he said, wrapping his arm around her waist. Brushing her hair aside, he kissed her on the neck.

"I've always done things like that. It's not just to make your dad happy."

"That's one of the reasons why it's so nice to be with you."

Catherine unpacked her clothes and put them in the little cupboards that lined the walls around the king-size bed, where Ruth had made her a space. Impressed, she ran her eyes over Ruth's simple wardrobe, made up almost entirely of T-shirts, white jeans, and light cardigans. Andrew's mother could have anything she wanted, Catherine ruminated, and she wanted this.

Once unpacked, Catherine lifted a beautiful white-leather

Dior bag out of its tissue wrapping. Remembering the etiquette guide she'd once read that had instructed, "A lady never puts her bag on the floor," she gently set it down on a freshly polished side table. As soon as she and Andrew ascended the stairs, Bernie went downstairs. Probably checking to see if we made a mess, she thought unhappily.

Minutes later, Bernie reemerged, shaking his head. "You should have put your purse on the floor."

"Oh, I—I don't usually put it on the floor."

"The bottom of your bag has round metal feet on it. If the boat moves, those feet are going to leave a mark on the table."

Catherine held it together while the group made light conversation, then excused herself to use the bathroom. She went downstairs, locked herself in, and sobbed. Three days, she thought. Three days I am stuck with this family and I can't do anything right.

Later that night, while she and Andrew were getting ready for bed, she brought up the purse. "I'm terrified of your father," she said.

Andrew threw back the covers on the bed and slid between the luxurious Frette sheets. "What's the big deal? He moved your purse. Seriously—ignore him."

That's right, she thought, as she settled into her boyfriend's arms and he kissed the top of her head. He moved my purse. It doesn't mean he thinks I'm an unsophisticated bumpkin, don't belong here, or that I'm not good enough for his son. He moved my purse. That's it and I can move on. Gratefully, she fell into a dreamless slumber.

It was a cloudless, perfect day at La Tonnelle, the only restaurant on tiny Île Saint-Honorat off Cannes. Early that morning, Ruth, Bernie, Catherine, and Andrew had sailed there and were now enjoying a lengthy meal with plenty of wine for all except Bernie, who never drank a drop.

"I don't care how much money you have, there's no way those langoustines are worth a hundred and twenty-five euros," Ruth said, snapping the oversize menu shut. "Forget it."

Instead of the overpriced shellfish, they ordered crudités and seared fillets. After lunch, they returned to the yacht, where Ruth lay down for a nap and Catherine opened her journal.

"I think Andrew is happy," she wrote. "When he first told me about this boat and about France and his parents, I had no idea that a year later I would be on this boat with him. Everything about this man is magic. We are going to come here every year from now on, and we are going to bring Sophie, and I'm going to learn French, and if I could cast a spell, it would be this one: God, let these people fall in love with me and with Andy and the promise and devotion we feel for each other."

They cruised into the sparkling sea. Ruth jumped off the boat and swam. Andrew followed suit, diving into the water and bursting out of the waves with a yelp. Catherine settled onto an enormous cushion on the back deck and opened her book, a memoir by Queen Noor. Bernie stood nearby, gazing out to sea, his clasped hands resting on a banister. Soon, the two fell into polite conversation. They talked about his work at the firm, and about Bernard Arnault, owner of LVMH and one of the world's richest men. Catherine had met him several times through her work with Dior.

"Yeah, he was a client of mine and really wanted to come into the fund," Bernie said. "Ruth was too intimidated to meet him because his wife is a piano virtuoso and they're both very cultured. But he's a fascinating guy." Throughout their two-hour-long talk, Bernie never asked her a single personal question: "He had no interest in me whatsoever," Catherine recalls. Nor did he change position, standing by the rail for the duration of their conversation.

Catherine asked if he had ever fished in South Africa, a destination to which she had recently been invited for a wedding and fishing trip.

"It's a beautiful place, but also dangerous," he said. "People have to have armored cars because of the violence. I could never live like that. That would be like being a prisoner in your own home, and I can't imagine anything worse than being in prison."

"I think you're safe, sir," she said, smiling as she referenced his sterling reputation. "But for all the Wall Street guys who end up in prison, there have to be plenty who never get caught." Catherine mentioned an article she'd read recently about informal economics and the "gray" market: "It said that there might be more money floating around in the informal economy, like poker games and con deals, than in the formal one. The money we actually see in banks is the tip of the iceberg; underneath, it's all black market money. What's your take on that? It's something I've been turning over in my head for a while."

"That's an interesting idea," he said, gazing out at the water and waving to Ruth.

The conversation didn't go any further than that, Catherine recalls. Bernie didn't flinch, shift uncomfortably, or end the discussion. They just drifted into a new topic, Andrew and Mark's exploratory trips to the Yellow Bar, the dangerous section of ocean where the preteens had fished unsupervised in a tiny boat, lacking any safety equipment.

"Those kids were fine," Bernie scoffed. "They talk about it now like we did something wrong, but that was the best time of their lives. They loved living on that boat—*loved* it." And she knew he was right.

That night, Catherine changed into a soft pink silk-charmeuse dress and a beautiful amethyst ring that had been loaned to her for the trip. As she emerged from the berth and into the salon where the family waited, Bernie let out a low, approving whistle.

Their reservation that night was at a Chez Tétou in Juan-le-Pins, *the* place to go, Andrew had explained—especially if you were affluent, Jewish, and from Long Island. Catherine had looked it up online: It was an authentic traditional Southern French restaurant right on the coastline. Bernie, always the designated driver, played chauffeur. They were seated at a prime table along the windows, where Ruth again complained about prices; bouillabaisse without lobster was 50 euros; with, 200 euros.

"Give me a break," Ruth said, peering at the menu through her reading glasses. "What is it with the *langoust?*" When the bouillabaisse arrived, sans lobster, Ruth tasted it and declared, "This would not have been any better with the *langoust.*" She swooned over the "fabulous" roasted tomatoes.

Wine was poured. Many glasses later, Ruth turned to Catherine.

"Let's talk about Stephanie," she said.

"OK," Catherine responded, feeling her nerves begin to tingle. Bernie, she noticed, was starting to blink rapidly.

"I know there's been a lot of back-and-forth and it's the nature of girls to fight," she started.

"Mom, they're not fighting," Andrew interrupted. "She and Mark are maligning Catherine. Catherine's not doing anything."

"Well, I know there was this e-mailing and 'cc'ing,' and I don't know how that stuff works, but it really upset Stephanie and I think it would be a good idea if you apologized to her."

"I will apologize, if that's what you think I should do," Catherine said, glancing at Andrew.

"Mom! That's ridiculous!" Andrew interjected.

"The girls fight," Ruth said, taking another sip of wine.

"I'm not fighting with her," Catherine said. "I have no issue with her at all."

"Debbie and Susan argued a lot, so while I think it's OK that you girls are fighting…" Ruth continued, as though Catherine hadn't said a word.

The conversation was interrupted by the appearance of a portly, bald older man, who appraised each of them with a smile.

"Saul!" Ruth and Bernie greeted him with warm familiarity.

"Let me buy you dinner tonight, Bernie, for all the things you've done for my family over the years," Saul said. "We couldn't live without you. You've made our family. It's so important to me. Let me buy you this dinner."

"That's ridiculous," Bernie said. "Saul, do you know this place is cash only? Who carries all that cash around?"

"I want to do this for you," Saul insisted. "It's a little thing."

"Who is that guy?" Catherine asked Andrew, under her breath.

"Oh, that's Saul Katz; co-owner of the Mets along with his brother-in-law, Fred Wilpon. He and my dad go way back; he's been an investor with my dad's asset-management business for a long time."

"Did you try the tomatoes?" Ruth asked. "You've got to try them. They are *fabulous*. In fact, we're going to send these tomatoes over to your table. We can't finish them all."

"You are not buying our dinner," Bernie insisted. They argued for a few more minutes, and Saul finally took his leave, smiling and waving.

"I did everything for that guy," Bernie said, watching him walk away. "Everything he has, he owes to me. The clients can be so ungrateful."

Catherine looked at Bernie, utterly confused.

On the way out of the restaurant, they passed the Katzes' table.

"How's Iris?" Ruth asked. "How's the foot?"

"Oh, you know, she had the surgery. It's healing," Saul said.

This is so not my world, Catherine thought. In her family, if you had any type of illness you didn't discuss it—in fact, it would be rude to bring it up. In Andrew's family, if you had any type of minor ailment, it was not only necessary to bring it up, it would be rude *not* to. She was starting to understand that the differences in their families were not only financial but also cultural. There was much she still had to learn.

When Andrew and Catherine fell into their rooms, exhausted, Catherine saw that the crew had turned down their bed and left a fresh carafe of water on a side table. The female mate appeared in the doorway.

"Is there anything I can do for you before you retire?"

"No, thank you, we're fine," Catherine said. The mate slipped away, and Catherine understood that she would be waiting for them, awake, no matter what time of night they wanted something. They crawled under the covers.

"Can I ask you something?" Catherine said. "I'm confused, because your father said the clients were ungrateful and what I saw was someone acting really grateful."

"Oh, that's just his rap," Andrew explained, slipping an arm around her. "You know, 'The clients are ungrateful. I do everything for them. They don't appreciate it.' I just ignore him."

"Well, he sure was appreciative of your dad, from what I could see," Catherine said, snuggling into Andrew.

"I have been living with that my entire life," he said. "People coming over and kissing the ring. Now you've seen it firsthand."

Andrew's parents waited for them at a tiny, nondescript beach club near their town house, one of the many that graced the Côte d'Azur. Catherine and Andrew cruised on the yacht to meet them, anchoring a hundred yards from shore. A tender from the beach club pulled up to ferry them ashore.

"I'm swimming," Andrew said. He dived into the water, his muscular arms cutting through the waves. Catherine watched, impressed by his virility and masculinity, as the little skiff whisked past him and deposited her on the dock. Then she waited for Andrew with Bernie and Ruth on a group of chaise longues.

Andrew pulled himself out of the water and onto the dock, his wet skin slightly bronzed from the previous day's swim. He trotted over to where they were sitting and sank onto a chaise.

"What are you doing?" Bernie snapped. "Put a towel under you. That's disgusting. You're getting water all over that chair. Nobody can use it now."

Catherine marveled that Bernie's first words to his son were a lecture about seawater on a beach chair. It seemed to her like a minor transgression. Andrew had told her his father often admonished him; he claimed the words rolled off his back. But it didn't seem like his father's comments were rolling off his back: She watched his jaw lock with tension as he stood up and searched for a towel.

They ordered breakfast.

"I don't even like this beach club because there are no good bodies to look at—well, maybe except for Catherine's," Bernie said, digging into his granola. "But she could be heavier on top."

Ruth sat working on the crossword, and Andrew continued toweling off. So this is an example of the famous Madoff family "openness," she thought: Someone says something awful and everyone ignores it.

The four ate and discussed the day's plan. Catherine and Andrew would go to Club 55, relax on the beach, then return to the boat.

"Not everybody can get in there; it's a very exclusive place," Bernie confided as he signaled the waiter for their check. "I made a call and got you in. There are going to be two beach mats waiting for you, called *matelas*."

He gave them pointers on the dos and don'ts of how to behave:

"Make sure if you go into the water, shower first; then go sit on the *matelas*. Don't sit on the *matelas* if you've been in the water but haven't showered."

It was the rules of the cabin shower all over again.

The most stylish way to come to Club 55 was via yacht. As Catherine and Andrew approached the dock in a tender, Catherine spotted a tanned older man with white hair sitting alone at the edge of the pier. As the man turned to watch them disembark, Catherine realized it was the fashion designer Giorgio Armani. An exclusive club, indeed, she thought.

As soon as they said the name *Madoff,* they were ushered over to prime *matelas* on the beach next to Liam Neeson.

"How many members belong to this club?" Catherine asked the waiter, when he arrived with their drinks.

He furrowed his brow. "The club isn't private, *mademoiselle*."

Anyone could get in, Catherine realized; you didn't have to be special. Bernie had simply made them a lunch reservation at a very nice place.

She and Andrew lay on the beach and watched as Armani's entourage took the *matelas* next to theirs. Two men in tiny Speedos "with bodies like Greek statues" played paddleball on the sand in front of them. Catherine recognized them from Armani's latest perfume campaign; it had been splashed across every bus in New York.

"That's it—I'm not even taking my towel off," Andrew joked as he watched them twist and dive to keep the ball aloft. The two laughed and lay back in the sun.

At noon, they stopped by the gift shop and bought a linen blouse embroidered with flowers for Sophie, then had "an amazing lunch that seemed to go on forever," with crudités, delicately sautéed fish, and *fraises des bois*. They snapped pictures of each other, then lay on their *matelas* and took a long nap.

They returned to the boat and dressed for dinner: Andrew in a charcoal suit and Catherine in an A-line Prada dress with plunging neckline and straw Bruno Frisoni heels. Their reservation at Alain Ducasse's latest restaurant had been booked at an unfashionably early hour. Only a few tables were taken, as most dinners in the South of France happened closer to 11:00 PM.

As they finished dessert, Andrew observed, "In a few hours, this place will be really hopping."

"It will definitely fill up," she said, smiling. "Let's go back to the boat."

In their berth, Bernie and Ruth had left them a split of champagne, and a mate asked if they wanted dessert. Catherine turned to Andrew, her eyes sparkling.

"No dessert, but can we anchor out?" she asked, suggesting they sleep out in the ocean, instead of moored at the dock. It was something Andrew had never asked of his parents, and they'd never offered.

"Why not?" he said. "I've always wanted to do that."

The boat dropped anchor off the coast, near the Îles de Lérins, and they sipped champagne under the stars. Andrew marveled at the gentle rocking of the waves and the warm Mediterranean breeze.

"Thank God you asked. This is wonderful," he said. Then they returned to their cabin and made love to the graceful movements of the ship.

"It was delicious," Catherine recalls. "Delicious, delicious, delicious."

As dawn approached, they fell asleep, "entwined like woodland creatures," while the *Bull*'s crew perched nearby, awake, ready to do their bidding.

Catherine and Andrew spent their last day walking around Saint-Tropez, browsing in shops and visiting an open-air vegetable market. At 6:00 PM, they met Ruth and Bernie at the famed Hôtel du Cap, on the French Riviera in Antibes, where they would be spending their final night. After drinks on the terrace, the foursome took their seats in the formal dining room, where a waiter dropped a black or white napkin into their laps, depending on the color of their pants.

"When I get home, I'm thinking of getting a Prius," Ruth mused, taking a bite of her fennel *mousseline*. "It's better for the environment and really saves on fuel."

Bernie laughed. "A Prius? Do you know how much fuel we burned going to Monaco so you could see your friend?"

"I wish you hadn't reminded me of that. Still, I'd like to get one."

"You're insane. We have a yacht; we are destroying the planet singlehandedly."

The four laughed good-naturedly and tucked into their dinners. As they ate, Catherine felt all of her fears from the previous week evaporate. Any questions they may have had about her were handled, she felt sure, now that they'd had a chance to spend time with her in person. It was a happy moment; she felt as if she'd hit all of her marks.

On the way home, when Catherine and Andrew checked in for their flight at the Delta counter, the attendant upgraded them to first class, citing Catherine's status as a platinum medallion customer.

Andrew shook his head as they sank into their comfortable seats. "This is the difference between you and my parents," he said. "They have to pay for everything; you don't have to pay for anything, simply because you're charming and people want to do nice things for you." In Andrew's world, he needed to be a Madoff, because status and money were his ticket for entry. In Catherine's world, nobody cared about his money—and nobody even knew her fiancé's last name.

They landed in New York and flagged separate taxis. Andrew returned to his apartment; Catherine got into her car and drove to her family's home in Saratoga Springs. She walked into the house, and her little girl leapt into her arms. Then she changed into pajama pants, poured herself a glass of the sulfurous "Saratoga" water that came out of her parents' tap, and curled up with Sophie on the worn plaid sofa. No high heels, no Giorgio Armani, no Bernie to impress. She was in heaven. For the next two days, she just spent time with Sophie and slept.

Chapter Eleven

THE BIG CRASH

You are my soul mate. We work together on every level. This is right and I know it.

Andrew had scribbled the words in Catherine's journal during their May trip to Key West. Those words had led him to this moment on a Saturday night in a restaurant in San Francisco, sitting across from the woman he adored.

It was September 27, 2008, and they'd traveled to the Bay Area for a lymphoma conference. It was exactly one year from the day that she had first noticed him looking at her while she sat poolside at the Sunset Marquis. Andrew had been acting strangely all day, Catherine thought. As they'd strolled through San Francisco, he'd kept looking at her and smiling, though he was "not a smiley guy." At one point, they'd passed a jewelry store and Catherine had looked in the window. When she looked up, she'd caught Andrew studying her. Later, when he'd said, "Is our reservation at a really nice place tonight? I want to make sure," she knew.

The waiter approached and poured two glasses of champagne. As Catherine reached for her glass, Andrew said, "Stop, stop, stop." He got down on one knee and pulled out a box.

"You are the woman of my life. Will you marry me?"

"Look in your breast pocket," she said. Andrew fumbled past his pocket square and pulled out a note no bigger than a matchbook that read, "Yes."

"You bitch!" he said as the two started to laugh hysterically.

"You were acting ridiculous all day—of course I knew!"

Still on one knee, still laughing, Andrew pulled her in for a kiss. The diners around them applauded. Catherine slipped the ring he'd given her—a simple circle of small diamonds—onto her finger and kissed him again. Her thoughts of never getting married again had evaporated. He was her soul mate. She knew.

When they returned to New York, Catherine and Andrew received "lukewarm" congratulations from Ruth and Bernie. They did not offer to throw the couple an engagement party, something that infuriated Andrew, though Catherine "didn't understand she was supposed to be insulted." Andrew confronted his parents.

"You're not even divorced yet," said Ruth. "Who knows when you're going to get married? We're just going to wait and see."

"That's ridiculous!" Andrew cried. "This is the happiest moment of my life and you won't even acknowledge that I'm in love. You need to welcome Catherine to the family or you're never going to hear from me again."

Eventually, the congratulations came. Three weeks after the engagement, Ruth and Bernie sent a case of nice wine and "all these people in my family started to make a fuss," Andrew says. Mark and Stephanie sent orchids, realizing, perhaps, that Catherine was there to stay. Cards arrived from Andrew's colleagues at the firm.

Andrew turned his attention to other things. In August, he and Catherine had started to look at apartments; Andrew had bemoaned that it was going to take them a year. The second one they looked at—a modern four-bedroom with giant floor-to-ceiling windows— turned out to be the one.

"I don't understand," Andrew had said. "In my first marriage, buying an apartment took forever. With you, everyplace feels like home." With a loan from Bernie, he'd made an offer on the $4.4 million apartment, which was still in the final stages of being built. He hoped to move in with Catherine by the end of the year.

Meanwhile, his divorce negotiations, though amicable, were hitting some bumps. In August, Andrew had offered Debbie half of what he believed to be his net worth, held in a mix of assets. While she turned down his offer, the negotiations were continuing; he figured they'd have a deal ironed out by early December. Then they could submit it to New York City Family Court for approval, and he and Catherine could start their new life.

Of course, he didn't—couldn't—know then that he and Catherine would be engaged forever: Andrew unable to get a divorce, Catherine unable to merge her finances with his because of the legal complications. Under New York state law, a divorce cannot be finalized until both parties have agreed to a financial settlement. Until Andrew reaches a settlement with trustee Irving Picard and his assets are unfrozen, he must remain married to Debbie.

September 27, 2008, will forever be the date that Catherine and Andrew refer to as their "anniversary of not getting married."

Even as Catherine and Andrew entered the happiest phase of their lives, the economy seemed headed for certain disaster. On September 15, Lehman Brothers filed for Chapter 11; it was the largest bankruptcy in American history. The insurance firm American International Group threatened to topple next; it had to be bailed out by the Federal Reserve, which had already poured billions into Fannie Mae and Freddie Mac. In a preemptive move that would bring it much-needed cash, Merrill Lynch merged with Bank of America. The stock market continued to plummet.

Despite the fear gripping Wall Street, Andrew was determined to live his life away from the trading desk, and to keep his focus on

Madoff Energy, Abel, the LRF, and his daughters. In October, he and Catherine flew to London and then drove north to Norfolk for a short visit with Catherine's friends Nick Zoll and his Spanish wife, the jewelry designer Monica Vinader. Catherine had met the couple in Argentina nearly ten years earlier, when Catherine wanted to spend every moment by the water and Nick and Monica were running a tiny lodge on the Rio Gallegos called Bella Vista. No one in Andrew's family had wanted him to make the trip, but as soon as Andrew stepped into the graceful gardens of Choseley Farmhouse, the English country estate where Nick and Monica lived, he was able to put his family out of his mind. Nick and Andrew toured the property with Nick's hunting dog nipping at their heels, and Andrew took in the earthy aroma of the vegetable patches and newly planted chestnut trees. Monica and Catherine pored over Monica's latest jewelry designs near the parlor fire inside.

The couple's hospitality was a panacea to the tension boiling in New York. Andrew felt he had Nick to thank, who months before had given Catherine a piece of advice that had helped bring the two of them together.

"Love is the answer to every question," he'd said when Catherine had lamented, "I don't know what to do with my career. I don't know if I should go to the UK for Sportfish or stay in New York or do something totally different."

Just a few miles from Choseley, she'd discovered the "I love you" graffiti written on Waterloo Street.

That evening, the couples changed into gowns and tuxedos for a benefit called the Best of Norfolk at Holkham Hall, one of the largest private estates in England. It was also the home of Nick and Monica's close friends, the Viscount and Viscountess Coke.

"You can call them Tom and Polly," Catherine assured Andrew. "They're our age and as comfortable as an old shoe."

Catherine wore a zebra-print gown from Dior and diamond

earrings designed by Monica that were up for sale in a charity auction that would be held that night. Andrew, wearing a tuxedo and a cashmere cravat, "felt like royalty" as he watched his fiancée glide around the room, showing off the earrings, even gamely sitting on a gentleman's lap so he could give them a closer look.

A day later, Andrew and Catherine hopped on a Ryanair flight to Pisa with Nick, Monica, and their close friends Katherine and Harry, then traveled to the tiny hamlet of Greve in Chianti, where Nick's mother had a home. They drove along winding roads through miles of vineyards, eventually coming upon a rustic villa set into the side of a hill, with a commanding view of the valley. For two days, they sat in front of the open hearth in the kitchen, drinking Super Tuscans and taking in the incredible landscape. At night, they cooked boar from a local butcher shop over open wood flames, then followed dinner with Grappa.

It all would have been perfect had the fairy tale not been interrupted again and again and again by the ringing of Andrew's phone.

"Where are you? I don't even know where you are."

"Mark is in crisis and you're not here."

"When are you coming back? *Are* you coming back?"

There were "certain realities" to running a family business, Andrew knew, and October of 2008 was a chaotic time in the market. Mark was feeling the stress and probably was highly resentful that his brother was off having a wonderful time. Bernie, as usual, played one brother off the other, telling Andrew that Mark was struggling without him, and constantly asking Mark where Andrew was, simply to highlight his absence from the desk. Peter, Andrew feels, "just missed me." He enjoyed working with his nephew and didn't like the fact that he was no longer around. Even Shana, the cousin Andrew deemed "his favorite Madoff," somehow got involved; that was just how his family worked.

"They all took turns manipulating and harassing me; they wouldn't leave me alone."

When Andrew returned to New York, he called his family into a conference room for a "big powwow."

"You've got to stop this," he said. "You guys are all making me feel terrible that I'm abandoning you, and it's not fair. Yes, I took a four-day weekend. That's not a crime, and I'm no longer running the trading desk. I'm running the energy business, which we've talked about at length and all agree has every hope of being hugely lucrative. The fishing business may not be lucrative, but I love it and feel entitled to do something I enjoy. So get off my back, OK? Mark is more than capable of running the desk without me, and he's got three people helping him. You don't need me here."

His father, brother, uncle, and cousin all denied their actions. They threw up their hands, feigned surprise, and told Andrew they didn't understand why he was feeling this way.

"They acted like I was crazy," Andrew recalls. He left the conference room in a furious huff, saying, "You're all insane."

But Andrew wasn't immune to guilt. In a conciliatory gesture, he agreed to spend a few days with his parents in Montauk and go fishing with his father. Catherine was relieved to stay behind. It was striped bass season, and he booked a few days of fishing with a guide.

On Friday after work, he drove out to Montauk. When he walked into the house, he found his father lying on the floor, groaning in pain.

"My back," Bernie said. *"Ohh."*

The television was turned to CNBC, where an analyst was talking about the economic crisis and what it meant for jobs in America versus abroad.

"Turn that fucking TV off," Bernie said, squeezing his eyes shut and gripping his back. "I am so sick of that fucking loudmouth."

★　　★　　★

By dinnertime, Bernie's mood hadn't improved. He was cranky and out of sorts, no matter what Ruth or Andrew said to try to cheer him up. Andrew hoped that the next day's plan—inshore fishing for striped bass—would do the trick. He'd checked the forecast; conditions were supposed to be ideal.

The next day, Bernie and Andrew rose early and boarded a twenty-foot fishing boat, along with a guide. The three sailed to a section of the water off Montauk Point called the North Rip, where the Long Island Sound meets the Atlantic Ocean. Depending on weather and tides, the rip can be rough, causing huge waves. This happened to be one such day.

Enormous twelve-foot waves washed up the side of the boat, and every time one broke, Andrew could see hundreds of striped bass surfing down the crest of the wave. Another wave would break, and the sun would shine through it, revealing the silhouette of hundreds of fish. They were so thick on the water, Andrew marveled, you could practically walk on them.

The guide was losing his mind. "This is incredible!"

With every cast, they caught fish after fish after fish—something Andrew knew was unusual.

Bernie, who'd begun the day fly-fishing but had switched to conventional tackle, said, "You think this is sporting? Look how easy they are to catch. There's like a thousand of them. Why even bother?"

Andrew turned to his father. "Even if you don't want to catch them, just look at them, OK? They're beautiful! You have experiences like this maybe once or twice in your life."

He turned back to the water, feeling his heart sink to his shoes. He'd built up in his mind a "father-son 'Kumbaya' moment," like the ones they'd had when he was a teen and Bernie had invited him for a day of billfishing. Once again, Bernie had managed to ruin it.

"Let's get out of here," Bernie said. "I don't like this. I'm uncomfortable."

Andrew bitterly put his rod down and they sailed back to shore.

"When I look back on it now, it's clear to me that he was miserable because his asset-management business was on the verge of collapse. He had complained at various points prior to that weekend about those 'fucking redemptions,' but he hadn't given any indication of how bad things actually were," Andrew says.

That afternoon, Mark and Stephanie drove up for lunch. As the five sat around the table, Mark pointed to a Jennifer Bartlett painting that hung on the wall. She was one of Ruth and Bernie's favorite artists.

"I really like that painting."

Ruth walked over to the painting and lifted it off the wall. "You can have it."

By Monday, they were back at work. Bernie sequestered himself in his office, staring at his computer screen, looking unhappy. Whenever Andrew peered through the glass, he saw his father poring over stacks of computer printouts. It went on through all of November.

Tired of shuttling back and forth between Long Island City and her work and Sophie's school in Manhattan, Catherine decided to begin moving things into her new apartment, even though Andrew's divorce papers hadn't yet been submitted to the judge. He would move in in December, when the divorce papers were scheduled to be filed. Catherine unpacked just enough to make herself a coffee in the morning and left the rest in boxes. She and Andrew felt like two young kids starting a life together, though in fact they were adults with entanglements and possessions to be merged.

Busy with work, Catherine asked Andrew if he thought Ruth's friend Susan might want to help decorate their apartment. Andrew told her that Susan had recently undergone treatment for cancer but that he would check with Mark to see if she was ready to go back to work.

"That's sick!" Mark shrieked when Andrew brought it up. "She's barely out of treatment, and your fiancée wants to force her to work? That's exactly like her. Never thinking of anybody but herself."

"You know what, Mark?" Andrew sputtered. "You've developed an unnatural fixation on Catherine as some kind of anti-Christ. By now, most of the people you've complained to have had the chance to meet her, and I hear all the time, 'What's Mark's problem? Catherine's nice. She's normal. What's gotten into him?' She's certainly not perfect, but there's no way she's responsible for whatever it is that is bothering you."

In the end, Catherine had found a decorator she wanted to use, a man named Paul Fortune, who'd designed the Sunset Tower Hotel in Los Angeles. Days earlier, he'd stopped by to see the apartment and take measurements.

"You're living in a fishbowl!" he exclaimed as he stood before the windows. "Everyone can see everything in here. Are you going to do curtain rods? You have to have privacy *sometimes*."

"If people see us sitting around eating popcorn and playing backgammon, so what?" she said. To her, the giant windows were a symbol of what she and Andrew had fought so hard for: Their love was finally out in the open, their lives an open book.

On the nights Catherine didn't have Sophie, she would turn out all the lights and sit on the floor of the living room, gazing into the apartments across the way. Then she would climb into her makeshift bed, a mattress on the floor, and think, If there's one nice thing about Andrew's money, it's that I'm never going to have to assemble IKEA furniture again.

Little did she know, she says, she was about to get her master's degree in assembling IKEA furniture.

★   ★   ★

On the morning of Thanksgiving, Andrew presented Catherine with a three-carat emerald-cut diamond set in platinum, wanting to give her a more traditional center stone ring. Even as she slipped it onto her finger, she thought, I cannot lose myself in Andrew's career, Andrew's money, Andrew's family, or Andrew's prestige. Mark and Stephanie were hosting dinner that night, and Catherine knew she had no choice but to go, but she couldn't wear the ring there. Mark would take it as a jab, given that Stephanie had recently announced she was pregnant and deserved maximum attention. This is what you signed up for, she told herself, as she miserably got dressed. She wore no jewelry but attempted an optimistic smile.

The bank-vault door swung open and Stephanie stood there, also smiling, with a glass of wine in her hand.

"Come in, come in!" she said, grinning and giving Catherine a warm hug hello. Whether Mark's wife was putting on an act or not didn't matter: She was just happy Stephanie was being so friendly. Catherine introduced herself to Mark's two older children, Daniel and Kate, then hugged her future stepdaughters hello. Ruth apologized on behalf of Bernie, who was running late.

An hour later, Bernie burst into the room.

"Sorry I'm late, everyone. My secretary, Eleanor, booked a meeting with some Spanish bankers without realizing it was Thanksgiving. Once we figured it out, they'd already booked their travel arrangements, so I couldn't cancel."

Catherine thought about those poor Spanish bankers, wandering around New York. "Are they really going to be able to find a place to eat on Thanksgiving?" she asked. "Can't you call them and invite them to eat with us?"

"No, no," Bernie said, brushing her off.

Catherine's parents would not have managed to throw such an opulent Thanksgiving, but anyone and everyone would have been welcome, she thought. They would have said, "It's Thanksgiving, this is our tradition; we insist you eat at our house."

Nobody knew, of course, that executives from Banco Santander were putting pressure on Bernie to redeem hundreds of millions of dollars in investments. Or that Bernie might prefer to have a frank, hostile meeting when his office was empty.

The meal was served. Catherine didn't interact much with Mark and Stephanie. Andrew quietly asked Mark if Paul Fortune, the decorator he and Catherine had hired, could come over to Mark's apartment and take a look for inspiration.

"No way," Mark said. "Stephanie is still mad at Catherine for saying that Susan Blumenfeld did the whole thing and Stephanie had nothing to do with it."

"What? Catherine didn't say that."

"It's what Stephanie heard," he acquiesced, softening.

When Catherine got home that night, she felt a little foolish. That was nothing, she thought. That wasn't so awful. If we can all just get through these kinds of events, smile and be sweet, sit in the right chair and manage our relationships, then Andrew and I can have happiness.

Two days later, Catherine and Andrew picked up Anne and Emily and drove to a hangar on Long Island where Bernie kept the private plane in which he owned a 50 percent share. The $24 million Brazilian jet had been delivered the previous summer and was painted dark blue and gray "like a United airplane." The sleek aircraft's interior looked like "the lobby of a beautiful hotel," according to Catherine, with its honey-colored woods and soft leather seats, or a miniature version of Bernie's yacht; indeed, he'd used the same decorator.

When they boarded the plane, Catherine and Andrew greeted Peter and his wife, Marion. The whole family was flying down to Palm Beach to extend the Thanksgiving holiday. Ruth and Bernie had already made the trip. Catherine was happy to have another opportunity to prove to Ruth and Bernie that she wasn't "awful, inappropriate, or a gold digger," that she actually loved their son. As was Peter's custom, he made everyone hold hands when the plane took off and again when it landed. At the airport, they parted ways.

As Ruth and Bernie's house came into view, Catherine was surprised by its modest size. Four bedrooms wasn't a cottage, but this house did not match the image in her mind evoked by the phrase "house in Palm Beach." Set on the Intracoastal Waterway, it had a beautiful banyan tree in front and a small, circular driveway. Bernie met them at the door and showed them to a small spare room to the left of the entrance. "Don't touch this; don't put anything there," he instructed, but this time, Catherine had anticipated it.

Andrew lay down on the bed, and Bernie said, "Don't touch the dress pillows!"

Bursting into laugher, Andrew said, "I'm sorry for laughing, Dad, but *dress pillows?* Really?"

As if on cue, a housekeeper came into the room and removed the white linen duvet cover and pillowcases, exchanging them with a set that looked identical.

"You have to do that every night before you go to sleep," Bernie instructed. "She's leaving for the day, so I'm having her do it early."

They put down their suitcases and followed Bernie into the main part of the house. It was lovely, Catherine thought: The floors were covered in large, terra-cotta tiles; the living room, kitchen, and bedrooms were surrounded by courtyards that let in a breeze. Outside, a swimming pool sat on a small patch of land that backed up to a fence.

Bernie disappeared, then quickly returned.

"Emily Madoff, put your things away right now! This is not ten Gracie. You cannot live in that same squalor in this house!"

Catherine realized he'd left to inspect their rooms. Leaning over, she whispered to Emily, "Just throw it all in the closet; he's not going to look in there."

Catherine and Andrew returned to their rooms to unpack. Tired, she sank onto the bed.

"Oh, my God, you're touching the duvet—you had the audacity to put your head on the pillow!" Andrew said, and they laughed.

That afternoon, Catherine chatted with Ruth in the kitchen while Ruth chopped vegetables for that night's salad. Every few minutes Andrew's mother would stop and take a drag on her cigarette. Anne walked into the kitchen. Suddenly Ruth bolted from the room.

Startled, Catherine asked, "What's going on?"

Anne rolled her eyes. "I know she smokes, but she thinks I don't know, so we have to go through this dance of her running out of the house."

Ruth is still like a teenager, Catherine thought. She picked up Ruth's abandoned knife and continued to chop tomatoes.

That night, the family sat outside by the pool, eating stone crab claws at a round table. The night was warm and breezy, and Catherine was enjoying the camaraderie she felt as they told stories and passed wine around.

Anne turned to her grandfather. "Papa Bernie, I noticed on the Madoff website there's a number for the firm's capital. What does that mean?"

Catherine felt her shoulders tense up. Anne, precocious, beautiful, and whip smart, was ever the provocateur. She had both an unparalleled knack for and her father's love of knocking people off their pedestals.

"Well, Anne, that's how much money the firm has in the bank. We have to reflect that on the website," Bernie said.

"But is that your money or the customers' money?"

"The economy is really suffering and we've had a lot of redemptions. The firm's capital goes up and down all the time."

"But is it going to go down a lot and you'll have to close the firm?"

"Everything is fine," he insisted. "Do you want more crab?"

"What if you have to close the firm? Lehman Brothers and Bear Stearns both failed."

Bernie, Catherine could see, was quietly growing more and more ticked. Stop, Anne, she thought. Just stop. Don't get too close to the flame.

"Seriously, could that happen?"

The more Bernie tried to change the subject, the more Anne poked and prodded. Bernie was her powerful grandfather whom the world respected, but to her he was a big teddy bear. She was, says Catherine, "just going for it."

Ruth got up and started carrying dishes into the kitchen. Catherine followed her.

"You don't have to do that," Ruth said.

"I'm happy to," Catherine insisted, wanting to be anywhere but at that dinner table.

"Back off and mind your own business!" she heard Bernie explode in the next room. "One day you can come and work at the company, and that will be your deal, but for now, it's *my* deal. So back off, OK?"

Anne flew from the table, sobbing. Andrew followed her. The rest of them finished their dinner.

It was their second day in Palm Beach. Ruth and Bernie had just returned from playing golf.

"Let me show you around the house," Bernie suggested to Catherine.

He took her up to the small master bedroom on the second

floor, with his and hers closets and bathrooms at either end. He opened the closet door and proudly showed her a three-foot row of crisply pressed pants. Then Bernie's masseuse appeared in the doorway—he was still having back trouble—and Catherine took her leave.

Later that afternoon, Catherine was in the kitchen, leaning over the counter and reaching for a paper towel, when she felt someone slap her on the rear end. She turned around, prepared to kiss Andrew. It was Bernie, his palms turned up apologetically.

"Sorry," he said and exited the kitchen. She started to wonder about that massage.

That night, when she and Andrew were going to sleep, Catherine told him what had happened.

"That is so creepy. That is so creepy," he just kept repeating.

When Catherine recounted the story to Shana, with whom she was slowly becoming friends, she said, "Yeah, he does that all the time at the office." Still, when Catherine really thought about his actions, they didn't *feel* so much lecherous as a display of his masculinity. For some reason he needed to prove to the young women present that he was still a man.

"All of my parents' friends will be there. It's going to be a huge scene," Andrew warned Catherine as they drove to the Breakers for lunch. "Everyone is going to fuss over you and ask embarrassing questions. You'll be fine, but I'm telling you, it's going to be stressful. You're going to be on display, whether you like it or not."

The Breakers was a large resort hotel complex in Palm Beach where the Madoffs and their friends had been meeting for years to have lunch, play golf, swim, and socialize.

Ruth and Bernie had rented a poolside cabana: Luxurious and private, like a stadium box, it had comfortable sofas and was generously stocked with snacks and sodas. When Catherine walked in, she spotted the bill for the cabana sitting on a sideboard and raised her eyebrows: It was the size of her monthly rent in Long Island City.

Just as Andrew had described, dozens of people he knew were milling about: relatives, family friends, guys he knew from college. The barrage of greetings started almost immediately.

"OK. That's Tom Lee. My parents know him. He's a private equity manager. We don't need to chat. Just say hi."

"See that woman talking to my parents? That's Ellen Shapiro. She's going to ask you lots of questions about yourself. Just roll with it."

Catherine had the distinct sensation that whenever she walked away, people were whispering. Who is her family? Where is she from? She's not even Jewish. Then she would admonish herself for being paranoid.

At lunchtime, Catherine and Andrew met Andrew's friend Monte inside the hotel. As they were walking back to the pool area, they saw Bernie with a tall, slender elderly man who seemed to have suffered a stroke; one side of his face drooped.

"There's Carl Shapiro," Andrew confided. "You're going to have to talk to him; he's a big client of my dad's." In fact, Carl Shapiro had been a client of Bernie's for decades. He was a retired garment industry giant who had invested the bulk of his considerable millions with Madoff. With him was his daughter, Ellen, whom Catherine had already met; his son-in-law, Bob Jaffe, a big figure in the feeder fund crowd; and his grandson Michael Jaffe, who had worked for the Madoffs. Everyone surrounded Grandpa Carl the same way Bernie's circle surrounded him.

Carl gave Andrew an effusive hug, surprising him. The two had met only a few times in Andrew's life.

"Wow, Andrew, you did good," Shapiro said, looking over Catherine admiringly.

★　　★　　★

On December 7, 2008, Andrew finally moved into the new apartment, and Catherine moved the last of her boxes from her old place, leaving behind a few big pieces of furniture that she wouldn't need once the decorator got to work. That night, Catherine's assistant, Katherine Dart, and her boyfriend, Nate Ratledge, came over for drinks. Nate, a noted environmentalist, was fascinated by Andrew's work in the energy sector. The four of them sat in the apartment, surrounded by boxes, debating policy and clinking glasses to Catherine and Andrew's new life.

Andrew was feeling optimistic. Debbie had agreed to a settlement, provided it was all in cash. Since most of Andrew's money was tied up in real estate and his accounts at the firm, any cash for a divorce settlement would have to come from liquidating his Madoff accounts.

The next day, he stopped by his father's office. During previous conversations on the topic, his father had kept stringing him along. This time, he was determined to pin Bernie down so he could get divorced and marry the woman he loved.

"Giving her cash is what's best for me," he started. "We've had this discussion before, and I don't see what the problem is. If I can't make this deal for some reason, you need to speak up now because we're at the point of no return."

Bernie stood up and closed the door to his office. When he turned around, his face was not the mask of concern it had been when Andrew entered. It was the smiling Bernie of their holidays in France. He held out his arms.

"Are you sure you can't work it out? What's the rush?" he said.

"What's the rush? How the hell can you ask me that? Debbie and I have been separated for a year and were miserable for years before that. We've been in therapy. It didn't work. I met someone new. I fell in love with her and now we're engaged. We moved in together.

These divorce negotiations have been going on since January and we're ready to press go. You knew all of this. What's the rush?!"

Bernie sighed. "If you insist on breaking up your family, we can do it, just not this week." Even at the brink of disaster, he was loath to deny his son, adding, "Maybe in two weeks."

"Two weeks is fine, but you have to let me know if it's going to be longer than that. We're supposed to sign the papers and file them with the court this week."

Bernie nodded and Andrew left his office.

It was the close of the trading day on December 8, 2008. Bernie had called Mark into his office.

"I need to know the numbers for the traders' bonuses," he said.

"Why?"

"Because I want to pay them."

"Pay them? Now?"

"Yes."

"But why?"

"I happen to be sitting on a lot of cash right now. The ... timing is right."

Mark was in charge of "closing out" the traders' bonuses, or figuring out what they were supposed to be paid. It used to take Bernie and Peter months to figure out those numbers, but since Andrew and Mark had made the system electronic, they could now figure it out in a day. Still, there was a process in place: Mark would figure out the numbers on the first trading day after the New Year. Then he would pass the numbers to Bernie and the person who did payroll. Even then, no one got paid until mid-February, since the other managers had slower systems and Bernie thought it unfair to pay the trading room first.

Mark stared at his father, who had returned to the pile of paper

Chapter Twelve
_____

THE CONFESSION

By 6:50 AM, Andrew and Mark were, once again, perched in the conference room behind the trading floor. They shot each other tense, worried looks, periodically breaking the silence to speculate, or to offer a new theory. One thing they knew: Something was terribly wrong.

By 8:00 AM, Peter still hadn't arrived.

Mark shook his head. "Let's wait at our desks."

Ruth, according to court filings, had taken out some $15 million in two separate withdrawals from her Cohmad brokerage account in the prior three weeks. Bernie had asked her to move the money into her Wachovia bank account, so he could use it to cover redemptions. She did his bidding unquestioningly, something that the media claimed as proof of her involvement, but then, the family moved millions of dollars around all the time: buying boats and apartments, making large wire transfers and multimillion-dollar donations to philanthropic organizations. Had Ruth questioned Bernie's directive, Andrew says, "Bernie would have barked at her and that would have been the end of the conversation."

It wasn't until 9:20 AM that Andrew spotted Peter making his way across the trading floor. He signaled to Mark and they hurried into the conference room. As Andrew took his seat, he felt the back of his neck grow hot with anticipation.

Peter stood by the door, his mouth a grim line. "I talked to your father. It's bad—he wants to talk to you himself," he said. Andrew's stomach dropped. He knew that his uncle tended to put a positive spin on things.

The brothers pushed their chairs back and followed their uncle onto the trading floor. They passed their colleagues—shouting orders at their desks—a row of administrative offices, a cluster of secretaries, a large conference room. The walk seemed to take forever.

When they arrived at Bernie's glass-walled executive office, they found him sitting behind his desk, leaning back in his chair, staring at a television set mounted on the ceiling. He didn't greet them, or even acknowledge their arrival. Andrew and Peter took the two chairs facing Bernie; Mark sat on a couch to the left of his desk. For a few minutes, the four sat in tense silence.

"I don't know where to start," Bernie finally began. His voice caught in his throat and tears started to well up in his eyes. Andrew felt a river of alarm rise through his chest. He glanced at Mark; he was studying Bernie intensely.

"Let's not do this right at your main desk," Peter suggested. "Let's move to the table in the corner." The four gathered around a small conference table at the far end of the room, where a wall offered a shade more privacy.

Again, Bernie started to talk and couldn't continue. Dumbfounded, Andrew watched his father struggle for words.

"I can't do this here," Bernie finally said.

Andrew looked at his father, feeling as though he had entered "the world of the surreal." What could possibly be so bad that he couldn't even discuss it at the office?

"Why don't we go to your apartment?" Andrew suggested.

"Are we all going up there?" Mark asked.

Bernie cleared his throat. "No. Peter, you stay here and run the show while we go up to the apartment."

Peter nodded and left the office. The coat closet was right outside Bernie's office.

As the three struggled into their winter gear, Bernie said to his secretary, Eleanor, "Have Lee bring the car around."

"Where the hell are you going? The market is open," Eleanor joked, liking to bust her boss's chops from time to time.

"Mind your own business!" Bernie snapped, immediately silencing Eleanor, who stared at her computer.

Andrew, Mark, and Bernie rode the elevator down in silence, then waited for Lee in the vast lobby of the Lipstick Building, watching the rain streak across the revolving doors. There was no small talk. Andrew tried to blend into his surroundings, wishing he could be teleported to his parents' apartment, so he could get whatever was going to happen over with. The anticipation was unbearable.

Their car pulled up in front, driven by Clive, not Lee. Again, they rode in silence, Bernie sandwiched between his two sons in the backseat, misty-eyed and shaken, struggling to hold it together, as though he'd "already received bad news and was trying to cope with it," Andrew says. Andrew stared out the window at the early Christmas shoppers, his brain "a dead zone."

Clive dropped them off on 64th Street, in front of the entrance to Ruth and Bernie's penthouse apartment. The three rode up to the eleventh-floor entrance, then removed their wet shoes in the foyer, obeying Bernie's shoes-off rule. They laid their coats across the banister of the staircase, taking care not to drip water onto the floor. Ruth greeted them at the door, her face grim. She, too, had no idea why her husband had rushed home in the middle of the day to talk to his family, but like her sons, she suspected the news was bad, somehow connected to the mayhem on Wall Street. Bernie had called her from the office and said, "I have something to tell you. I can't tell you on the phone. I'm coming home with the boys." She'd gotten off the phone, shaking, and had waited for them in the kitchen.

Together, the family entered the sitting room, a forbidding room that Andrew had never liked, with dark green walls, khaki carpeting, dark leather club chairs, and a heavy desk. Bernie sat by himself on a large leather sofa. Ruth sat on a club chair next to the couch. Andrew took the ottoman and Mark the desk chair. The four faced one another, sitting a considerable distance apart.

"I don't know where to start," Bernie began again. He started to sob. "The firm is insolvent. I'm broke."

"How is that possible?" Andrew asked. "I don't understand."

"The money is gone. It's over."

"I don't understand," Andrew repeated. "How can that be? We're having an OK year. What happened? Is this about the redemptions?"

Then Bernie said something more terrible than they could have imagined.

"It's all been one big lie. It's a giant Ponzi scheme and it's been going on for years, and there have been all these redemptions, and I can't keep it going anymore. I can't do it."

Andrew stared at his father, his mind a jumble of disconnected thoughts and phrases. He was trying to piece together what his father was saying, but the sentences kept evaporating. He grabbed at them, frustrated, as they continued to disappear.

Ruth lit a cigarette. Her hand shook. "What's a Ponzi scheme?"

"It means the asset-management business was fake," Andrew said.

"I've been lying to all of you for years. I've been lying to your mother, I've been lying to you, I've been lying to the customers, I've been lying to myself.

"I have an appointment to meet with Ike Sorkin on Monday," Bernie continued, referring to the family lawyer, "and I'm probably going to jail." He broke down then, really sobbing.

Andrew rose from the ottoman, crossed the room, and awkwardly draped an arm around his father for a few seconds. At that, Andrew started to cry, too. He got up and returned to the ottoman. Through his tears, he said, "But there was all this money. Where did it go?"

"The money is gone. I've got fifty billion in liabilities. . . ." His voice trailed off.

Andrew stopped. "Fifty million?"

"Fifty *billion*."

Andrew now glanced at his brother, who hadn't yet said a word. He recognized that look. Mark's face was red, his jaw clenched. A vein worked in his temple.

"I still don't understand. How is all of this going to unfold?" Andrew asked, his mind racing to process what it all meant, how it was going to affect him, what was going to happen.

"I've got a couple hundred million in cash left. There are certain accounts I'm going to redeem with that money—friends and family. I have a large redemption coming next week; that's when it's all going to unravel."

"What are all these people going to do, Dad? What about Susie West?" Andrew asked, referring to his widowed mother-in-law, who'd invested her life savings with him. "What about Roger's widow, Jen? Are they going to get their money back?"

"I'm doing my best. I have a list of people—"

"Wait," Andrew interrupted. "How can you even do that? They're not going to get to keep that money."

"They will," Bernie explained, and patiently started to outline other situations where firms had failed and investors were made whole.

Andrew stopped him, sickened, not wanting to hear more. "How long has this been going on?"

"Oh, God, it's been going on for years."

Much has been made of when the fraud started, and the truth is, no one really knows. Bernie started the firm in the sixties, when computers weren't even in use. The records from that time are thin. Even modern regulatory requirements don't require records that go beyond six years. Bernie claims his Ponzi scheme began in 1992, that any questionable behavior he engaged in before then was "at worst, a gray area" involving "synthetic" trades to defray income tax costs for his most important clients. And there is evidence that he executed actual trades into the eighties. But whether the original Ponzi scheme started when Bernie said it did or much earlier, only Bernie knows.

"And what about me and my family, Dad? What's going to happen to us?"

"I've been doing the math," Bernie said. "I've been looking through all the records, and at the end of the day, the amount of money I've taken in and paid out over the years is about a wash."

Mark stood up. "This is *bullshit!*" he yelled, and stormed out of the room.

"I'm going with him," Andrew said and ran after his brother. Mark was in the foyer, fumbling with his shoes, yanking his coat over his arms.

"I'm leaving," he repeated.

"OK, let's go," Andrew said. He followed his brother into the elevator and out into the fall drizzle.

Clive stuck his head out the window. "What am I doing?"

Andrew shouted into the wind: "The old man is still upstairs. You're waiting for him."

Mark had already stepped off the curb and had hailed a cab. Andrew slid onto the seat, next to his brother.

The cabdriver turned around. "Where to?"

"Just drive," Andrew instructed. The driver started to inch down Lexington Avenue, which was congested with cars. Andrew felt grateful. It would buy him time to think.

He turned to Mark. "What do we do?"

"We need a lawyer. Right now."

"How? What do we do? Walk into the lobby of Skadden, Arps and scream, 'Help'?" Andrew asked, referring to the white-shoe firm, famous in corporate law.

"No. We need a *real* lawyer—a criminal defense one. Let's call Marty; he'll know what to do." Mark's father-in-law, Marty London, was a retired senior litigator at Paul, Weiss; he'd represented Spiro Agnew during the Watergate trials, and Jackie Kennedy in her lawsuit against Ron Gallela. He and his wife, Pinks, were staying at the Beekman Tower Hotel while their apartment was being renovated.

Mark leaned into the partition. "Take us to Forty-ninth Street and First Avenue." The cab turned left as Mark punched a number into his cell phone.

"Stephanie. What are you doing right now? You're with Susan Blumenfeld? Get her out of there." He listened, his face growing red. "Make up an excuse. Just get her out of there." He hung up the phone.

Mark and Andrew rode the rest of the way in silence, each in his own world of fear.

Ruth sat at the banquette in her kitchen, smoking one cigarette after another. Bernie had returned to the office. There had been no agonizing embraces or recriminations. He'd told her that he had two more checks to deposit. That he was planning to go to the office in the morning to pay the traders. She'd nodded numbly. Yes, yes. OK. After he left, she just sat there, a complete zombie. Eventually, she rose and made her way into the bedroom to dress for the office Christmas party, which was scheduled for that night, at Rosa Mexicano. For the occasion, she'd bought a black Prada blouse, tailored like a man's shirt, with silver detailing on the collar. As she fumbled with the small buttons, her fingers trembling, she had the thought, I'll never wear this again. She paired it with a black skirt that fell just below the knee and a pair of tall, suede boots with a heel; she'd never liked her legs.

The thought of not attending the Christmas party didn't cross Ruth's mind. Of course she and Bernie were going. Before he'd left, Bernie had said, "We have to show up and act like everything is fine." Yes, she'd nodded again, numbly. Yes, OK.

It was noon when Andrew and Mark entered Marty London's suite at the Beekman Tower, though Andrew felt as though he'd been slogging through that day for a year. A pile of suitcases sat by the front door.

Marty greeted them: "What happened? What the hell is going on?"

Mark strode past his father-in-law into the room. Andrew followed. Now it was Mark's turn to do the talking.

"My father just confessed to a huge crime; he said his whole business is a Ponzi scheme and that the firm is insolvent and there's fifty billion missing."

"Fifty million?" Marty asked.

"No, fifty *billion*," Mark said in what would become a refrain.

Marty paused. "Oh, boy, I need to sit down. My whole retirement fund is with him."

"Your hair?" He struggled to remember if they'd spoken, then vaguely recalled texting her.

"For the party. Are we going?"

"Oh, yeah, yes, we're going. I think. I have to run."

He walked out of his office without knowing that the next time he would return would be six months later, accompanied by his attorneys and the FBI so he could recover his personal effects.

Marty Flumenbaum and Andrew Ehrlich arrived at 3:00 PM sharp. Flumenbaum was short and stout, in his fifties, with a side part and glasses. Ehrlich was tall, slender, and young. The lawyers shrugged their arms out of their raincoats; both were wearing suits and ties.

Marty London immediately started to recap the story for his colleagues. "Are you familiar with Bernie Madoff? The boys just told me this incredible story, that he's running a Ponzi scheme to the tune of fifty billion dollars."

"Fifty million?" asked Flumenbaum.

"Billion, with a *B*."

"Do you think he was sane? Was he telling the truth?" he asked, repeating the same questions London had posed.

No one, from family members to the top lawyers in the country, could wrap their head around that figure. It would dwarf the WorldCom scandal, which involved $11 billion. It would mean Bernie Madoff had committed the biggest financial fraud in history.

Over the next hour, Flumenbaum asked Andrew and Mark to describe in depth who they were, their jobs at the firm, their relationships to their parents, their wives. He asked them repeatedly if they were involved in the fraud.

"We had no idea," they kept repeating. "None whatsoever. We were completely blindsided."

They wrapped up the story and Flumenbaum closed his note-book. "We need to report this and I'm not even precisely sure how to do that. We have a new partner at the firm who came on board from the SEC. I want to bring him in and get his thoughts on this." Flumenbaum picked up the phone.

Paul, Weiss's offices were only a short walk away, so five minutes later, Walter Ricciardi, the firm's expert on regulatory procedure and someone intimately familiar with the command structure at the SEC, entered the suite.

"We need to report this," Flumenbaum repeated. "What are the channels? What is the chain of command?"

The clock was ticking. It was already 5:00 PM. Soon the SEC's offices would close. They needed to get someone on the phone—but it had to be the right person.

"You'll want to call the division of enforcement at the SEC," said Ricciardi. "Linda Thomsen. After that, you might try the head of their New York office and maybe the FBI."

Flumenbaum turned to Andrew and Mark. "Are you both comfortable doing this?" he asked. There was a clear sense that Flumenbaum was in charge; he knew the right thing to do and wasn't going to give them any other option but to do it.

"Yes, let's do it," Andrew said.

"Let's do it," Mark repeated.

Andrew looked at his brother. "We're doing the right thing."

Mark nodded.

Reflecting on that moment today, Andrew says, "I would love to say that Mark and I were waving the flags of justice in the air, but the bottom line is that we were absolutely terrified. We knew that what we were doing was going to send our father to jail, and the feeling was awful—absolutely awful."

"Give me a minute," Andrew said.

He walked out of the living room and into the bedroom, feeling his knees crumble as he crossed the threshold. Sinking to the ground, holding on to a radiator, he let out enormous, racking sobs that tore through his chest and burned his throat: guttural animal sounds, so alien he wasn't even sure they'd come from him. Doubling over, he clenched his stomach, trying not to vomit.

When the sobs subsided, he wiped away his tears roughly with the back of his hand and stood up on wobbly legs. He cleared his throat, returned to the living room, and sat down. Pulling out his phone, he sent Catherine a text: "We're definitely not going tonight."

Then he turned to Flumenbaum. "Make the call," he said.

Ricciardi tried to get Linda Thomsen on the phone but couldn't. He left an urgent message instead. The group sat around in tense silence, waiting for the phone to ring. Eventually someone from the SEC called, but it still wasn't the right person. Flumenbaum turned to Mark and Andrew: "OK, you guys, you can go home. There's nothing else to do."

With instructions to share nothing with their wives, Andrew and Mark left the hotel suite. Without exchanging a word, they got into separate cabs. Andrew headed uptown, to the apartment he'd moved into just two days earlier. He walked in the front door, turned into his bedroom, and lay down on top of his bed. He was still wearing his overcoat, suit, and shoes. For the next four hours, he lay there, completely numb, while a live feed ran across his brain.

I've just turned my father in for securities fraud. He's going to go to jail. I have no idea what's going to happen with my life. My entire family is invested with him. Every friend. Many of the employees at the firm. Everyone I know. Who knows how many others. I just turned my father in for securities fraud. He's going to go to jail...

As Andrew stared at the ceiling, he racked his brain for some inkling that he could have seen this coming. How could he possibly have missed something this big? But nothing came, other than the image of his father rotting in jail because he and his brother had turned him in.

He had no idea how much time had passed before Catherine slipped into the room. She sat down on the edge of the bed: an innocent woman with a beautiful daughter who'd brought so much joy to his life. He couldn't allow her to get sucked into this frenzy; it wasn't fair to her. She waited, her huge blue eyes searching his. Her last moment of not knowing. He couldn't bear the thought of living if she left; he couldn't ask her to stay.

Andrew sat up. Leaned over and turned on the light.

"You need to decide whether or not you want to stay with me."

He doesn't remember what he said after that. But when Andrew and Catherine crawled under the covers at the conclusion of the longest, most painful day of his life, Catherine said something that would be forever seared into his memory: "Listen, I'm not going anywhere. Wake me up if you need me. I'll be here all night." She wrapped her arms around him, her cheek resting against his back. In that moment, he says, those words saved his life. He wouldn't have to face this alone.

He has said those same words back to her every night since.

Weeks after Bernie and Ruth celebrated their forty-ninth year of marriage, the couple went to the office Christmas party. In a daze, Ruth "put one foot in front of the other," smiled, had a glass of wine, and left. Beyond that, she doesn't remember a thing. That evening was lost forever to trauma and terror; she has no interest in getting it back.

The only memory that she cannot erase is the image of her son, Mark, fleeing from her home: The "golden child," the "mama's boy" who'd called her every day from college, who'd given her three beautiful grandchildren and had one on the way. It is the image of his back that is burned into her brain, since it is the last vision Ruth would ever have of her son.

She never saw him again.

Chapter Thirteen

CATHERINE AND ANDREW'S NEW NORMAL

D id he tell you when the Ponzi scheme started?"

"What was your role at the firm?"

"Who are some of your father's clients?"

Andrew was sitting in a conference room at his lawyers' offices at Paul, Weiss, being grilled by government officials. Gathered around a long, glossy table were his lawyers, Flumenbaum, Ehrlich, and an associate named Hannah Sholl; Marty London, who was there to provide moral support; an FBI agent; a representative from the SEC; and a representative from the U.S. Attorney's Office. A few other officials joined them via speakerphone. Exhausted and frightened, Andrew answered their questions while Mark waited his turn outside.

"Until I stepped down, I was head of equities. I ran the firm's NASDAQ desk in the late nineties, added the rest of the market-making desk in 2001, and moved to the proprietary-trading desk in 2003. I handed that off to my brother in 2007 or 2008. I don't remember the exact dates."

"Jeffry Picower was a big one; Fred Wilpon and Saul Katz; Carl Shapiro, Norman Levy..."

Ted Cacioppi, the FBI agent who appeared to be in charge of

things, had been kind. When he'd led Andrew into the room that morning, he'd explained that Bernie had already been arrested. He was the one who'd put on the handcuffs. Bernie had "gone quietly, as though expecting us. He seemed relieved." Once again, for the umpteenth time in two days, Andrew had broken down.

After twenty minutes of intense questioning, the FBI agent said, "Thank you. You're free to go." Andrew left Paul, Weiss, got into a cab, and went to his former home, 10 Gracie Square. He hadn't set foot in the place since he and Debbie had split, almost a year earlier, and it felt terrible to return there under these circumstances. But the situation was going to affect everyone, not least his children. He was going to need Debbie's help if they were to come through it all in one piece. He recounted the story of the last twenty-four hours to Debbie, then went into his former study and dialed the headmaster of Dalton.

"Something terrible has happened. My father has been arrested and I need my kids to come home right away." The headmaster was deeply sympathetic, saying she and the school would be there to help in any way they could.

Debbie, too, was immediately supportive. "I'm sorry this happened to you," she said. "I know you had nothing to do with this, and no matter what happens between us, I will always defend you, and if need be, testify on your behalf."

Andrew offered his soon-to-be ex-wife a sad, grateful smile. He still needed her support to accomplish the difficult task of breaking the news to their kids. In spite of everything that had happened between them, he hadn't expected anything less: There may have been an air of mystery surrounding his father, but there was none surrounding him. There were no shadowy business dealings, no strange meetings, no secret clients.

Anne and Emily were pulled out of class and sent home in a cab. A half hour later, Anne burst in the door, her sister close on her heels. Anne was sobbing, screaming, tearing at her hair.

"Who died?" she sobbed. "I know somebody is dead. Is it Papa Bernie?"

Andrew took her into his arms. "Nobody died. Your grandfather's been arrested, OK? Mark and I turned him in for securities fraud, and he's going to go to jail. It's going to be huge news, a massive scandal, and it's going to be terrible. But we're going to be OK."

A fresh round of wailing ensued. When Anne's sobs subsided, she asked, "Are you going to go to jail?"

"*No*. I'm not going to go to jail. This has nothing to do with me. I'll be involved in this mess because I'm his son and work in the business, but I'm not going to go to jail."

They moved over to the sofa in the living room. It was a grand space that commanded gorgeous views of Carl Schurz Park and the East River. Andrew recalled with some irony the real-estate broker commenting that he would be able to see three bridges without moving from that spot. Somehow that no longer seemed very important.

"What's going to happen?" Emily asked. She, too, was crying, and Andrew sat her down next to him, holding her hand.

"I'm not sure how this is going to unfold, but there's going to be a lot of media attention on us in the next few days. It won't be focused on you guys, but there will probably be reporters outside the building. And if you need to talk or ask questions, I'm right here. You can share all of your thoughts and feelings with me. It's going to be difficult, but I promise we're going to be OK."

After more tears and more questions, things settled down. Andrew hugged his daughters good-bye and returned to his new apartment and his bleak new life.

That morning, Catherine had woken up to find the *Wall Street Journal* on their doorstep. There were front-page stories about the housing crisis and the economic meltdown — but not a single mention, yet, of Bernie Madoff. How strange, Catherine remembers thinking: I know what tomorrow's headline will be. The feeling was surreal, as if she'd already experienced the future and was waiting for the world to catch up.

At 7:00 AM, Sophie called out from her bedroom. Her three-year-old's sweet, high-pitched voice offered a fresh jolt of reality: Months earlier, Sophie had begun her first year of nursery school. Catherine had just started to become friendly with one or two of the other mothers. But few Chelsea Day School moms even knew Catherine's last name; they certainly didn't know the name of her fiancé. Maybe not tomorrow, but soon, Catherine thought, all of that is going to change. At some point, people are going to identify me in relation to this scandal, and people are going to talk. They'll know Andrew's financial status, our family dysfunctions, details about our courtship — things you'd never discuss.

Catherine fed Sophie her oatmeal, and the two went downstairs and hailed a taxi. In front of the school, in a sea of mothers, she kissed her daughter good-bye. Then she went to meet her assistant, Katherine, to tell her she needed to find a new job.

A tall, willowy brunette who resembled the *Sports Illustrated* model Marisa Miller, Katherine had been debating, of late, whether to stay in New York or move to Colorado with her boyfriend. She also needed to work more hours than Catherine was able to offer. When they greeted each other at Jamba Juice, Katherine's face immediately registered concern.

"What's wrong?"

"I can't tell you all of the details yet, but someone at Andrew's company did something wrong. It's not Andrew, but I can't tell you who it is. I'm not going to be able to give you any additional work, and I'm probably going to have to resign my job at Dior, and you need to get on a plane to Colorado and get as far away from this story as you possibly can."

Katherine's eyes widened. "What about all the projects I'm in the middle of doing for you? The shelf paper for your apartment?"

"Anything you have for me, just throw in a box and send. Then get out of Dodge. Go home, pack your stuff, get on a plane, and leave New York."

Katherine covered Catherine's hand with her own. "Are you and Andrew going to be all right? Is there anything I can do for you?"

Catherine smiled gratefully. "Yes. Please don't talk about us. I know your best friend works at *Vanity Fair,* but please don't answer reporters' questions. I can't tell you any more than I already have. You'll know everything tomorrow; it's all going to be in the paper."

"But what could be so big that you would have to resign from your job? And that I should go to Aspen?"

Catherine answered with a tight-lipped smile. They hugged good-bye and Catherine rushed back to her apartment. She figured she had twenty-four hours before the paparazzi arrived. With her hands on her hips, she surveyed that bank of windows she loved, the crowning jewel of the apartment. Dragging a ladder out of the supply closet, she started to measure them.

When she was done, her calculations made, she headed not to the expensive decorator showrooms that she and Paul Fortune had planned to visit, but to Bed Bath & Beyond. The curtain panels on sale for $19.99 each were made of polyester gauze. They would be exactly what she wanted: a "caul," like the gestational layer around a fetus, protective but still transparent, so she and Andrew and the girls could look out. Gathering up two shopping bags, she returned home. The curtains, she knew, would be closed for a long, long time.

At 5:00 PM, the news broke on WSJ.com. It was a tiny item, no bigger than an inch: "Bernie Madoff arrested." Andrew came home soon afterward. Exhausted from his day with the authorities, he showered and went straight to bed. Catherine closed her office door and called her friend Jack Hearn, whom she always affectionately referred to by his last name. The two had met in 2002, when they'd started chatting in line at City Bakery and realized they both knew Bob Scott, an investor at Urban Angler: Hearn in his capacity as a bank executive, and Catherine through her work with the store. They'd been having lunch almost every other week since.

"Sweetheart!" he greeted her when she called. "I'm so glad you called."

"Hearn—"

"I know we haven't talked since San Francisco, and it's my fault—"

"Hearn—"

"I know you saw our friends Rosanna and Zoli while you were out there, and I felt left out that all of you were seeing each other and never even called me—"

"Hearn! Andrew's father was arrested."

For the first time in their one-sided conversation, Hearn was silent.

"What happened?" he eventually managed.

"I don't know what happened, but Bernie used the words 'Ponzi scheme' and 'fifty billion dollars.' The story is up on WSJ.com."

She heard him type in the URL and waited as he read.

"Sweetheart, sweetheart...empires fall. That's what they do. Empires fall."

Her hand holding the receiver started to shake.

"What are you and Andrew doing for lunch tomorrow?" Hearn asked.

"I don't think—"

"We'll go early, and we'll go someplace where nobody knows

Andrew and nobody knows you. I have to leave early to go downtown for Maria's show anyway."

Catherine saw the two paths laid out at her feet: Were they going to isolate themselves and bunker in, or were they going to face the world? Andrew had nothing to hide, she thought. In fact, he'd done something beyond brave. Not only had he confronted the reality of what had happened, he'd marched to the authorities and turned his father in. Not everyone would have done that. The stress of the past two days had been overwhelming, and she cherished the idea of seeing her good friend over lunch. But how was she going to get Andrew to agree to come along?

"Let's do it," she agreed. They made a plan to meet at Papillon, on 54th Street and Madison Avenue, at 11:00 AM the next day.

News of Bernie's arrest spread quickly. On December 12, 2008, Catherine and Andrew awoke to find the story dominating the headlines. "Invest Big 'Fesses to $50B 'Fraud,'" blared the *New York Post*. "Look at Wall St. Wizard Finds Magic Had Skeptics" was splashed across the *New York Times*. E-mails and text messages started to flood in from friends. For the first time, the implications of what had happened were becoming clear: Ninety percent of the notes were from Catherine's loved ones. Most expressed concern and support, then confusion. None of Catherine's friends had any idea of Andrew's wealth—let alone that he was connected to anything totaling $50 billion. An e-mail from her former assistant, Katherine, read: "When you said this would be big news, you really weren't kidding!"

Andrew also received supportive messages from friends, but nowhere near as many as Catherine. The finances of the firm were closely tied to Andrew's colleagues, relatives, and friends; fearful of putting themselves in legal jeopardy, most had lawyered up immediately. The advice they received was universal: Don't talk to anybody, especially in the Madoff family.

Again, Catherine took Sophie to preschool, and again remained under the radar. Andrew waited for her in the car, then drove her to Gracious Home, where she picked up the curtain track, screws, and a new drill bit. Then they headed to Papillon to meet Hearn. Andrew hadn't wanted to go.

"So when will be the day when you leave the house again?" Catherine had asked him. "Because if you hole up now, it will be that much harder later."

"But today will be the worst day."

"So do it on the worst day. Then you know it will only get easier. You're going to have to show your face eventually. I know it may feel terrible, but you have to force yourself to do it."

Reluctantly, he'd agreed to go. After he dropped her off in front of the restaurant, he left to find parking. Five minutes later, Andrew joined Catherine, Hearn, and Hearn's former assistant at their table.

"Are you OK?" Catherine asked.

Andrew looked around. "Yeah. I don't think anybody recognizes me here."

The four ate their burgers, listened to Hearn's stories about his recent travels, and avoided mention of the scandal. But at the end of the meal, Hearn enclosed Andrew in a massive bear hug.

"You take care of this girl," he said. "And let her take care of you. She's always made my life interesting, but it sure as hell got a lot more interesting yesterday."

Hearn, Catherine knew, was leaving their lunch to go down to CNBC. From time to time he appeared on *Closing Bell* with Maria Bartiromo; she would definitely ask him something about the Madoff news. But Catherine trusted him entirely: He would never allow himself to be pulled into wild speculation on air.

After lunch, Catherine ran into a little bodega across the street from Papillon and bought a copy of the *New York Post* and the *New York Daily News,* to see how the coverage was unfolding. When Andrew tried to withdraw cash from the bodega's ATM, his card didn't work. Frowning, he switched to a credit card. It didn't work. He tried another, then another, inserting and reinserting them, as a thin layer of sweat gathered on his forehead.

None of his cards worked.

Unbeknownst to Andrew, the government had sent a letter to financial institutions: "Freeze all accounts related to Bernard L. Madoff." The banks had interpreted the order to include all relatives of Bernard L. Madoff. Mark, Shana, Debbie, Peter—none of their credit or ATM cards worked. It had taken less than a day for the banks to execute the freeze order. It would take weeks to clear it up.

Andrew carried the curtain track up to the apartment while Catherine dragged the ladder into the girls' rooms. She assembled her mounting hardware, got out her drill, and spent the next five hours putting up the track and hanging curtains as she listened to the entire season of NPR's *RadioLab* on her computer.

Once again, Andrew left to meet with Mark and his lawyers. The legal team needed to educate themselves about Mark and Andrew, as well as their careers and families, in order to gather technical detail about the business. The brothers discussed the pros and cons of joint legal representation. Overnight, Andrew's relationship with Mark seemed to be back where it had been: Whatever had been going on between them no longer mattered—they would get through this together.

When Andrew returned home, he started to unpack boxes. While he was stacking his bicycle gear in the hall closet, Flumenbaum called. Andrew leapt to answer the phone.

"I got a call from your father's lawyer. They need two more signatures on his bail bond. Will you and Mark sign?"

"Absolutely no way," Andrew said.

"That's what I thought. Thanks."

It was already dark when Anne and Emily arrived. They were spending their first weekend in the apartment, something Andrew had fretted over; he wanted it to go well. That was before his entire world had imploded. Catherine opened the door with the drill in her hand, goggles on her head, and gloves sticking out of her back pocket to the sight of "two girls who looked like urchin children, with the weight of the world on their shoulders."

"I just put curtains up in your rooms," she blurted out. She had no idea what else to say. Both girls started sobbing and fell into her arms. Andrew and Sophie joined the group hug. In that moment, all the normal hardships of blending a family, the anxieties of divorce, were erased. The five of them stood by the door, hugging and crying.

Catherine ordered dinner from Flex Mussels. With Andrew's credit card frozen, she was now covering their household expenses. Andrew expressed relief that the order would not be in his name.

"Well, I'm changing my name," Anne said.

"That's crazy," Andrew said. "I understand your impulse to do that, but it's way too soon to know if that's necessary."

"I don't want to be prejudged on who I am."

"All your friends at school know who you are, and if you change your name today, they'll *still* know who you are. If you want to make a fresh start in college, that's up to you. That's three years away. Let's cross that bridge when we come to it."

"I'm not going to Gabby's bat mitzvah tomorrow," Emily piped up.

Andrew turned to his younger daughter. "You need to go. You need to face the world. Your friends are going to be very supportive."

"I'm not going."

"You're making a mistake. It's better if you don't run away from this."

Andrew's phone rang. He held it up to show Catherine: Ruth.

By then, he'd expressly been instructed by his lawyers, "You cannot speak to your father, your mother, your cousin, your uncle, or anyone who can affect your case." He and Ruth hadn't spoken since he'd left his parents' apartment. He answered it anyway.

"You need to sign that bail bond!" Ruth shouted, causing Andrew to jump. "Your father is in jail!" Her voice was shrill and aggressive; it seemed to come from a woman he didn't know.

"How can you ask me to do this—after what he's done?" Andrew cried.

"I can't believe you're turning your back on your father!" she screamed.

"That's the craziest thing I've ever heard—there's no way I'm doing this!"

Anne and Emily emerged from their rooms and peeked anxiously into the kitchen.

"You have to sign for your father's bail! You have to!" Ruth was apoplectic.

"There's no chance!" He hung up and threw down his phone; it bounced off the table. Andrew felt a swell of emotion. His chest started to heave. Pushing past his frightened daughters, he ran into his darkened office and again sank to his knees. Howls rose from his body. His mother had never gotten angry with him like that, not once in his life. He'd tried to be the perfect son. And he'd thought she'd been the perfect mother.

Catherine followed him into the office but, seeing him collapse to the floor, quietly backed away. His wails ricocheted through the empty apartment and echoed off the walls. She imagined the neighbors could hear, even in the apartments across the way.

"Should we go in there?" Emily asked, her lower lip starting to tremble.

"No, let him cry."

The girls retreated to their rooms. Eventually, Andrew emerged from the office.

"That might be the last time I ever hear my mother's voice," he said, rubbing his red, raw eyes.

Ruth was going to stay with Bernie; she'd made her choice clear.

Ruth sat with her lawyer as he patiently explained the conditions of her husband's bail bond. He needed two more signatures in addition to Ruth's and Peter's. She couldn't go to any of her friends, all of whom had been burned in the scandal. That left Mark and Andrew. Her sons' futures had also been destroyed and their lives upended, but somehow Ruth was unable to process that.

Now, looking back on the conversation, Ruth remembers calling Andrew and saying, "Could you please sign the bail bond?" She didn't yell, she says, more surprised by that claim than anything else.

"I don't get angry. That's a problem I have."

She stares into the distance, frowning, in thought. "They had to sign something…I don't even remember why. Maybe Bernie wanted them to put up their apartments."

Another long pause. "Angry? No. I don't recall that."

It had been four days since Bernie's confession. The curtains were up. Emily had decided to go to Gabby's bat mitzvah. Catherine and Andrew waited for the cable guy to arrive.

"Are you sure you want cable?" Catherine asked. "Shouldn't we tell him to wait?"

"No, let's get it," Andrew said. "I want to make life as normal as possible for the girls."

While they waited, Catherine composed a memo for the door-man of their building: "Until further notice, no one is to be admitted up to our apartment under any circumstances, except for the following people..."

Cable was installed. Emily returned from the bat mitzvah, breathless with happiness: Dozens of friends had circled her and folded her into a giant tween hug. Emily and Anne disappeared into their rooms to navigate the hundreds of supportive Facebook messages they'd received from friends. That afternoon, the girls' friends poured into the apartment, the rooms alive with chatter. The buoyant teens watched *The Notebook* while Catherine and Andrew unpacked boxes. For a few hours, they all pretended life was as it had been. Even Mark displayed some humor, calling Andrew to laugh that the *New York Post* had gotten it wrong, that it should have run the headline "Made-off with the Money." (Most people then were still mispronouncing the name "*Mah-doff.*") He had always enjoyed the clever headlines in the *Post,* and for years had harbored fantasies of joining the team that wrote them.

By December 14, the thunderclouds had once again rolled in. "You could not turn on the television; it was like someone sticking you in the eye with an ice pick," Catherine recalls. Yet despite all their efforts they could not possibly escape the story, which was in every newspaper and every tabloid, and even on Taxi TV: complete, nonstop, blanket coverage.

That day, Emily went to visit a friend; Anne, Andrew, and Catherine went to Five Points, a bistro on Bond Street, for brunch. When they returned to their apartment, they spotted a man standing in front of their building, an expensive camera slung around his neck.

Anne scrunched down in the backseat. "What are we going to

do?" she cried. "He's going to put my picture in the paper, and everyone's going to know..." She started to cry.

"They're not going to take a picture of you; you're a kid," Andrew said, turning around in his seat and squeezing his daughter's knee. "I'm the one they want."

He pulled into his parking garage and shut off the ignition, then turned to Catherine. "Do I walk backward? Should I try to hide my face?"

"No. You didn't do anything wrong. You walk like a man." Catherine knew this was easier said than done. "Let's get out of the car, split up into different directions, and enter the building separately," she suggested.

Anne was not photographed. But when Catherine walked into the building, the man leaned in: click, click, click. Then Andrew approached: click, click, click, click, click.

By the following day, their photos were on the cover of the *New York Post,* and the crowd of paparazzi around the entrance of their building had mushroomed to fifteen. Andrew pushed past them, steering his bike with one hand, his backpack slung over his shoulder. Flashbulbs exploded around him. He shielded his eyes from the blinding light.

"Did you know?"

"Have you talked to your mother?"

"Did Ruth know?"

Swinging a leg over his bike, he rode as fast as he could away from the hostile crowd, pumping his legs and leaning into the wind. Blocks flew by as he picked up speed. He felt a swell of anger rise through his chest. Earlier that day, he'd gotten a call from a board member at the Lymphoma Research Foundation requesting his immediate resignation.

"I understand you guys are embarrassed about all this," Andrew had said. "But you need to give me the benefit of the doubt. I am telling you I am not involved in this crime. My term is up in a few weeks anyway. I am not resigning."

Andrew pedaled harder. Rounding the corner on 23rd Street, he dropped his bicycle against a wall, ripped open his backpack, took out his brand-new cable box—he'd unplugged it as soon as he'd gotten home that morning—and "practically threw it into the open doorway" of Time Warner Cable Express.

Then he hopped onto his seat and rode back into the eye of the storm.

Chapter Fourteen

BOMB SCARE

Bank of America closed Andrew's accounts. An envelope arrived, containing a check and an official letter: "Here's your check. We won't do business with you anymore," Andrew recalls. Wachovia closed Mark's accounts. In the days and weeks following the confession, Andrew had to make more visits to banks than he ever had in his life, in order to move money from accounts that had just been closed. Each time was "humiliating, scary, embarrassing." Andrew would stand in line, feeling his pulse quicken. Approaching the teller, he would smile and pass her his slip. She would return his smile, look down, and tap on her keyboard. Her smile would disappear. A manager would discreetly be summoned. Offering Andrew a clipped smile, the manager would consider the screen, which trumpeted the words "LEGAL HOLD." A more senior executive would appear. The two would confer in whispers, before politely declining his request. Andrew would wish he could sink through the floor.

After numerous unsuccessful attempts to find a bank willing to take his money, Andrew tried the small local bank where Catherine kept her accounts. It billed itself as the "friendly bank," and this moniker was true even for the sons of Bernie Madoff. Andrew and

Mark were each able to open personal checking and business accounts there. But every day they lived in fear that they'd receive an official letter from the "friendly bank," too.

For Andrew's entire life, he had been very proud of his name and the cachet it carried, particularly when it came to banks and brokerage firms. Whenever he'd visited the Chase bank down the street from the Lipstick Building, a bank executive would rush out from behind his desk, clasping his longtime customer's hands in greeting.

"Mr. Madoff! How are you? Is there anything we can do for you today?"

Now, overnight, no one would make eye contact with him. He couldn't blame the tellers, who were behaving no differently "than if Osama bin Laden had walked in and tried to make a withdrawal." But that didn't make the experience any easier: "It probably seems silly that I would care so much about this, but boy, did I care," Andrew recalls. Whenever he had to leave for the bank, he would shore up his shoulders, take a deep breath, and say to Catherine, "OK, honey, I have to go to the bank."

"I'm sorry," she would say, offering a sad smile. When he returned home, he always had to nap.

The ignominy continued. On December 16, 2008, Andrew's divorce lawyer from Hogan & Hartson dropped him as a client, citing a conflict of interest. Andrew's legal team explained the truth to him: Hogan & Hartson was a big firm and had done a simple calculation that it would be more lucrative to represent throngs of burned investors than a single Madoff. For them it was a business decision, but for Andrew it was another stick in the eye, not to mention a waste of the tens of thousands of dollars he'd already paid them. Between the other firms hired by Madoff victims and the divorce lawyers Debbie had seen in 2002, Andrew was left with few choices for representation. So this is what life will be like from now on, Andrew realized. Soon after that, the U.S. Attorney imposed financial restrictions on both brothers: They signed a "voluntary" consent order agreeing not to fritter away their money, take out any loans, or transfer their funds to Switzerland. They were to report every penny they spent over a certain dollar amount and submit meticulous billing details—an order in place to this day. Originally, the U.S. Attorney's Office had submitted an extremely low number; Flumenbaum came back with a more reasonable amount for men supporting families with children and charged with maintaining the assets in place. That number was approved. While the details of the order were not made public, the U.S. Attorney's willingness to negotiate what Andrew and Mark considered a fair and reasonable agreement was the first indication that the government didn't see the brothers as a problem. The government did need to place restrictions on them but wasn't looking to punish them.

In February, Andrew and Catherine drove to Connecticut to clean his boat. On the way, they stopped by the summer home he'd owned with Debbie to check the messages on his machine.

"Hi, this is a producer from the David Letterman show," one began. "We'd like to invite you to come on the show and read the top-ten list of reasons why it sucks to have the last name Madoff." The producer, of course, had no idea he'd reached a *real* Madoff. Andrew and Catherine shared a grim laugh, then deleted the message.

A box had arrived for Catherine. She'd just come home from yoga class, pushed through the throng of paparazzi, and was inside her front door, waiting for her heart to stop racing.

Hurrying from behind his desk, her doorman showed her the box. Clearly, it had seen better days: Wrapped in yards of packing tape and streaked with sticky black goo, it had no return address and an incorrect ZIP code and was lettered in an unfamiliar, messy hand.

"It's kind of strange," the doorman said, in his thick Slavic accent. "Do you want me to throw it away?"

"No, that's OK, I'll take it," she said, hoisting it onto her hip. Everything is fine, everything is normal, she'd been telling herself for days. If she acted like everything was fine, she thought, maybe life *would* go back to normal.

When she walked into the apartment, she found Andrew talking to his childhood friend Ari.

"You've got to stop leaving the house," Ari was saying. "Stop talking to your friends. Just clam up. You have to go into your shell."

"I'm not doing that," Andrew argued. "I'm not running from this. Why should I be ashamed to show my face? I didn't *do* anything." He was unpacking groceries, angrily stacking cartons of yogurt in the fridge.

"It's not that. You've got to understand: People don't want to see you living a normal life. They want to see you suffering. If they see you living a normal life, it's going to make them really mad."

What Ari was suggesting was exactly the approach Mark was taking. He'd been bunkered in his apartment since the confession: blinds closed, phone off, door triple-locked.

"Someone could shoot you!" Ari added.

Catherine sighed and put the box down on the living room floor.

"Nobody is trying to shoot us," she said. Then she felt a flash of alarm and thought: What if someone tries to shoot us?

The phone rang. Catherine picked it up as Sophie tore through the kitchen, her babysitter, Josie, close at her heels.

"Sophie!" she admonished, leaping out of the way. "Hello?"

It was Sophie's dad, Jon. He was breathless.

"One of my clients is very high up in the government; he

works in national security. And he just called to tell me that the Israeli Mossad has a contract out to kill Andrew."

"Who said that?"

"It was a person very high up in the government. I don't want Sophie in that house!"

"Nobody is trying to kill Andrew," she said, as Ari wildly nodded, pointing to the phone. See? See?

She got off the phone. Eventually, she was able to hustle Ari out of the house. She turned to Andrew.

"What are we going to do about this sketchy box?"

"Someone probably took a dump in the box and sent it to us," Andrew said.

"But what do we do? Should we call the police?"

"I don't know," Andrew said. "Do we bother them for something like this?"

They both considered the box, walking around it. Sophie was sitting on the sofa, watching *Kipper* on TV, while Josie brushed her hair. Catherine glanced at her daughter.

"I think we should call them. It's probably nothing, but I don't want to take any chances. Let's leave it to them."

"OK."

Andrew dialed the local police station. "I'm Andrew Madoff. I'm the son of Bernard Madoff. I just got a box in the mail and it's a bit suspicious-looking. Should I open it, or...what should I do?"

"Don't touch it; leave it exactly where it is," the officer exclaimed. "We'll be there in a minute."

The moment Andrew hung up the phone, Catherine heard sirens.

They met a young patrolman by their elevator. "Phew, that is bad news," he said, peering into the living room. "Come downstairs with me right now." He pushed Catherine and Andrew into the elevator. When they reached the ground floor, he said, "You can't go back up."

"But my daughter is in the apartment!" she cried, thinking he'd been planning to write a report and accompany them back upstairs.

"Ma'am, she's on the other side of the box, and protocol says that you can't walk past the box. You've got to stay here and let the bomb squad take care of it."

More police had arrived. Fire trucks pulled up in front of the building, sirens wailing.

"So you're telling me that since my daughter and her babysitter are on the other side of the box, they have to stay in the apartment with a bomb, while we're down here?"

"I'm sorry, ma'am. You shouldn't have taken it upstairs. If it was sitting here on the sidewalk, they would have been able to come out."

Catherine turned on her heel and in a flash was running up the stairwell, taking the steps two a time. She faintly heard people calling her name. When she entered her apartment, she found Josie still brushing Sophie's hair. Catherine called to Josie to bring Sophie downstairs and quickly picked up the box. She marched back down the stairwell with determination. As she walked out of her building, the newly formed ring of fifty firefighters and policemen, some in riot gear, slowly backed away from her. Catherine deposited the box on the sidewalk, went back into her building, and ran up the stairs again. She gathered her daughter into her arms and bundled her into her shoes and coat. Then Catherine, Josie, and Sophie made their way outside, and Catherine transferred Sophie into Andrew's arms, where she burrowed into his neck. By then, the entire block had been cordoned off with police tape and wooden barricades. Traffic on the nearby avenues had slowed to a snarl.

Catherine dialed Jon. "I need you to come uptown right now."

"I'm closing up the store; I can't get there for an hour," he said.

"We might have a bomb outside our building."

A noise escaped from his throat. "I'll be right there."

Catherine took Sophie from Andrew and walked toward the wall of firefighters. One stopped her as she tried to walk past him.

"You can't leave the cordoned area, ma'am," he said.

"The hell I can't! I'm taking my daughter out of here." She pushed past the firefighter and carried her sleepy, pajama-wearing daughter to a café on York Avenue that she and Jon had designated as a meeting place.

"Why are we here, Mommy?"

"It's a fire drill, sweetheart."

Jon was waiting under the awning; they didn't exchange two words. Catherine transferred Sophie to her father's arms, kissed her daughter, and walked up the street. There, Josie was huddled next to Andrew, shaking, near tears. Catherine walked her out of the line of firefighters again, put her into a cab, and returned to the scene.

A man with "an air of authority," wearing an overcoat and a badge, was inspecting the box. He looked up at Catherine. "Do you know what this is?"

"No, I don't."

"You don't recognize anything about it?"

She shook her head.

"OK, I don't think it's a bomb. I'm just going to cut it open. You OK with that?"

Catherine nodded and stepped closer to Andrew. He circled an arm around her waist.

Taking a multi-tool knife, the agent cut through the side of the box. He carefully peeled back the cardboard and tape and turned it over.

Out fell a bundle of woven raffia—the shelf paper her assistant, Katherine, had promised to send.

★   ★   ★

In her haste to "get out of Dodge," Katherine had taken her former boss at her word: *Anything you have for me, just throw in a box and send.* The same day they'd met at Jamba Juice, she'd scrawled what she'd thought was Catherine's new address on the front of the box—actually an amalgamation of Andrew's old address and Catherine's new one, hence the incorrect ZIP code. The box had then bounced from post office to post office, growing more and more battered as the postal service tried to figure out where it should be delivered.

A few detectives gathered upstairs to take Andrew and Catherine's statements. One of them, Efrain Curet, said, "By the way, I'm on your dad's detail over at Sixty-fourth Street."

Andrew swallowed. "How's he doing?"

"He's OK."

"May I have your card?" Catherine asked.

After the fireman had left, the barricades had been removed, and all the reports had been filed, Catherine collapsed into her desk chair in her office. She opened her computer and typed an e-mail to Katherine Dart.

"Hey! Thanks for the shelf paper. You just cost the City of New York a lot of money."

At least I still have a sense of humor, she thought grimly, powering down her computer for the night.

Chapter Fifteen

HOUSE ARREST

At 7:00 AM on December 11, 2008, the FBI knocked on Bernie Madoff's penthouse door. His doorman had called up to announce their arrival, and Ruth and Bernie changed out of their pajamas and into T-shirts and jeans. Bernie left the apartment quietly; the sensitive agent waited to cuff him until he was out of view of his wife.

Ruth went into her kitchen, made coffee, and stared at the front page of the *New York Times*. She lit a cigarette and started to cry. She had known since the previous day that this moment was coming but hadn't realized it would come so early.

The night before, Bernie had told her that he was going to pay the traders, see his lawyer, and send the checks he had in his desk drawer. He needed about a week—then he'd turn himself in. She'd nodded, numbly. Yes, OK. Then the FBI showed up. "It must have been the boys," Bernie guessed.

Ruth wasn't angry at her sons. If anything, she was "scared to death...in a state of terror." Instantly, the blinds were drawn, the doors were locked; the unused penthouse terrace was now in paparazzi crosshairs.

In the afternoon, Ruth made her way on the subway to the federal court at 500 Pearl Street for Bernie's bail hearing. Sharing a bench with her husband of nearly fifty years was an assortment of drug dealers. Judge Louis L. Stanton, she noticed, treated the accused assembled before him as human beings, making sure they had their health papers in order and understood the proceedings. "He handled everyone so fairly it was a pleasure to witness," says Ruth. From the moment he took the bench, she loved him. It was a small respite from the nightmare unfolding around her, though certainly not an indicator of things to come.

Bernie's bail was set at $10 million. Ruth was allowed to put up her Montauk and Palm Beach homes. The judge eventually modified the requirement for four signatures on the bond and accepted the two they had. Bernie was escorted home. There, with a policeman standing watch in the kitchen, Ruth prepared dinner for Bernie, just as she always had. They'd had a special indoor grill installed in the kitchen when they moved into the apartment so that Ruth could cook Bernie's steaks the way he liked them: black and blue. On autopilot, she put it to use that evening.

That night and the next day, the apartment was outfitted with highly sophisticated surveillance equipment, and Ruth and Bernie hired a security firm, one of the conditions of his bail. Ruth was astonished by the staggering cost of the service: $30,000 a month.

"It was a fortune and came from money he'd been accused of stealing," Ruth says, amazed. "He paid his lawyers and security firm out of that money and was free on bail. A poorer person would not get the same treatment. It was incredible to me."

In the weeks that followed, Ruth went through her days "like a robot." She and Bernie would go upstairs to the kitchen, have breakfast, put the TV on, and read the newspaper. They watched "a lot of TCM." At night, she cooked grilled chicken, hamburger, turkey burgers, chili—Bernie was a meat eater. Afraid to put even one "toe out the door," she placed herself under house arrest, too, leaving only to go to the Food Emporium or to borrow books from the library.

Any semblance of normal life was out of the question, Ruth soon learned. When she needed to get her highlights touched up, she called her longtime colorist, Giselle, at Pierre Michel salon, to make an appointment.

"You know you can't come here; some of our clients have lost money."

"Can you come to the house?" Ruth asked.

"No, they wouldn't let me do that."

Ruth's housekeeper of many years continued to come every week, refusing to accept money. Then Ruth had to let her go. "I wasn't allowed to pay her and I couldn't *not* pay her," she says.

No one visited. Those who weren't muzzled by lawyers or consumed by rage were simply too afraid. Ruth understood: "What does one say? How does one behave?" Even the policemen and security officers waited downstairs in their cars. "Once in a while, one of them would come up and kibitz," Ruth recalls.

It didn't matter: She didn't feel like seeing anyone except lawyers. She was too miserable.

Yet unwelcome visitors managed to find their way into her home. Ruth once answered a knock at the door to find a dark-haired stranger standing before her. "He wore jeans and a T-shirt," she says, "and looked like he was about fourteen years old."

"Are you Mrs. Madoff?"

"Yes."

"I'm a real-estate agent. I've come to look at the apartment."

"No, you're not." She firmly closed the door on the young man, who turned out to be a reporter from the *New York Post*. Shaking, she'd called the police, who promptly arrested him. He was charged with trespassing and issued a summons.

An envelope arrived, bearing a Fifth Avenue address. Ruth did not recognize the name of the sender or the "gorgeous" cream-colored stationery nestled inside. In beautiful cursive, a woman had written, "When your husband goes to prison, I hope he gets fucked with a big, black cock." Crying out, Ruth tore it to shreds. After that, she ripped up every letter she received without reading it.

When the paparazzi outside her building swelled to several dozen, Ruth started to exit through William-Wayne & Company, an antique shop on the ground floor—until the owners stopped allowing her to use it. Then her doorman acted as sentry.

"I wouldn't come downstairs right now."

"OK, they're gone, Mrs. Madoff."

Once, her doorman had mistakenly given her the all clear and a paparazzo, who'd been hiding in a doorway, chased her all the way to the supermarket. The building's super, Jose, immediately vacated his post and accompanied her to the store.

Most of the tenants, says Ruth, were "incredibly decent," accosting the paparazzi on her behalf, checking to make sure she was OK. Some, though, feeling burned not by the fraud but by Bernie's arrogance as building president—"he was very particular about the way things looked and wanted control over the lobby," Ruth says—tried to get the disgraced couple kicked out.

In the immediate aftermath of the confession, feverish rumors swirled in the press. It was reported that Ruth spent $2,500 a month at her gym; that she'd never settled bills she owed at fancy restaurants. She never considered hiring a PR company, thinking they were expensive and useless. In retrospect, Ruth calls this "a huge mistake."

"I was a moron," she says. "At the time Al Gore was getting a divorce, you read about it once, then never again. I didn't know who to call. I had no network. And when I finally did try to hire someone, they would refuse to take me on as a client, claiming a conflict of interest with another client."

People stared at Ruth on the street—she hated that. She didn't expect anyone to say "poor Ruth" but didn't expect them to hate her, either, and was deeply hurt by it. Nothing stung like the public's loathing when she'd always been so well liked: It was an entirely new and shocking source of pain.

Ruth couldn't have known that Catherine, blocks away, was often writing e-mails to her—only to delete them before sending. Conflicted about the prospect of her future mother-in-law living under self-imposed house arrest, knowing in her heart that Ruth hadn't been involved in her husband's scheme, Catherine wanted to reach out to her but knew it would seem disloyal when Andrew's feelings were in such turmoil. She came closest to pressing "send" when the editor with whom Ruth had worked on her cookbook released a statement to the media that Ruth had not actually worked on the book.

"It made me so mad," Catherine recalls. "I knew that cookbook was the only personal accomplishment of which she was truly proud." *Hang in there,* Catherine would write, then erase the words from her screen. Who knew how Ruth would even take the gesture? Perhaps she would just be angry, Catherine thought.

As for the man who had done this to her, Ruth wasn't angry at him. Watching Bernie sit in front of the television, day after day, sobbing, she felt her "heart was breaking for him." She knew what he'd done was "horrible," but she couldn't "process it to the monster level." She simply couldn't feel hate in her heart for the man she'd loved for nearly fifty years. He'd "gotten in over his head," he'd explained, and she believed him. How could she not? And anyway, how could *anyone* know how they would have reacted in her situation? "Well, my husband wouldn't have done such a thing," friends had said. Ruth thought: Oh, no? Really? Was your husband one of the most respected men on Wall Street, given numerous awards, and appointed president of NASDAQ? Was your husband unfailingly loving and kind? Sure, Bernie had his quirks, but he'd been a wonderful husband and father. Ruth had never doubted for one second that he loved her, "no matter what was going on." Mistakes he'd made in their marriage were now water under the bridge. How could she *possibly* have seen this coming?

As she had done throughout her marriage, Ruth asked Bernie only the most perfunctory questions during those four lonely months. A story would come out in the paper; she might bring it up.

"I never should have said fifty billion," Bernie scoffed. "There never *was* fifty billion. I just tried to figure out what the accounts would have been worth and that became the number. I don't think it's correct. That Picard is a lunatic."

Bernie picked up the remote and changed the channel. That was the end of the discussion. It was how they'd communicated for nearly fifty years, since Ruth had been a teen, struggling to make her fastidious new husband happy.

The truth is, Ruth did get angry. Just not at Bernie.

Though she doesn't remember it, she was angry with her sons for not signing the bail bond. She was angry at the paparazzi. Angry at the press. Angry at her friends for deserting her. Angry, in fact, at the entire world.

Just not at the man who'd ruined her life.

That is why, on Christmas Eve, separated from her children, on the brink of losing her only connection to the outside world, in the depths of a bottomless depression, Ruth decided she'd had enough.

"I can't do this anymore," she told Bernie, through tears. "I want to kill myself." And the couple who had spent their entire lives together decided to end them together, too.

Since the confession, thoughts of suicide have crossed her mind many times, she later admits. "To slog through being miserable for no good end—what's the point? But I can't...do anything because of my grandchildren. I couldn't do that to them. So it's really a conundrum. It's terrible. But maybe that will change. Maybe I'll want to stay alive. I can't see it right now, but maybe. I've been optimistic my whole life."

Even when the specter of having to leave her current, temporary home loomed, she mused, "If I have to leave here, I'll kill myself."

Back on December 24, 2008, though, the statement was a real wish.

In a small safe in the bedroom, Ruth kept "carefully chosen, beautiful pieces of antique jewelry" with far more sentimental value than the many more costly pieces she owned. She'd planned to give them to the grandchildren someday. Now she found herself on her knees, opening the safe and taking the pieces out. Hands trembling, she spread them on the carpet and separated them into four piles. Gathering up handfuls of jewelry, she wrapped them in paper towels and shoved them into plastic bags.

She'd been impulsive her entire life. Once she made up her mind to do something, she "had to do it." Sending the jewelry was mindless work, and she had no thought that what she was doing was illegal—or that the property was technically no longer hers. Get it out, get it over with, she thought, fumbling to stuff the jewelry into four envelopes: one for Catherine, one for Stephanie, one for Susan, and one for Debbie. Closing each envelope with "yards" of masking tape, she lettered the addresses of her daughters-in-law in a sloppy hand.

It was already 4:30 PM and she was racing against the clock. The post office was going to close for the holiday and she needed stamps. Certainly, she couldn't send the packages FedEx or weigh them at the post office, so she would have to estimate how many stamps each package required. After she did this and found a place to buy the stamps, she stuck dozens of them crookedly all over each package. Then she ran out one last time, to drop them in the mailbox on the corner.

Ruth and Bernie went downstairs to a small second kitchen they'd installed near their bedroom, took out two glasses, and filled them with water. Each had a bottle of a hundred Ambien on the counter. Ruth looked at the bottles of Ambien, feeling terror start to creep in. She wasn't sure if she was doing the right thing. She wasn't sure she wanted to die. She was, she says, "a complete wreck." She had no idea whether Bernie was going along with her plan because he wanted to die, too, or because he simply couldn't refuse her this one request after what he'd put her through. Shaking out the pills into her hand, she lifted her glass.

Ruth took ten Ambien and "maybe some Klonopin." She didn't drink alcohol, because she didn't want to vomit and neutralize the effect of the pills.

Bernie gave her his signature smirk, took more, and "got very sick." Somehow, they made it to their bedroom; Ruth doesn't remember how.

Then, for the next fifteen hours, Ruth and Bernie slept the sleep of the dead—but didn't actually die. When they awoke, they looked at each other and said, "Well, we're still here."

Ruth spent the rest of that groggy morning berating herself. She should have drunk wine and *then* taken the pills. She felt like a moron. Who knew Ambien couldn't actually kill you?

In February, Ruth's sixth grandchild, Nick, was born to Mark and Stephanie. Her lawyer called to deliver the happy news.

It was Wednesday, March 11, 2009, the night before the verdict was read. Ruth and Bernie had changed into their pajamas and climbed into bed. They held each other, terrified. She could feel his electronic monitor rubbing against her ankle, a sensation she found "creepy." Eventually, the Ambien they'd taken—only two each this time — took effect. They had no idea if Bernie was ever going to spend another night at home.

Ruth didn't attend the hearing. A few people had called to ask if she was going. She said no. They asked if she wanted them to come over. Again, she declined. She felt so ashamed of what was going on that she couldn't bear to be with anybody.

While Bernie stood before the judge, a frenzy of angry victims outside the courthouse, Ruth read and watched TV. She knew her husband was going away for good. He was old: seventy. Both of his parents had died in their sixties. He was going to get a sentence of twenty-five years, she figured; there wasn't a chance it would be anything less. She was resigned to that fact. But still, she held on to a glimmer of hope that first he'd come back home. That they'd get to spend a few final weeks together.

Bernard L. Madoff was found guilty and remanded to the Metropolitan Correctional Center in downtown Manhattan to await sentencing. The judge ruled that he would not be able to serve that time at home. The woman who'd never been alone a day in her life "freaked out" when her lawyer delivered the news: She sat on the edge of her bed, sobbing, clutching the phone. To her, it was like someone had just told her that her husband was dead. She couldn't believe she was never going to see him at home again.

When she hung up, she stared into the abyss of her new life. How she was going to start over — why she would even begin to try — was beyond her. She was sixty-seven years old. She'd never cultivated a career, established a name for herself, or even made her own friends. Her sons weren't speaking to her. She was about to get kicked out of her home.

As Andrew had just a few months earlier, Ruth sat frozen in place for hours, afraid to move.

Chapter Sixteen

THE NEWS GOES FROM BAD TO WORSE

If the first few days of the scandal were taxing for Mark and Andrew, they were nothing compared to what followed. Overnight, the brothers found themselves out of work. With nowhere to go during the day, they spent hours in marathon meetings with lawyers, who needed to know everything about what they knew and when, what information the government might have, what they might be accused of, and what they had been exposed to. Their legal team went over the facts of their lives and careers in excruciating detail. When Andrew wasn't with lawyers or at home, he spoke with other dislocated employees of the firm, meeting up for lunch or a game of squash to talk about the struggle of moving on.

Though their lawyers tried to be as reassuring as possible, Andrew could "tell" by their questions that they weren't presuming the brothers' innocence. Often, criminal defense attorneys have clients who are guilty—or, at the very least, telling half-truths. But over the course of several weeks, continually impressed by the amount of information Mark and Andrew had provided, the lawyers began treating the brothers differently. Every story checked out; every detail turned out to be correct. Andrew says this "went a long way toward building our credibility and convincing our lawyers that we were completely uninvolved in the fraud."

That kind of work didn't come cheap. Though Mark and Andrew's expenses were somewhat defrayed by the joint representation— each footed half of the bill—their legal costs came to $200,000 a month.

Flumenbaum and his team had one goal: to prove the brothers' innocence. To that end, they advised both Mark and Andrew to steer clear of press and hire a PR firm to manage the hundreds of media inquiries flooding in daily. The only statement the brothers would make was a generic quote written by Flumenbaum: "Mark and Andrew knew nothing of their father's crimes. They are innocent victims like so many others." Andrew hated the quote, which he felt did nothing to convey the depth of his despair, the empathy he felt for the victims, or the contempt he felt for his father and his crimes. As the brothers' PR firm turned down every request, Andrew and Mark watched their formerly pristine reputations get utterly destroyed.

It was the "paper of record," the *New York Times,* that was the worst, says Andrew, printing stories with "shocking inaccuracies" in its haste to break news. The *Wall Street Journal* did a much better job in terms of accuracy: "Their reporting was spot-on, almost from day one." Though the stories printed in the *Times* and the *Journal* were "the only ones [Andrew] cared about," the Madoff scandal had captured the imagination of the media at large, from television to newspapers to tabloids to blogs. It was dissected everywhere, and as a result, a number of rumors surfaced that the brothers were never able to dispel.

One such rumor was that the U.S. Attorney was hot on their tails and the brothers were about to be arrested. In fact, officials had combed through their files, taken apart their computers, and grilled their colleagues at the firm. Certainly, if any of Bernie's cohorts in the scheme had been able to hand over the brothers and reduce the sentences they themselves were facing, they would have. Of course, with so many other falsehoods flying—their kids were being shunned! Catherine had a tattoo of Andrew's name on her derriere! the whole Madoff clan was secretly gathering for expensive late-night dinners at Bernie's!—that crucial argument was overlooked.

Another devastating rumor claimed that Mark and Andrew were being investigated for tax fraud. "I know there wasn't a nickel I made over the course of my career that wasn't fully taxed, but no one from the U.S. Attorney's Office would step forward to say, 'The rumors are untrue,'" says Andrew. "It wasn't in the government's best interest to do that, because they were hoping it *was* true."

A week after the confession, Catherine's mother called. "Why don't you come to Saratoga this Christmas? Come home. Get away from all this."

Gratefully, Catherine and Andrew accepted her invitation. Days before they left, they drove to SoHo to pick up some gifts for their kids, their nieces and nephew, and Catherine's teenage brothers. They parked in front of Mark and Stephanie's building to drop off gifts with the doorman, then walked to some nearby stores. At a store called Evolution, Catherine bought a stuffed rat for her high-school-aged brother, Nick, an inside joke about a pet rat he'd had. Then she went to Kidrobot, a store that sells limited-edition toys by artists, to shop for her youngest brother, Jake. Carrying the purchases, they made their way back to their car. Just as they rounded the corner in front of Mark and Stephanie's building, three men jumped out from behind a parked car, cameras flashing.

"What's in the bags?"

"Have you spoken to your parents?"

"When are you going to turn yourself in?"

As Catherine and Andrew increased their pace, mouths set, the paparazzi ran backward in front of them, hunched over and snapping pictures furiously. Catherine and Andrew reached the car, put their bags in the trunk, and hurried off on foot. Bystanders craned their necks. One called out, "Are you famous?"

The photographers fell away. They were there to take photos of Mark and Stephanie, who lived nearby. But Catherine knew that they were in Connecticut that weekend, where they still kept a home. Catherine and Andrew slipped into the coffee shop inside Alessi to catch their breath.

"How are you going to feel if we're on the cover of the *New York Post* tomorrow, under some smarmy headline?" Catherine asked.

"I can't feel ashamed about that. I'm not going to feel bad that you bought something for your brother at Kidrobot." Andrew looked up at the coffee menu, contemplating it angrily.

The next morning, Catherine woke up to an e-mail from her friend Alexandra Lebenthal, a financier and "chick lit" author who'd written a book called *The Recessionistas*. The subject line read, "Good News and Bad News."

Uh-oh, Catherine thought. She clicked on the message.

"The good news: You look really good. The bad news: You're on the cover of the *Post*."

"Shopping Gall!" screamed the headline, over a large photo of Catherine and Andrew with their Kidrobot bags. Catherine was misidentified as "Debbie Madoff," though the reporter managed to correctly identify the make, model, and license-plate number of their car.

On Christmas morning, Catherine's brother Nick presented Andrew, whom he was meeting for the first time, with his gift: a kit of disguise mustaches, so he could move about New York unnoticed. The whole family cracked up as Andrew tried on various models. Then Catherine gave her brother Jake the bag from Kidrobot: "It's like a grown-up toy store," she said.

"I know. I Googled it after I saw that picture of you in the *Post*."

Days later, Catherine was visiting Seaside, Florida, alone when Andrew called to tell her about the packages Debbie, Susan, and Stephanie had received from Ruth.

"Did she send one to me?" Catherine wondered aloud while watching two preteen girls stroll along the boardwalk, giggling and holding ice cream cones. A part of her still wanted acceptance from Ruth, a phantom mother-in-law she might never see again.

"I don't know. I'm looking through the mail now. I don't think—oh, wait a minute, wait a minute, wait a minute..."

He opened the battered envelope his mother had sent. A Cartier watch, diamond necklace, and bracelet fell out into his lap.

"Can I keep them?" Catherine asked, still seeking, in some way, evidence of Andrew's mother's acceptance. "It's not like I have anything to do with this..."

"Catherine, they're stolen property! No!"

"Oh. You're right. What was I thinking? Of course I can't keep them. I'm sorry."

The next day, Andrew and Mark turned over the contents of the envelopes they'd received to their attorneys. They were now turning in a member of their family for a second time.

In Seaside, Catherine had searched for a book on how to navigate crises. Beverly Smallwood's *This Wasn't Supposed to Happen to Me* offered a road map for surviving a crisis with one's spirit intact. Catherine bought copies for Andrew, his daughters, and Shana—anyone who had shared with her their personal concerns about how to make it through the woods.

But books were not Catherine's only comfort. In the ensuing weeks, she found solace in the Mothers of Young Children group she had joined at her church. None of the energetic, soulful moms with whom she spent an hour every Monday morning brought up the scandal, and consequently, neither did she. Instead of talking about headlines and investigations, they talked about bedtime and bath rituals, effective discipline strategies, finding time to care for the men in their lives, and maintaining a spiritual core. Catherine wondered if they knew about the bigger drama in her backstory and were just too polite to mention it. But it was so refreshing each week to focus on other people's daily dilemmas and joys that she didn't much care.

In late January, on their way back from promoting Abel at a consumer show in New Jersey, Catherine and Andrew drove to East Side Poultry to pick up dinner. Catherine waited in the car while Andrew ran inside. She spotted a strange-looking man on the street, eyeing her through the car window. He was wearing a hockey jersey and banana yellow sweatpants with one pant leg pushed up and one down; his messy hair stuck up in a "fauxhawk." Feeling her hackles rise, she watched as he shifted his glance to Andrew, who was standing inside East Side Poultry.

Minutes later, Andrew emerged, carrying their dinner. He saw the man, paused, and looked surprised.

"Hey!" Andrew said, smiling broadly.

Oh, so they know each other, Catherine thought. She felt herself start to relax.

Reed Abend was a former Madoff trader who'd served as the "office clown." One of Andrew's last hires on the prop desk before he'd turned things over to Mark, Reed had once dyed his hair fire-engine red and liked to talk loudly about his exploits on the Jewish Internet dating site JDate. Andrew had never had the opportunity to bond with Reed in the trenches, but they knew each other well enough. Days earlier, Reed had called Mark for a job reference, which Mark had agreed to give him.

At first, the conversation seemed friendly enough. Then, Catherine noticed, Reed started to speak heatedly. Andrew's smile disappeared as he listened; then he started to frown. Catherine felt her adrenaline pumping again.

"But it was your name on the door!" Reed shouted.

Calm down, Andrew indicated with raised, open palms.

"You should make it right! You should make it good!" Reed's face was bright red.

People emerged from a bar and stood on the street, watching. Oh, God, Catherine thought, how long is this going to take?

They argued back and forth, Reed hurling insults. As Reed grew shrill, Andrew shook his head and walked around to his side of the car.

Reed ran over to Catherine's window. Bending down, his nose near the glass, he screamed, "Is this your whore? I see you, whore!"

Catherine recoiled in her seat, terrified. Andrew put the bag of chicken on the hood of the car and walked over to where Reed was standing.

"Back away from the car, Reed."

"Fuck you and your fucking whore!" he shrieked. He made a move toward the car and gave Andrew a shove; Andrew hauled back and clocked him across the jaw. Reed fell to the ground. As Andrew walked back around the car, grabbed the bag of food off the hood, and entered the driver's side, Reed stood up.

"Whore!" he shouted.

Andrew started to climb out of the car again.

Catherine touched his arm. "Just go," she whispered. "Just go."

Andrew started the ignition and pulled away from the curb.

Catherine, shaking, thought: Did that just happen?

"Sorry," Andrew said. "This guy, Reed, used to work at Madoff. But he was one of the few traders who made money this year. He was complaining about his bonus."

Catherine couldn't speak. I just dropped off my daughter, she thought. What if Sophie had been in the backseat?

"Does he think you were in on it?" Catherine croaked.

"No. He just wants his money."

When they got to the apartment, Andrew called the police and attempted to turn himself in.

"You don't need to report yourself for hitting this guy," the policeman told Andrew. "Unless he was lying in a puddle of blood, incapacitated, you didn't do anything wrong. But you do need to make a statement about him harassing you. That way, if it happens again, you'll have a record." Andrew elected to report himself and to file a harassment report, though no charges were ever filed. The incident promptly made its way into the papers the next day.

The school break Catherine had planned for herself, Andrew, and Sophie became, like the rest of the plans they had made in happier times, something Andrew decided he was better off sitting out. In February, Catherine and Sophie flew to London on their own. Their first night there, they had dinner with Colin Rutherford of Sportfish. He entered the restaurant to meet them with his trademark swagger.

"How are you?" Catherine said, embracing him. She introduced Sophie.

"Delightful! I think I might be getting a divorce."

"Oh, so sad! I'm sorry."

"Don't worry about it; it's been a long time coming. More importantly, how are *you?*"

"I feel kind of bad telling you this, given your news, but...I'm engaged to be married."

"When's the happy day?" he asked, signaling the waiter for champagne.

"There are some complications. I don't really know when we're getting married."

"Then he's not good enough for you," Colin said with a shake of his head.

"No, it's not like he's stringing me along. We're very much in love, but a couple of months ago, he came home and told me that his father had just confessed to—"

"Madoff?" Colin interrupted.

"Yes."

"Oh, Catherine. Are you sure you want to do this to yourself?"

"But he wasn't involved."

"If you like and approve of this guy, I have no doubt he wasn't involved. But do you really want to go down this road with him?"

It was scary, Catherine says, to have someone whose judgment she trusted telling her, "Maybe you leave anyway, because you have a life to live." It was something she'd never considered, and she tried to push the thought away.

But she couldn't escape the sentiment: Upon returning to New York, she heard it repeated. Brooke Travis, Dior's marketing director, had asked her to sit for a portrait as a favor to a fashion illustrator working for the company. Since Catherine had a meeting a few blocks away—coincidentally, across the street from Ruth and Bernie's apartment—she agreed to do it.

As the artist Bil Donovan made a watercolor sketch of Catherine, Brooke ventured, "I have to be honest with you. Our friends are placing odds on when you are going to walk. Catherine...you would have to be a saint to stay with him."

Catherine kept her eyes focused on the artist.

"It's OK," Brooke continued. "You can lose it. You can break down. I'm your friend."

When Catherine left, she saw an army of photographers, their cameras pointed up to the sky. A few smiled and made catcalls. One held up a camera, grinning and saying, "Want your picture taken, pretty lady?"

"We're trying to get a shot of Bernie's place," a producer explained as he hurried by. He had no idea of her connection to the story that was currently making news, and she had no plans to enlighten him.

In March, Catherine and Andrew flew to Charleston, South Carolina, to visit Andrew's cousins Steve and Debbie Brown. Andrew didn't know them well; Bernie had never made extended family a priority.

"You can't see your mother. You can't see your father. And you keep saying, 'I lost my family,'" Catherine had said. "So were your parents it? There's no one else?"

"I have these cousins in Charleston," Andrew had acknowledged. Urged on by Catherine, he reached out to them.

Now they were walking through security at JFK. When she handed her boarding pass and license to the TSA agent, he looked at her photo and handed it back to her. Andrew had just walked ahead. "Is that Mr. Madoff with you?"

She braced herself. "Yes."

"He's the son of Bernie Madoff?"

"Yes."

"My name is Raul. I just want you to know that me and my mom have been praying for him and his dad. I hope he finds Jesus and I hope you guys are OK."

Thank you, Raul, she thought, feeling her eyes well up with tears. Catherine caught up with Andrew and recounted the story. He turned around and gave Raul a warm, grateful smile.

In Charleston, as they were driving from the airport in their rental car, Mark called, livid. A Reuters story had surfaced that said Mark owned fifteen houses.

"I can't believe a journalist could be that sloppy and stupid! He did an address search and turned up every house I've ever lived in over my entire life..." He continued to rant loudly until Andrew turned off the highway and started driving through a sleepy suburb. Finally, Andrew hung up the phone.

"We're in Charleston now," Catherine said. "Can you try not to talk with your brother every fifteen minutes about every news story?"

"Sorry," Andrew said, adding the coordinates to Steve and Debbie's house to the GPS. He turned to Catherine. "I'm so glad we did this."

Within minutes of turning in to his cousin's driveway, Andrew's phone buzzed with an incoming text.

"Don't answer it; I'm sure it's Mark," Catherine said.

Andrew glanced down. His eyes widened: "Bernie." It was their first communication since the confession.

The text read: "I love you and Mark very much. Please take care of Mom."

Andrew pulled over and fumbled with his phone, wildly dialing Mark. His hands shook. When Mark answered, Andrew covered the phone and looked at Catherine: "He got the same text!"

"What are we going to do?" Andrew yelled into the phone. "This is a suicide note." He ran a hand through his hair, then gripped the steering wheel, listening to Mark. "I know, but—"

"Call Efrain," Catherine mouthed, referring to the detective they'd met during the bomb scare who was working Bernie's detail.

Andrew nodded. "I'm gonna do that right now."

Hanging up the phone, Andrew quickly dialed the number as Catherine read it to him from her phone.

"I'm really worried that my dad is going to kill himself."

He listened. "OK. OK."

He hung up. "He's going to look into it."

Andrew's head dropped forward onto his chest and his shoulders started to heave. Catherine could see his cousins starting to emerge from their house. She leapt out of the car and walked up the driveway, waving them off.

"Steve! Steve! Stop. Andrew needs a minute. Can you give him a minute?" Then she awkwardly introduced herself to the gentle, friendly pair. Eventually, Andrew came into the house, red-eyed but calm. Efrain had checked on Bernie, who seemed perfectly fine. If Bernie contemplated suicide more than once, that text was Andrew's only clue.

Hard news on the story waned, but chatter about the case continued, from sources ranging from bloggers to the most well-respected figures in media. In the springtime, Catherine, Andrew, and his daughters took their first family trip to Seaside as a way to reclaim their lost vacation. While they waited in the airport, a Madoff story flashed across the television monitor. Catherine glanced at the girls, hoping they weren't listening, but she could see that they each had one eye on the screen. The camera panned to Diane Sawyer. Oh, good, I trust her, Catherine thought; Diane Sawyer is my idol. She'll see through all of this over-the-top coverage. She doesn't care about anything but the truth.

As the story concluded, Sawyer turned to her cohost and said, as Catherine recalls, "The more you learn about this family, the more disgusted you become," she said.

This family, Catherine thought, meaning these two teenage girls I love, too. Anne and Emily continued to read their magazines, pretending not to hear.

Even the judge overseeing Andrew and Debbie's divorce proceedings felt the need to weigh in: "Just so you know, I think you were in on it," she said to Andrew as he sat, stunned, across from the judge in her chambers.

Debbie immediately jumped in to defend her ex. "I want it put in the record that he didn't know," she said. "He was not involved, and the dissolution of our marriage has absolutely nothing to do with that."

By Halloween, there would be Bernie masks in the stores where Anne and Emily searched for their costumes. He had been reduced from their beloved grandfather—a man they had once thought worthy of immortality on the side of a coin—to a rubber mask in shops, used for cheap laughs, then discarded.

Chapter Seventeen

Two Paths, Two Realities

In the wake of Andrew's separation from Debbie, his social circle had shrunk, and after the scandal, it grew even smaller. Some friends couldn't speak to him because they'd been told not to by lawyers; some were angry or suspicious, others Andrew simply didn't want to see.

"Before all this happened, I had a lot of friends by default," he says, "people I met through work or my parents or who I knew from the girls' school. But after everything fell apart, my willingness to spend time with people I hadn't chosen as friends vanished."

Catherine, though, had assembled a new crop of friends — people Andrew actually enjoyed getting to know. Her friends became their friends, as did the people she was constantly meeting in line at Whole Foods, in the stacks at Barnes & Noble, or at yoga. In the early months of 2009, Catherine and Andrew filled their calendar with dates for coffee, lunch, and drinks; often, they saw three groups of friends in one day. Instead of shrinking from questions about the scandal, they made openness a policy, answering every curious query thrown their way. More often than not, the person grilling them for details came back with his or her own tale of woe.

"I had a cousin who stole my identity," they would say, or, "My father lied to me, too."

"My dad had a second family two towns over. We didn't know until he died."

By reaching out to new people and refusing to hide, Andrew learned that the world was, in fact, not such a terrible place. It was possible to change people's perception of him, with a little patience and time. That gave him hope that one day, down the road, life might return to normal, albeit a new normal.

Mark, too, encouraged people to probe for the truth: "Ask me any question you want," he would say. But his challenge was laced with a taunt; it was bait, daring the person sitting across from him to admit they suspected he was involved. Mark had managed to learn the opposite lesson about the world—and deliberately went searching for evidence that would reinforce his worldview.

Each time he came home, from the moment he locked his doors and closed his blinds, Mark spent nearly every waking moment scouring the Internet for news stories about the case. Everything he found—whether it was a *New York Times* cover story or a post by an unknown blogger—was given equal weight. All day long, he would e-mail the offending items to Andrew. "Did you see this??!!!" he would write. Their relationship, says Catherine, was defined by "constant communication but no warmth," like a "professional partnership between two people who didn't really know each other." It was a painful departure from the easy intimacy they had shared years ago.

A typical day for Andrew would start with a text message from Mark at 5:30 AM. At 6:00 AM, Andrew would receive an e-mail from his brother. At 6:30 AM, Andrew would pick up his brother's call. At 7:00 AM, Andrew would get two more text messages from Mark, then at 7:30 AM, three more e-mails. On and on it went throughout the day.

Mark appeared to be in severe pain, says Catherine, and he

didn't want to experience it alone. She guesses that "his identity was completely enmeshed with Andrew's, so constantly updating Andrew on every little thought he was having was a way of keeping the self complete." Certainly, it was a strategy he'd learned from his family.

If Mark and Andrew had had a strong emotional bond and communicated frequently as a result, says Catherine, she would have understood. But that wasn't the case. Catherine and Andrew were not invited to see Mark's children Audrey and Nick and, indeed, had met Nick only once—in a stiff, formal visit days after he was born. They didn't know when Mark and Stephanie traveled or where they went. They had no idea who their friends were. Andrew recalls once walking into his lawyers' offices with Mark. One of the lawyers turned to Mark and said, "I'm so sorry I couldn't make it to Audrey's birthday party yesterday. How was it?" Avoiding Andrew's gaze, Mark had mumbled a response about the party being "small."

By February 2009, Andrew had had enough of Mark's constant news feed. "Stop e-mailing me about the case. I don't want to know this stuff."

"You don't understand," Mark complained. "You live in Never Never Land. You have no idea what people are saying about us."

"I don't care what they're saying. Shut off your computer and forget about that. You have to ignore it."

Unable to share his bad news with Andrew, Mark started bombarding the other people in his life with e-mails, calls, and texts. Susan, his ex-wife, received dozens of missives a day. So did his father-in-law, brother-in-law, and friends. The media picked up on and reported Mark's press obsession. Soon commentators began addressing him directly.

"Hi Mark!" started a typical blog post. "Since I know you're reading this, why don't you kill yourself?"

The onslaught of comments, instantly available to Mark, chipped away at his equanimity. The more he read, the more despairing he became, yet he walked into commentators' flying fists day after day. Andrew's strategy was to ignore, Mark's to obsess. And blog posts were one thing, but he couldn't believe that a revered publication like the *New York Times* was printing "speculation, lies, and bullshit," says Susan. "They would reprint 'news' from blogs as fact." Mark felt the need to dissect every article, riding a roller coaster of emotion that depended on its content.

"There's an article coming out today," he would say to Susan. A few hours later, she'd get a call: "I think it put me in a good light." Or he would call and say, "I don't think it's too bad; I'm happy it named those guys because that looks better for me."

Friends like Jeff Wilpon, whom he'd known since high school, "supported him from a distance," says Susan. "Jeff never said a bad word about Mark, but he wouldn't come out and say, 'Mark Madoff is my friend and I know he's innocent.'" Mark really resented that, according to Susan, and wouldn't acknowledge that Jeff was "completely muzzled" by his lawyers—Jeff couldn't have made a comment if he'd wanted to.

There was only one thing more upsetting to Mark than the lack of support from friends and the daily torrent of abuse he endured from the public—and that was Ruth's decision to stay with Bernie.

Mark adored his mother. His entire life, she'd "walked on water," says Andrew. So when Ruth chose Bernie over her children, as Mark felt she did, the blow was staggering.

"How could you not see this coming?" Andrew tried to explain to his brother. "Mom has always put Dad first." But what Andrew accepted as a fact of life was unthinkable to Mark.

"What kind of mother doesn't protect her children?" he kept saying.

"We're grown men in our forties. Have you considered that she thinks we can get through this without her help?"

Susan, one of the only family members still in contact with Ruth at that time, said, "You have to understand. Your mother is not in her right mind. She doesn't love your father more than she loves you, but she's completely alone."

"We would have taken her in—she knows that!" Mark said. "My brother and I discussed several times that if she wanted to leave him she could come live with us."

"I don't know that she does know that," Susan insisted.

Mark had become furious with Susan when he found out she was allowing Ruth to talk on the phone with her grandchildren.

"They've lost more than half their family, and this connection is important," Susan had argued. "You want me to be a good mom? Well, that's what I think being a good mom is."

"She didn't protect us," he repeated stubbornly.

All those factors—the pummeling from the media, the perceived desertion of his friends, and especially his mother's betrayal— became kindling for a long-smoldering anger within Mark, who felt as though he'd followed a straight and narrow path his entire life and had gotten "screwed" for it. Susan remembered something he'd said to her after 9/11, when one of his closest friends perished in the World Trade Center.

"I don't believe in God at all anymore. First my marriage falls apart. Then Schwarty dies. I've lived my life very black-and-white. I went down the road and I didn't look left and I didn't look right. And look how screwed I got."

Mark, considering himself "screwed" seven years before he and the world would learn about his father's crimes, was already beginning the dangerous habit of seeing life's tragedies in Technicolor, and life's blessings in grainy black-and-white.

While Mark's life was unraveling, Andrew was trying to rebuild his. Madoff Energy, the oil company Andrew had had such high hopes for, was dead. It still needed at least $5 million to $10 million in start-up capital, and finding new investors was out of the question, as was borrowing the capital from the now-defunct BLM. Andrew loved his work with Abel, but the company was located in Camarillo, California; with his children living in New York City, relocation was not an option. So, at forty-three, with a résumé worth no more than the piece of paper it was printed on, Andrew had to start thinking about a new career. And, having voluntarily resigned from Dior after the scandal, so did Catherine.

"I can't live off my investments forever," she confided to Andrew one morning. She had gone five months without a salary. She occupied her days cooking and caring for the three kids at home, assembling the IKEA furniture she felt lucky they could still afford, and being relentlessly social to avoid depression.

Years earlier, post–Hurricane Katrina, Catherine had come up with the idea of launching an emergency preparedness business. She'd written a set of procedures for creating a rudimentary preparedness plan and tentatively titled the company the Contingency Group. Now Andrew asked her if she wanted to dust off the idea. They hauled out her notes and read through them, then tried to secure the domain name. But the company name she'd chosen turned out to be too close to ones that already existed, so they came up with a new one: Black Umbrella.

Both Catherine and Andrew liked the word *black* for its tactical appeal—as in black ops—and *umbrella* as a representation of protection and status in many cultures across the globe. In combination, they felt, the phrase symbolized stealth and safety—a fitting description of their objectives for the business.

Over that summer of 2009, busy developing Black Umbrella and watching his brother flounder, Andrew had come up with an idea.

"Why don't you take over responsibility for Abel?" he'd asked Mark.

The two had been chatting on the phone, discussing their dead careers. Mark was "clearly desperate" for something to do.

"I'll step back and you can take over my role," Andrew offered.

"That sounds interesting," Mark mused. "Can you give me some time to think about it?"

A day later, he'd called Andrew back: "Let's do it," he said.

Mark's new role lasted about a week, Andrew recalls. While Andrew had taken a hands-off approach to running the business, Mark "went in there like a ton of bricks and completely alienated the guys in California." Wanting to "take over everything," he was "immediately in their face," grilling them about their sales process. It was an area Mark knew about and was perfectly suited to fix, but his heavy-handed approach created conflict. Top brass at the company called Andrew and said, "You've got to get him out of here. This isn't going to work."

Catherine, meanwhile, had planned a trip to California to visit Abel, work with one of Black Umbrella's employees in LA, and have coffee with entrepreneur and philanthropist Lynda Resnick. When she cc'd Mark on an e-mail she'd sent to company executives, informing them of her arrival, he "lost it."

"This is bullshit!" Mark yelled over the phone to Andrew. "You told me you were going to let me be responsible for the company. Now Catherine is undercutting my authority and going out there to do things behind my back."

"That's crazy, Mark," Andrew said, exasperated. "She's an owner of the company. She paid for her equity just like we did. She's going to be in LA for a bunch of things, and whenever she travels to California, she visits Abel. It's rude if she doesn't. These guys have known her for a dozen years; she's not undercutting your authority."

"If you don't want me to run the company, just tell me," Mark shouted and hung up the phone.

One day later, Andrew's doorman informed him that a box had

arrived. Inside, Andrew found Abel baseball hats, T-shirts, pens, and bags—all the company paraphernalia Mark had in his possession. A letter from Mark followed, tendering his resignation from Abel's board of directors.

Andrew accepted his brother's resignation, called his executives in California to apologize, and appointed Abel's director of sales to Mark's position on the board.

"He never had anything to do with the company after that," Andrew says. "It was unbelievable to me how fast he messed that up, considering he had no other options."

It was, says Andrew, an illustration of so many things about Mark: self-destructiveness, paranoia, an inability to get out of his own way. Andrew wanted to help his brother, but Mark made it impossible. Helping Mark with his career would be like offering his leg to a drowning man in the middle of the ocean. When it came to their professional lives, it would be best, Andrew realized, to steer clear.

Naively, Catherine assumed that as soon as she hung out her shingle, business would appear, and she would replace her previous income within a matter of months. Andrew and Catherine spent their spring and summer laying the foundation for their new venture, reading and rereading every book on preparedness they could find. They made a list of people who might be able to consult with them or become employees: a friend from Los Angeles, who had walked around with a length of rope and a pocketknife in his backpack since the age of six. An acquaintance who had a background in Special Forces. Tom Brown III, one of the preeminent survivalists in the United States. Two sisters who ran a women's self-defense school in New York. They rewrote the business plan, outlining new tactical modules, different levels of service, and operational procedures. By the time the one-year anniversary of Bernie's confession arrived, they were booking space for the company's first employee-training session. All of it was done on a "shoestring" and in the hope that when the "rug was yanked out from under" Andrew post–divorce settlement, he and Catherine would have built a business that could soften their landing.

Of course, the sole owner of Black Umbrella would be — could only be — Catherine. Andrew, whose assets were all up for grabs by bankruptcy trustee Irving Picard, couldn't possibly invest in or own a new company. And he knew that should she walk away from him at some point, his work to build that safety net would be worthless. Yet even though the world as he knew it had been turned upside down and his own father had "committed a betrayal of biblical proportions," Andrew "trusted Catherine with [his] life."

He had to.

Bernie at his wedding, in 1959.

Ruth prepares for her high school prom in 1958. She would be engaged to Bernie a few months later.

Ruth (right) and her sister, Joan, in 1954. Ruth met and fell in love with Bernie that same year.

Joan and Ruth at Copake Lake, New York, 1949.

Long Island Daily Press

MONDAY, DECEMBER 8, 1958

Madoff—Alpern

The engagement of Laurelton students Ruth Alpern and Bernard L. Madoff was today announced by her parents, Mr. and Mrs. Saul Alpern of 137-25 224th St.

Both are graduates of Far Rockaway High School.

Miss Alpern is now attending Queens College.

Her fiance, the son of Mr. and Mrs. Ralph Madoff of 139-54 228th St., is in his senior year at Hofstra College.

RUTH ALPERN
Wears New Ring

Ruth and Bernie's engagement announcement. Fifty years to the day after it was printed, Bernie would unnerve his children by announcing he wanted to pay out the trading bonuses early.

Bernie with his parents at his bar mitzvah, in 1951.

Bernie's parents at their apartment in Hollywood, Florida, in 1968.

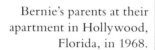

Ruth's parents in the late 1970s at their summer cottage in Sunny Oaks, near Monticello, New York.

The trading floor of Bernard L. Madoff Inc.'s legitimate market-making operation in 1994. Andrew is leaning over a monitor (right of center), phone to his ear.

Peter Madoff congratulates Mark on his wedding to Stephanie Mikesell, in 2004, as Andrew looks on.

Bernie and Ruth at the firm's 2008 Montauk summer party.

Catherine (far right) and Andrew with Bernie and Ruth at the Hôtel du Cap, France, 2008.

Catherine and Andrew at the finish line of their 210-mile ride to Saratoga Springs on their "anniversary of not getting married," in 2010.

Catherine with a Bahamas bonefish in 2007. *(Courtesy of Brian Goulart)*

Mark and his first wife, Susan, enjoy a quiet moment at home in 1993.

Debbie West Madoff in Idaho in summer 2002 during her and Andrew's attempt to reconcile.

Stephanie Madoff in Cabo San Lucas in 2008.

Catherine and Andrew
at an East Hampton
birthday party, 2009.

Andrew points out his parents'
apartment to Catherine in 2008.
(Courtesy of Emily Wilson)

Catherine and Andrew during their
courtship, spring 2008. *(Courtesy of
Emily Wilson)*

Andrew with Catherine at an event at
Holkham Hall, England, in October 2008.
They had been engaged for one month.
(Courtesy of Debbie Rowe)

Chapter Eighteen

LIFE AFTER BERNIE

The apartment was quiet: There was no hum coming from the television set in the study. No faint trace of cigar smoke in the kitchen. The day before, Bernie had been escorted into the high-security wing of the Metropolitan Correctional Center to await sentencing. Ruth had decided not to accompany him to the courtroom to listen to the verdict.

"Why would I go there?" she asks. "To be photographed? It was a free-for-all, a zoo. He didn't need me to hold his hand, nor would I."

For more than four months, Ruth had been living in an "ivory tower" with her husband, going about life in a protected bubble. When she'd gotten the call that Bernie wasn't coming home, she had broken down, sobbing, in her bedroom. Soon after, the security guards took their surveillance equipment and left. Now, for the first time since Ruth was a teenager, she was left alone with her own thoughts. That day, she did what she always did: She smoked, watched TV, and drank wine.

For Andrew, that day was a nonevent: "I was absolutely aware that my father was going to prison that day, but I barely noted it. I understood the full scope of what my father had done and how many lives he'd destroyed. I refused to allow him to ruin my life like he had Mark's and so many others."

Catherine, though recognizing that photographers might arrive as they left to take the kids to school, still elected to wear a favorite T-shirt that said "Buon Viaggio."

Only later, when rumors about Bernie's prison life started to leak to the press, did Andrew feel small flashes of emotion. When the *New York Post* printed a story saying that Bernie had been diagnosed with cancer, Andrew called his mother to see if it was true; it was only the second time he'd spoken to her since the confession. As soon as she denied the rumor, he thanked her and got off the phone. On another occasion, it was reported that Bernie had been beaten up in prison. That upset Andrew more, he says: "Somehow, the thought of him getting beaten up was worse than the thought of him going to prison."

Within a day or two of the verdict, it dawned on Ruth that she would eventually be forced out of the apartment and needed to clear out her things. Until Bernie left, she'd existed in a state of suspended animation, pretending, for the moment, that life within the walls of the apartment was normal. Once he was gone, she "had to get out." She moved through the rooms of the penthouse, surveying decades' worth of possessions. Ruth was a pack rat; every closet was jammed with clutter. Overwhelmed, she picked up a Hefty bag and shook it open, trying to figure out where to begin.

Ruth would be allowed to keep enough clothing and toiletries to take care of her basic needs, she'd been told. But instead of carefully going through her possessions and choosing the things that might carry her through the rest of her life, she mindlessly jammed items into bags. Once they were full, she threw them into a pile in the corner for the U.S. Attorney's Office to catalogue. For her wardrobe, she chose sweaters, jeans, and cardigans at random, throwing them into a suitcase. She set aside a small pile of evening jackets, which she ended up forgetting to take.

In the bottom of a drawer, Ruth came across a bound leather book: her wedding album. Sitting cross-legged on the floor, she turned the cardboard pages, looking at images of her teenage self alongside her handsome groom. There they were cutting the cake; posing with their parents; enjoying their first dance. One by one, she pulled the stiff photos from their backings and broke them into pieces, dropping them into a garbage bag.

Other beloved personal effects went into that garbage bag: love letters from Bernie. Photographs of her family. She couldn't bear to have those items featured on the news.

That night, at 11:30 PM, she rode the elevator down to the street, clutching the garbage bag in her hand. Lexington Avenue was empty, save for a few lonely cabs. Looking left and then right, she hurried to the corner, seeing puffs of her breath form in the cold winter air. She dropped the bag into the city-owned trash can, blew on her hands to warm them, and hurried back into her building, satisfied that the most intimate scraps of her life had been discarded. There was nothing of real value in the bag; she'd already learned her lesson about disposing of "assets." This was about keeping her most personal items out of the pages of *Vanity Fair*.

Ruth spent those last weeks at home watching TV, reading books from the library, and packing. She was allowed to take her everyday dishware, but things like her gorgeous Royal Crown Derby china, with its hunting motif, had to stay stacked in the china cabinet. The U.S. Attorney's Office had told her, "They'll want all your underwear and nightgowns." That, she says, was "unthinkable to me. As if I had fancy underwear. If anything, I was embarrassed because it was nothing." But she had no choice. She left them behind.

For the first time in months, Ruth started to venture out of the apartment. She went to the movies by herself, something she'd always preferred, not liking to "go to the trouble of making arrangements" with people. But paparazzi stalked her constantly. Whenever she went to the Food Emporium, they "jumped up and down in the street like lunatics, nearly getting killed by cars" in an effort to take her picture. A "kid that looked like a twelve-year-old" followed her with a point-and-shoot camera, identifying himself as a reporter from *Inside Edition*. Exiting CVS one day, Ruth was pounced on by paparazzi. As she dodged them, a woman on the street screamed at the photographers, "Will you leave her alone already!"

"I didn't have time to thank her because I was in such a frenzy," Ruth says.

The famed photo taken of Ruth sitting dejectedly on the subway was snapped by a paparazza who'd followed Ruth from her lawyer's office. She started to take photos on the platform; when the two boarded the train, she squatted in front of Ruth, snapping mere feet from her face.

"Does your mother know what you do for a living? Do you get pleasure out of humiliating people like this?" Ruth asked, enduring the stares of passengers. "It's the most degrading thing you could be doing with your life. It's shameful."

The woman seemed embarrassed, Ruth recalls. "She said she was normally a studio photographer. But she wasn't too embarrassed to sell the picture."

Loneliness wasn't a problem...except when it was. She stopped answering the phone. No one called anyway. Some nights, she refreshed her Internet browser over and over, thinking a new e-mail might appear, but it never did.

"If I had been allied with Mark, Andy, Stephanie, and the children, I could have managed without friends. But I had nobody. And no one reached out to me, when I needed people so badly."

Not that Ruth really expected her friends to contact her. After all, every one of them had been a victim. Their attorneys had instructed them not to speak to her, her own lawyer explained, but what if they'd sent her a letter? Who would have known?

Well, she wasn't going to speak to any of them again. Ever. She didn't care what their lawyers had told them.

When Ruth thought about her friends, all the anger she wasn't able to feel at her husband burbled to the surface with force. They have *no* idea what they would do in my shoes, Ruth thought.

In fact, Andrew suspects that her friends would have taken her back but likely felt the same way he did: It's Bernie or us.

Ruth hurried into the Metropolitan Correctional Center for her first visit with Bernie. Paparazzi had been alerted to her arrival; now they swarmed around her as she entered the building.

"What are you going to say to your husband?"

"When are *you* going to jail?"

The doors closed behind her, and she took a deep breath. She wore drawstring pants with no zipper, as she'd been instructed. Waiting in a long line of mostly women and children, she slowly inched her way toward the metal detector. A mother holding a baby got turned away, sobbing, because she wasn't wearing the proper shoes. The guards "didn't care how long you were waiting or how long things took," Ruth recalls. The crowd was ushered into a glass-enclosed waiting area, "like a bus stop," where Ruth smiled at a little boy standing by the vending machine.

"Someone handed him something from the machine, and his mother said, 'What do you say?' And he said, *'Gracias.'* He was the sweetest thing; he must have been about two and a half years old. You'd watch the fathers come out and cry when they saw their kids. It was heartbreaking. Nobody looked like a criminal. It was all so normal."

Ruth chatted with some of the women; when they found out who she was, all expressed concern. One handed Ruth her number.

Bernie was housed in the maximum-security wing, where

visitors could go up only one at a time, via a separate entrance. A mother was there with her children, waiting to see her husband; Ruth let her go first. When it was Ruth's turn, she exited the elevator and saw a row of small cells. There was a "fellow" housed next to Bernie: "A terrorist, I forgot his name. A sheik. I don't even remember. I sort of recognized his picture. He smiled. Everyone did."

Bernie was in the next cell, wearing a standard-issue prison jumpsuit with his hands, legs, and waist wrapped in chains.

As she shares that chilling detail, Ruth pauses. "I can't bear for my grandchildren to know that Bernie was wearing chains."

The chains were removed. They were allowed to hug once, then instructed to sit across from each other in chairs. Ruth told him about packing up the apartment. He told her about life in the cell. Beyond that, she doesn't remember their discussion. Everything was monitored by a hovering prison guard. As Ruth left the prison, she was again besieged by a throng of paparazzi. She pushed her way back to her car.

During that period, the only people Ruth spoke to were her sister, Joan; her lawyer; and Bernie. Ruth visited him once a week, which was "like having a husband who had died but you could visit," and occasionally talked to him on the phone. Since Bernie was only allotted a certain number of minutes on the phone per month, they kept their conversation perfunctory. Mainly, they fretted over which prison he would be sent to; one, Ruth had heard, required three buses to reach, and the government had seized her car.

Ruth missed her sons terribly but says she was glad not to be in contact with them, because she didn't want to be a burden.

"They didn't need my misery on top of their own. Their lives were hell. I knew it because I was living in the same hell."

Mark, Ruth had heard, believed she was "out playing golf," something he'd read in the press.

"I had nobody! I was hiding in the house by myself. But he started to believe the garbage that was written in the papers. What was he thinking? But I knew I couldn't address it until we met face to face."

On "automatic pilot" when she first stood by Bernie, when Ruth "felt abandoned by everybody," she reasoned "there was no reason not to" remain loyal to him.

Urged on by her lawyer, Ruth started to look for a one-bedroom rental. She found one she liked on the Upper East Side. After filling out a form, she was told she'd been accepted. Then the Realtor called and rescinded the offer.

"Maybe it was because they were worried about paparazzi, but I think someone in the realty business put the kibosh on me," says Ruth. Next, she found a small, furnished condo in Battery Park Plaza, near playgrounds and a bike path.

"I loved it," Ruth said. "I thought, This is for me." She signed the lease and made a deposit.

"The broker told me there was no chance they could not let me in the building, but when it got back to the owner of the property, I was rejected. The owner of the apartment was having a nervous breakdown. I don't know if what they were doing was legal or not, but I wasn't going to go to court over it."

Two more offers on apartments were refused. "I was shunned and rejected everywhere I looked," she says.

Ruth's lawyer knew someone who owned a building in Long Island City, just one train ride away. They agreed to accept her, and she prepared to sign a lease.

Then, Irving Picard initiated a "clawback" lawsuit against Ruth for tens of millions of dollars in money she no longer had, and, unsure of the outcome, she withdrew from the lease in Long

Island City, too. With the deadline to move out of her apartment looming, Ruth accepted her niece's offer to move into her home in Hewlett, Long Island.

"I thought I would die," she admits. "I never thought I could live with anybody. How could you be a guest in somebody's home? You'd have to adhere to whatever rules they had."

Ruth had no choice. Thanking her niece profusely, she prepared to leave her home of twenty years.

On June 29, 2009, in the federal courthouse in New York City, Judge Denny Chin sentenced Bernie to 150 years in prison. His lawyer had asked for 12; Ruth had expected 25; the judge gave him the maximum allowable by law. By then, says Ruth, she was "not the least bit surprised."

Three days after her husband's sentencing, Ruth spent her last day in the apartment, with dozens of reporters and paparazzi crowded outside her building. Given the cozy relationship between law enforcement and the press, there was no way to keep her moving date a secret.

The marshals who oversaw Ruth's exit from the apartment sat down and proceeded to criticize the décor of the homes they'd been in. Ruth, who was sitting silently by on a nearby chair, finally piped up, "I can't imagine what you're going to say about me behind my back when you meet the next person you're assigned to."

Eventually, the FBI arrived to escort Ruth from the building. Jose, Ruth's super, had hired a nondescript panel truck to remove the belongings she was allowed to keep and parked it in an alleyway on the side of the building. The marshals exited first, "making a big show" that Ruth was about to come out. But the FBI agents, who were "kind to [her] all along," led her down a back staircase and whisked her into a waiting car. At 72nd Street, they switched cars to throw the paparazzi off track, then drove her the rest of the way to Hewlett.

When Ruth arrived, Diane Hochman, the daughter of Ruth's sister, Joan, greeted her aunt at the door.

"They adjusted their whole household," Ruth recalls. "I had my own bathroom and felt very safe there. I never saw a single reporter outside, ever." Diane and her husband worked, so Ruth walked every day to the supermarket a half mile away. She walked to CVS, to the local library, to a nearby park.

At night, Ruth would help fix dinner and talk to the children. Diane's daughter, Jessie, was a senior in high school, with aspirations of becoming a journalist. She asked Ruth if she could do a mock interview with her, swearing she wasn't ever going to use it. Ruth said yes and gave her a "perfectly honest" interview—one every journalist around the world would have killed for, then. "She was fantastic," Ruth says.

Ruth had thought it would be horrible to live in someone else's home, but it was perfectly pleasant, she says. "They were so easy and laid back, fun to be with, and as welcoming as could be." Getting to know her sister's children was a "huge awakening" for Ruth, who'd kept her distance from family at Bernie's behest.

"It was a waste that it hadn't happened sooner," she says. "I realized how wonderful they were and how much I liked them—I wished I'd gotten to know them all throughout their lives." She felt guilty for having stayed away for so long. In all the years she had lived under Bernie's rules, it simply hadn't occurred to her to take a stand with him and demand they spend time with her family.

It was just another one of the many lessons she'd been forced to learn in those grueling six months.

In late July, Ruth left Long Island and moved in with Joan and her husband, Bob, who lived in a gated community in Boca Raton, Florida. The couple, then in their early to midseventies, had lost every penny to Bernie. Afterward, they traded in their cars for two black Fords, printed up business cards, and started running a taxi service, shuttling snowbirds to and from the airport. Their day started at 3:00 AM. Obsessed with making every dime possible, they worked twelve hours a day and refused to turn down a fare. Sometimes, that meant they would hop up in the middle of dinner. Bob also often transported cars from Florida all the way to New York, taking rest breaks by the side of the road.

Ruth tried her best to be helpful, cooking and taking care of things around the house. The two were "incredible," Ruth says, never once getting angry at her for the circumstances they found themselves in. "They bent over backwards for me; there was not a day they didn't ask how I was doing. And they included me in a million dinners that they were invited to, picking and choosing friends they felt I would be comfortable with. They were beyond anything."

In mid-July, Bernie was transferred to Butner Federal Correctional Complex, a medium-security prison set on seven hundred acres in Butner, North Carolina. His new designation: Inmate Number 61727-054.

Ruth was glad when Bernie was sent to Butner, though she'd been hoping for Otisville, New York, a minimum-security "camp." Bernie, she was told, would sleep on a bunk bed and could freely move about the building. The nonthreatening visitation room was set up "almost like a nursery school," with tables and chairs. Inmates were allowed to hug and hold hands with their visitors, though they had to sit in separate chairs.

In August, Ruth made the first of four visits, driving up from Boca Raton. Visiting was expensive: "The motel was eighty dollars and I was having a heart attack over every cent." Ruth, whose liberal politics were still firmly entrenched, couldn't help but notice the scores of "young drug dealers, who were given no rehabilitation and had no way of making a living."

Sometimes Ruth cried. "No one paid attention; everyone had their own problems." And she never stayed the allotted four hours; usually she stayed only two.

"I don't think Bernie wished I stayed longer," she muses. "It's a long time to sit in that chair."

No doubt he was squirming on the day when, horrified by what she'd read in the papers, Ruth brought up the subject of Bernie's affairs.

"All those things I kept accusing you of, they're probably true," she ventured. "I never settled that with you and I really regret that."

His response, she says, was to "deny, deny, deny."

Only once did Bernie say he was sorry—a "very broad 'sorry,' that could have been for anything."

"I felt stupid to start dealing with that after I let it go for so many years," she admits. He was going to lunch with this broad, going here, going there. But I never said anything; I just let it go. I'm not proud of that, because it makes me look like a dope. But I was afraid to hear the truth."

Eventually, a friend of Ruth's offered to let her stay in her unused condo in Florida, just a few miles away from Joan. Gratefully, Ruth moved into the small but airy apartment, and soon established her routine. She read, watched TV, did the crossword, and smoked. She got her exercise by walking briskly through the neighborhood, staring at her shoes. From time to time, she talked to Bernie on the phone. She was still scared—she was always scared. But a feeling emerged in those months that surprised her: She liked living alone. In fact, she preferred it. Sitting on her borrowed furniture, watching the sun set over a man-made lake and smoking a cigarette, she thought: Maybe I can have a new life.

Chapter Nineteen

MARK SPIRALS

ndrew and Catherine were deeply asleep when their phone rang at 4:30 AM on October 15, 2009. A police officer identified himself.

"Is this Andrew Madoff?"

Alarmed, Andrew pulled himself up to a sitting position.

"Yes."

"I'm calling to ask if you've seen your brother."

"No, he's not here. I haven't heard from him. Why?"

"His wife has reported him missing. They had a fight. He left the apartment and she hasn't seen him since."

"OK, I'll let you know if I hear from him. Please keep me posted."

Andrew turned to Catherine and groggily explained what had happened. An hour later, just as the two were falling back to sleep, the phone rang again. Andrew leapt to answer it and heard the voice of Mark's father-in-law, Marty London.

"Mark just walked in the front door. Apparently, he'd checked into the Soho Grand Hotel."

Andrew covered the phone and whispered to Catherine.

"They found him; he was at the Soho Grand Hotel. Probably sleeping one off." The luxury boutique hotel was just blocks from Mark's apartment.

She rubbed her eyes, then propped herself up on her elbows.

"The Soho Grand? Given that this is going to make the papers, couldn't he have checked into some fleabag motel instead?"

But Mark wasn't sleeping off a night of overdoing it.

"I have some bad news," Marty continued. "We think he attempted suicide. He took a bottle of Ambien and another of Klonopin. The police brought him to the emergency room at New York Hospital. They just pumped his stomach."

Andrew jumped out of bed, scrambling for his clothes. "I'll be right there."

Susan Elkin, Mark's ex-wife, had received the news in the middle of the night, too. She was alone in her king-size bed when the phone rang at 4:00 AM. Rolling over, she peered at the clock; her husband, Richard Elkin, whom she had married a year after Mark and Stephanie's wedding, was out in the city with clients. Although not particularly prone to worry, she felt a faint stirring of dread in her gut when the man introduced himself as a detective.

"I'm wondering if you know where Mark Madoff is."

"Mark Madoff?" She scrambled to process the detective's words.

"He's been missing for a few hours."

Susan sat up and turned on the light.

"Have you tried his mother?" she asked.

"No, ma'am, we haven't."

"Do you need me to go over to his house?"

"No, we're at his house in Greenwich."

"OK, well, thank you. Please keep me informed."

She hung up the phone and sat there for a minute. Perhaps she'd just been subjected to a hoax. Before she made any phone calls, she wanted to make sure the story checked out. She dialed Mark's apartment, and a man answered the phone.

"Hi, this is Susan Elkin."

"Oh, yeah, I just spoke to you."

"I need to speak to Stephanie Madoff." In the background, Susan could hear Stephanie shriek, "I don't want to talk to her!"

The detective returned to the phone. "She doesn't want to talk to you."

"I'm not getting off this phone until she talks to me," Susan said, hearing her voice start to grow shrill.

Stephanie's voice became louder. "She's the reason we were fighting! She's the reason we were fighting!"

Stephanie picked up the phone. *"What?!"*

"Is it true—is Mark really missing?"

"Yes, he is." Stephanie began to cry.

"Have you talked to his mother?"

"You should know; you're the one in cahoots with her."

"Stephanie," Susan pressed, "do you need me to call Ruth?"

"No. I have her number." Stephanie hung up the phone.

At 9:00 AM, Susan's phone rang again. It was Stephanie, in hysterics.

"He's safe, he's safe," she kept repeating, through tears. "I'm so sorry. I'm so sorry. I'm so sorry."

"Stephanie, just go be with your husband," Susan said, trying to soothe her. "It's fine; I'm so happy to hear he's OK."

Susan scraped the rest of her eggs into the garbage. She wasn't going to be able to eat.

Andrew followed a nurse down a gleaming hallway at New York Hospital, through the doors of the bustling emergency room. In a private room, in a special section of the ER reserved for psychiatric patients, lay his brother, Mark. Still experiencing the residual effects of the pills, Mark was "out of it," moaning and twisting in the thin hospital sheets.

Their family doctor, Adam Stracher, joined Andrew at Mark's bedside.

"How could he have taken two bottles of pills and not died?" Andrew whispered.

"It's a little-known secret about these drugs, but they're designed so that it's very difficult to overdose on them," Adam explained quietly. "As long as you don't drink, you'll sleep like a bastard, but you're not going to die."

Andrew put his hand on the metal railing of the bed. "Mark. What happened?"

Mark started to cry. "I had a big fight with Stephanie. I found out that...that she's been talking to a divorce lawyer. Why'd she do that?" He cried harder. "I'm so embarrassed about this. Please don't tell my kids. I'm so embarrassed..." Moaning, he turned onto his side.

Andrew exchanged a look with Adam.

"OK, buddy, I'll be right outside," Adam told Mark.

"Mark, this can't be all about Stephanie," Andrew offered.

"It's not. I'm also so angry at Dad. How can a parent do this to his children? I just don't understand. He needs to know how awful this is." Mark sobbed.

"You have four children who need you. You can't abandon them to send Dad a message about what a horrible person he is."

"I know, I know. I'm so sorry."

The nurse knocked on the window, indicating it was time for Andrew to leave.

Marty London showed up, and the three visitors gathered in front of the nurses' station, along with the doctor who'd treated Mark.

"Don't worry about privacy," the doctor was saying. "We have experience with this sort of thing. We have a whole routine in place to deal with famous people." The doctor suggested they check Mark into an in-patient facility at New York–Presbyterian Hospital in White Plains; there, he could receive twenty-four-hour psychiatric care. They could book him under an assumed name; the press would never get ahold of the story.

Incredibly, the doctor was right. The press only managed to find out that Mark had gone missing; the true story went unreported. The next day, the cover of the *New York Post* announced, "Madoff Son 'Runs Away.'" It was reported that Mark had fought with Stephanie at 8:00 PM, hopped on his Vespa scooter, and "sped off." At 11:30 PM, his worried wife had reportedly called the police, and the following morning, he'd returned to the apartment, telling her he'd checked into the Soho Grand under a different name and paid cash. End of story.

Mark's Vespa, in fact, was still parked outside the Soho Grand, the day after his suicide attempt. Andrew and Stephanie's brother, Rob Mikesell, had been strategizing about how to retrieve it. They decided that Andrew and Catherine would drive to SoHo, stop by Mark's apartment, and pick up the keys, then retrieve the scooter and return it to the apartment.

Now Andrew and Catherine were circling Mark's block in the car, on the lookout for paparazzi.

"Drop me off in front of the building and wait for me three blocks away," Andrew instructed. The coast seemingly clear, Andrew hopped out of the car and disappeared into Mark's building. Catherine drove a few blocks to Crosby Street, where she miraculously found a parking spot.

Just as Rob had described, Andrew found the keys in a little dish by the front door. Mission accomplished, he walked out onto the street. But the paparazzi had "come out of their hidey-holes," and he was immediately blinded by flashbulbs. Throwing his hand in front of his face, he attempted to shield his eyes from the glare.

"What happened to your brother?"

"Why did he have a fight with his wife?"

"Is Stephanie planning to leave him?"

Andrew hurried down Mercer Street toward Prince and Broadway. Paparazzi jogged alongside him, snapping pictures and shouting questions. He quickly abandoned any thought of retrieving the scooter and made a beeline for the subway. Gratefully, he darted down the stairs. Paparazzi followed, pushing aside commuters in their haste to stay on his tail. Andrew changed trains at 14th Street but was unable to shake them. They trailed him through the underground tunnel and onto the Lexington line. At Hunter College, Andrew leapt off the train, paparazzi in hot pursuit, and ran the six blocks to his building. They snapped photos of him all along the way.

Andrew closed his apartment door and leaned up against it, trying to catch his breath. A rising anger displaced his immediate concern for Mark. It had been almost a year since his father's confession. The press attention had just started to die down. And now, once again, he was getting harassed on the street, this time thanks to his brother.

Catherine waited for Andrew in SoHo for an hour and a half. In his flight from the cameras and the turmoil of the moment, he hadn't remembered to call her. While he lay at home alternately sobbing and fuming, his phone still in his coat pocket in the hall, Catherine dialed him again and again. Where could he be? Once again, she attempted to text him, and received no response. Starting the ignition, Catherine inched out of the lucky space she'd found and headed home.

After Mark's suicide attempt, when he was still at the hospital, Andrew had called Susan to discuss breaking the news to Mark's kids. Mark had asked him not to tell them, but Susan disagreed; the kids needed to know. When they got off the phone, Susan called her therapist to ask how to handle the situation. Certainly, it was a place she'd never found herself in before.

"You tell them the truth," her therapist had said. "You tell them simply and completely. But you tell them the truth."

Kate, then fourteen, had been visibly upset. Daniel, seventeen, had received the news more stoically. Susan answered all of their questions and reassured them that things were going to be fine.

Hours later, Susan received an e-mail from Mark.

"You can't imagine how embarrassed I am to be here," the message began. "Please don't tell the kids I'm here. It would break my heart if they knew that this had happened. Tell them I went fishing for a couple of weeks."

Susan wrote back right away: "I can't tell them you've gone fishing. I already told them the truth. Your children can handle this. They love you. They're not angry with you. There's nothing wrong with them seeing their father vulnerable and in pain."

Andrew had the same concerns when it came to telling his own children. Having been raised in a world where messy truths were often concealed—especially from children—he had no road map to navigate this series of unfolding crises. And yet their family had been destroyed by lies; he could no longer stand for duplicity of any kind.

But when Anne came home from school that afternoon while Andrew was at the hospital, Catherine saw for herself how hard it was to deliver the whole truth.

Anne dropped into a chair in Catherine and Andrew's shared home office. "Where's Dad?"

"He's at the hospital, visiting your uncle Mark."

"The hospital?" Anne sat up in alarm.

Catherine took a deep breath. Though she knew it was the right thing to do, she didn't want to say the words.

"Uncle Mark tried to kill himself. But he's going to be OK. And now, because of this, he's going to get the help he needs."

"Why? Why? Why? Why did he do this?" Anne cried out.

"Because he's not well. He hasn't attended to his own health— his mental health."

Anne sobbed even harder.

"What about Daniel and Kate? What about Audrey and Nick? How could he do that to them?" Suddenly Anne's sobs abated. "I have to call them."

"Call them right now." Catherine nodded. "You guys need each other."

Later that day, Andrew continued the discussion with both his daughters.

"You should know exactly what happened. Uncle Mark took a few bottles of pills," he said.

"Are you going to kill yourself, Dad?" Anne asked with her usual frankness.

"No," Andrew said, putting a firm hand on her forearm. "I would never, ever do that. Even in my darkest moments, I haven't considered it. I have never felt that impulse—not once."

"Is Uncle Mark going to be OK?" Emily asked, her eyes starting to fill with tears.

"Yes. He's sick, but he's safe now, and getting the help he needs. He's going to be OK."

The three hugged, and Andrew breathed in the scent of his daughters. How much longer would it be, he wondered, before their childhoods completely slipped away?

The White Plains branch of New York–Presbyterian Hospital is housed in an old Rockefeller estate. Formerly a private home, it has since been converted into an in-patient psychiatric facility with a warren of musty rooms. Doctors are dressed casually and patients wear street clothes, though shoelaces are forbidden. It was there that Mark Madoff quietly checked in for three weeks, following his suicide attempt. During his stay, he sent e-mails to Daniel and Kate, telling them how much he loved them. They wrote back, saying, "Please don't worry, Dad. We love you. Get better. We can't wait to see you."

Their differences set aside, Susan and Stephanie talked frequently over that three-week period, working together to support the man they both loved.

Now Andrew strode purposefully through the hallways of the facility, eyeing the Ping-Pong table where patients hit a ball back and forth; the TV room, where some lounged and others played board games; and the kitchenette with its vending machines. A nurse led Andrew to a small private room at the end of a hall.

Mark sat up in bed, his arms folded. Andrew sat down in a chair across from him, and the nurse left the room.

"How are you doing?"

Mark looked out the window.

"You did this because of the fight you had with Stephanie?"

Mark whipped his head in Andrew's direction. "No, I didn't say that. Things with her are great."

"But in the hospital you said—"

"This has nothing to do with her." He paused, then repeated his mantra. "How else am I supposed to make Mom and Dad understand what they've done to me?"

Andrew's eyes widened. "That's ridiculous. This is how you're going to try and make them understand? You've got four kids! You cannot leave your children fatherless because you're trying to send a message to Mom and Dad."

"I'm *furious* at them. I can never forgive him for what he's done—or Mom for staying with him."

"Mom is living in a fantasy world," Andrew said. "You have to understand that. OK? It's very painful and I wish they loved us enough not to hurt us like this. But you know what? They don't. And I have accepted that. This is not going to send a message to them. You're forty-five years old, and if you want to help yourself, you've got to recognize that and move on with your life."

A nurse poked her head into the room. "Everything OK?"

"We're fine," Andrew said.

"Good. I'll be back to do another check in five minutes." She slipped quietly out of the room.

"I just don't understand how she could choose him over us."

"It's not about Mom making a choice. She doesn't get it. She doesn't recognize that all the horrible things that have happened are Dad's fault. She's like a cult member—one that has a leader but only one follower. She's not holding him accountable for what he did in general, let alone very personally, to her, to us, and to everyone we know. It's completely unforgivable. But what you're doing now is *not* going to help. All it's going to do is take your kids' father away from them. And that's horrible. I cannot watch you do that."

Mark turned over and stared out the window.

"You know, part of this is your fault, too. Maybe I did this because of you."

"Make up your mind!" Andrew exclaimed loudly. "First you blame Stephanie, then you blame Mom and Dad, now you're blaming me? When are you going to take responsibility for your *own* actions? Huh? I'm not taking responsibility for this. I did not put you here."

"You abandoned me. You totally disappeared."

"If you think you're going to score points against me with that one, forget it. It's not gonna happen. I love and support you and will do anything I can to help you. But first, you need to help yourself. You need to take responsibility for your actions and talk about what's actually bothering you. Please open up to me and let me know what you're thinking. As soon as you're willing to do that, I'm here for you. But if all you want to do is yell at me, then forget it. I'm not going to take that."

"You can't understand what it's like for me. Everything's fine with you because you have *Catherine*," he said, practically spitting her name.

Andrew stood up. He glared at his brother.

"I'm done. *We're* done. You're never going to talk about her that way again." Gathering up his coat, he stalked past the pretty nurse who'd once again entered the room to check on Mark.

"Sign here. We'll need your signature there as well." The associate pushed a legal document across his polished desk, and Andrew once again scribbled his name. He was sitting in his lawyers' offices, officially removing his brother as his children's caretaker and trustee in the event of his death.

Andrew was angry: first and foremost with his father, for destroying everyone's lives. He was angry with his mother, too, for the role that she'd played in the months following the confession. But he was particularly angry at Mark, for trying to kill himself. Andrew loved his brother very much, and in spite of their differences over the last few years, he felt the bond of brotherhood trumped everything else. It was a confusing set of emotions to have, and it was hard to focus on which ones were real, but the anger shone through most brightly. And because Mark had been unsuccessful in his suicide attempt, Andrew had been able to tell him all the reasons he felt angry. But Mark didn't want to hear it.

If anything ever happened to Andrew, Mark was supposed to take care of his kids. After Andrew's bout with lymphoma, this wasn't some vague hypothetical notion. For Mark to abandon that responsibility—not to mention the responsibility for his own children—was so foreign a concept to Andrew that he was unable to process it.

When Mark heard the news that Andrew was removing him as trustee and legal guardian, he was furious.

"I'm sorry," Andrew said, once his brother had calmed down. "Something could happen to me at any moment, and I cannot risk having you in charge of my kids' future. You've proven yourself untrustworthy in that regard."

Mark was absolutely incredulous that Andrew cut him off after his suicide attempt, says Susan. "I remember calling Andy and saying, 'I know you're mad at him—just fake it.' And Andy would say, 'I'll try.' Time and perspective have shown me that this was Andy's [own] desperate attempt at survival."

The brothers' long march toward estrangement resumed.

Susan had just taken a basket of clothes out of the laundry room when Mark called. He had been out of the hospital for a week.

"You're going to keep seeing a therapist, aren't you?" she asked.

"Yeah, oh yeah. I am."

"And do they have you on meds?"

"Yeah, I've been on antianxietals, but now they're going to put me on antidepressants as well."

"Good," she said. "How are you feeling about everything?"

"OK." There was silence for a moment, while Susan screwed up her courage to pose the question she'd been waiting to ask.

"Have you considered seeing your mother? She's really concerned about you."

"My therapist said I don't have to see my mother until I'm ready."

"That's true." She paused. "But I know you and I know it will help you."

"Well, I'm not ready." Susan felt she could hear his anger ratcheting up through the phone. "I tried to kill myself and she *still* hasn't left him."

"You have to understand her state of mind, Mark...," Susan said, repeating her oft-stated argument.

"I know what kind of mother you are, and if someone said to you tomorrow, 'You have to choose between your children and Rich,' I know what you'd do."

"She's not choosing between the two of you; she's doing this for herself."

"My whole life was a lie. My father is a scumbag, so who knows if anything he ever said was true. Who even knows if he loved me?"

He continued bitterly, "If at any point my father had told me not to work at the firm, I could see my way through this. But he never suggested that—not even once."

"Maybe you should talk to your father, to get some closure," Susan ventured. "Don't you think that would be helpful?"

"No. I never want to talk to my father ever again in my life."

They got off the phone, and Susan resumed folding clothes. She wished she had the power to help Mark get past his pain, but it seemed no one did. He'd never been able to see the gray areas in life, and when things didn't go well, he just shut his feelings down. That was how he'd plowed through their divorce, she now realized. At the time, she would have told people he had a lot of strength. Now she saw through that lie to the truth: The strongest people were the ones who allowed themselves to feel.

Chapter Twenty

PICKING UP THE
PIECES . . . AGAIN

The pressures that had led Mark Madoff to check into a hotel under an assumed name and down two bottles of pills were still very much in play when 2009 drew to a close. Since the beginning of that year, he'd been grasping for a way to carve out a new profession, something that would give his life meaning. Mark had wanted to work at BLM for the remainder of his life. He'd hoped to take over the business from his father, usher it into a new age, and eventually put his own name on the door. Whatever his flaws, at BLM his future had been bright. And with his brother inching his way out the door, the sky was the limit for Mark.

Now here he was: forty-five years old with a name that made him a pariah and four children to support, ranging in age from less than a year to seventeen. He had no means of income. No business degree. No appreciable skills, aside from what he'd learned as a trader. And no clue where to begin.

Mark was trying to let Stephanie down from their luxurious life slowly, Susan says, continuing to employ full-time help and never asking Stephanie to give up boxing classes, the gym, or travel.

Susan was more than happy to do her part, chipping in for more than her usual share of expenses. When she called Mark and said, "Kate's camp bill is due," he might say, "Can we split it this year?" Or she would tell him, "Daniel just went to the orthodontist. The bill came to one thousand dollars." And he would say, "I'll pay for it; I can get it this month."

"The man never nickeled-and-dimed me one time, even after we got divorced," Susan says. "He bought my children anything they needed."

Behind the scenes, though, Mark was struggling. A mutual college friend had introduced him to Geoff Bartakovics, a former investment banker who'd launched a wildly successful e-mail newsletter called *Tasting Table*. Together, they'd cooked up an idea for a new Internet business using Geoff's name only, but at the last minute, the funding had fallen through. Mark, who'd pinned his hopes on this new venture, was crushed.

A good friend who ran a consulting company offered Mark a job in his office, but he insisted on the caveat that they keep it very quiet, fearful that his business would suffer if the news leaked. Though Mark was happy to be working again, he felt underutilized and underpaid.

Susan would call him at work and ask, "How are you doing?"

"Oh, peachy," he would respond, with sarcasm in his voice.

The job did offer opportunities to network, and people seemed happy to meet with him—but no one was able to point him in a specific direction. Who would offer Mark Madoff a job at the level at which he felt qualified—or even give him an informational interview? No one in the banking industry, certainly. Discouraged, Mark told Susan he felt like he was "walking around under a shame umbrella."

"Networking was not Mark's strength," says a close friend of his, "but he went out of his way to meet with many senior-level executives in real estate and other industries. Let's remember, this is a guy who never had to put a résumé together, go on a job interview, or worry about money. The fact that he was able to get out of bed every day, network, and earn money to support his family was amazing."

And it couldn't have been easy for Mark: That same friend recalls telling him, on one occasion, "I spoke to a guy who will meet with you, but he's positive you were involved in your father's scheme, or at least had to know something." Mark, he recalls, responded, "No problem—get me a few minutes of his time, and I promise he will be convinced I had nothing to do with the scandal."

He was right: Two days later, Mark's friend received a call from the executive, who said, "Now I get it. I'm convinced. He had nothing to do with what happened."

Eventually, his conversations with people in the real-estate industry sparked an idea for another newsletter, and for the first time in months, Mark felt a stirring of excitement. He developed a search engine to gather the most important real-estate news and compiled it in a newsletter that he called *The Sonar Report*. A list of one thousand friends of friends became his first test clients, and he delivered the issue for free.

The response was overwhelmingly positive. No one knew that the person behind the newsletter was Mark Madoff, and his beta clients seemed to love the service. For nine months he worked around the clock, feeling that he'd finally found the ticket to supporting his family. Eventually, his friend had to let him go from his job; someone had gotten wind of the hire. But believing things were about to turn around, Mark took the news in stride.

By February of 2010, Andrew and Catherine were in the thick of launching Black Umbrella, and despite plenty of negative attention from the blogosphere, their first few clients were trickling in.

Andrew saw Mark periodically at their lawyers' offices, or talked to him quickly on the phone if a legal issue came up.

But it wasn't until April, with his life starting to approximate some semblance of "normal," that Andrew finally felt ready to reach out to his brother in a meaningful way. He sent him an e-mail asking if he wanted to meet in Central Park.

On the appointed day, Mark and Andrew rode their bikes to the northeast corner of Columbus Circle and sat on a bench, watching throngs of New Yorkers stream into the park. It was a beautiful, sunny spring day, and the two chatted casually about their lives while cyclists maneuvered around strollers, couples held hands, and women debuted their new spring dresses. Andrew told Mark about the launch of Black Umbrella, and Mark shared a few cryptic details about *The Sonar Report*.

"It's easier for you," Mark said at one point. "You have all these things going on."

"Easier in what way?"

"You have Catherine." For the first time, he didn't say it with malice.

"Are things OK with Stephanie?"

Mark frowned. "Of course they're OK. Why wouldn't they be?"

He drew a circle in the dusty earth with the toe of his sneaker, and the two sat in silence for a moment.

"I'm kind of pissed off that you didn't invite me to participate in Black Umbrella," Mark admitted.

Andrew looked at his brother. "That would have been a bad idea on several fronts."

"Why?"

"Because it's better for our relationship. We've finally separated for the first time in a healthy way. And...it just is."

That was never going to happen, Andrew thought. No way. Not after how Mark had treated Catherine, the suicide attempt, or what had happened with Abel. It was something he wouldn't even consider.

They chatted for a few more minutes and parted ways with an awkward pledge to speak more often. Mark, Andrew could tell, was still angry. He was every bit as angry as he had been with their parents. He was angry with Andrew because things came more easily to Andrew. He was angry at the press, at the public, at the friends who'd abandoned him, as well as the ones who'd stayed by his side but were unable to help.

What had been difficult for Andrew to see before, when he'd been so enmeshed with his brother, was now crystal clear: If Mark was going to crash and burn, he wanted Andrew to flame out with him.

The channel now open, Andrew and Mark started talking on the phone again every few days, sharing tidbits about the case, their various work projects, and what they'd heard about their mother. A discussion started to form around whether or not they were going to see her. Ruth, they knew, was planning to come to New York for Christmas to see her grandchildren.

Andrew wanted to see her; Mark was on the fence.

"I'm still so angry with her," he said.

"I think your anger is misplaced," Andrew argued. "It's Dad you should be furious at."

"I'm furious with him, too. But I just don't think I'm ready to see Mom."

"Well, I think we should consider seeing her at Christmas. I'd like to. But when we do see her, we should do it together."

"Maybe. I don't know."

In fact, unbeknownst to Andrew and their lawyers, Mark had been exchanging e-mails with Ruth for over a year.

"Mark and I e-mailed for a long time, but never spoke on the phone," Ruth says. "He said, 'Happy Birthday,' 'Happy Mother's Day,' 'I love you,' that kind of thing."

It was Ruth who reached out first, in June 2009, writing, "Hi, Mark, just want to say hello. I love you, Mom." He responded that he was not sure how to begin, but that "the distance between us has been agony for me." He and Stephanie were "hiding" in Nantucket. He closed his note, "Have you found a place, neighborhood? I love you very much. This has made my day nicer."

Ruth replied:

> 22 River Terrace. I'm not sure that's the address. I love the area. There's a terrific playground for Audrey and Nick. I can't wait to take her there. The kitchen is minute and I won't have room for my favorite pots, but the closets are decent. I'll be living like a poor college kid. I have no furniture. Right now I don't even have a bed. Anyway, to answer your question, I'm really pleased with my decision. I saw a gorgeous apartment in Tribeca but I was probably too old for the building. Way too hip for me but I liked it. I made a budget but there are probably many things I forgot to include. I never lived on my own before. Once I get settled I know it will all come together. Right now it is a big hassle but that will change. I'll be off the computer unless I can set it up at Diane's. I'm going there for the weekend, and then Monday hopefully I'll be in my new apartment. Love, Mom.

Mark wrote again, saying, "This is the best news I've heard in a long time. I'm crying with sadness and happiness at the same time." He assured her that Audrey was going to be "all over that playground." The casual tone of the e-mails, says Ruth, shows that they had no idea, then, how much worse things were going to get.

When Ruth moved out of her penthouse, Mark assured her that he knew the day "sucked," but that she should "try to look at it as a new start." Ruth responded, "If I can make it through this week, I can handle anything."

She added, "I'm pretty numb by now but not numb enough. How did I become the focus of all this? I am probably the most boring person on the face of the earth. And it's the media that is ruining anything I might have left of a life. There is nowhere I go that I'm not recognized after that giant picture in the 'Style' section. No one believes in my innocence no matter what happens. I just can't manage with all that ancillary meaningless stuff. Love, Mom."

Then, somewhere around October 2010, when Ruth was still trying to organize a meeting with her sons, the tone of the e-mails changed. Ruth attributes the shift in Mark's feelings to the fact that the Madoffs remained in the press day after day, making it clear to Mark—and the rest of the world—that the story wasn't going away. When Ruth attempted to reach out to Stephanie in an effort to see her grandchildren, Mark's response was swift and furious. He told her to stop trying to contact them. The most difficult thing, he said, was her "continued relationship with someone who has inflicted such pain on your children." He closed his note, "It is agony to hear from the kids that their grandfather writes them cheery letters so they can hear how he is doing. I can assure you that it may not be so cheery if I have to tell my son that he can't go to college because his grandfather stole from his own children and that their grandmother still talks to him. . . . I continue to be humiliated publicly, and I have no idea if I will be able to support my family. I had hoped that things would be further along and I would be able to get on with what is left of my life."

Ruth wrote back to Mark, explaining that she felt sorry for

Bernie no matter what he had done, and that she couldn't abandon her husband:

> I need to clarify my position to you, so maybe you can understand what is going on for me. You accuse me of choosing Dad over you and Andy. I don't believe that I've made that choice. I have not chosen Dad and not you. I've never condoned or diminished the agony that Dad has caused to everyone that I know and love. Clearly our lives have been destroyed. What we are going through now is unbearable and would be no matter what choice I make. This is a tragedy beyond anything imaginable for all of us. I just don't see how my abandoning him would make anyone better off. And I don't think my doing so is any proof that I don't understand or sympathize with what you are going through or would help you in any way. You must know what this is doing to me. I write one or two letters a week and get a few phone calls from him. I don't see this as a decision to give up my family. You have given me up and I pray that one day you might understand that I have not chosen one over the other. I miss you all terribly. Why can't you understand? He is still a human being, suffering, and is only going to get worse. I don't expect you to pity him, but I just can't let him rot in there.

"I didn't visit Bernie often," she says. "I went maybe four times in two years. Mark seemed to think I was making a choice between him and Bernie. I tried to explain that I wasn't abandoning Mark, or choosing one over the other. The boys wanted me to hate Bernie right off and I couldn't. I just couldn't. Mark never forgave me for that, and I don't know if Andy ever will."

There were people who said, 'You're crazy—who would abandon their children over a husband who's in jail?' But I didn't look at it as abandoning my children. I didn't want to abandon any of them. Mark and Andy had their families, too. It just didn't feel like a betrayal of them."

Most difficult for Ruth was the fact that Mark was willing to communicate only by e-mail. In the best of times, she didn't express herself well via e-mail; under these circumstances, she found it nearly impossible. "I was trying to explain my terribly complicated feelings about the man I was married to for fifty years—that I couldn't let him rot away in prison. I never saw that I had an option. I just didn't." She desperately tried to reason with her son, writing, "I do not want to go back and forth by e-mail. This is a situation that is far too complicated and requires a lot of discussion. When everything is settled we can spend the time trying to understand what the other is feeling." Once she realized her words were having no effect, she would try playing by his rules. In one e-mail, she backed down after pushing to see her grandchildren: "Hi Mark," she wrote. "I love you too much to put you through this decision. I'll see them soon enough. Not martyrdom. I really can wait."

Once or twice, Andrew had confronted Mark, suspecting he'd been talking to their mother behind his back, but Mark vigorously denied it.

"I got the sense that nobody was being up front with me, which I really didn't like," says Andrew. "Finally, I just gave up."

What had been Mark's great hope, *The Sonar Report,* became one of his biggest disappointments. The moment he started charging for the service, the subscriptions dropped dramatically. Once again, he found himself out of work with few prospects and facing an insurmountable climb. His self-esteem plummeted still lower.

Susan started to have daily powwows with several friends of Mark's. After each had gotten their requisite daily phone calls, e-mails, and texts, they would call one another to compare notes on Mark's state of mind. Every evening they repeated the ritual. All knew that Mark tended to compartmentalize: He would tell Susan one piece of information, his friends another, and Stephanie another, unable to have a completely honest relationship with any one person. Susan hoped that by taking a "tag-team approach," she and his friends would have a better chance of stabilizing Mark emotionally.

And yet, despite the circumstances that had transformed him into a person his family didn't recognize, Mark tried his hardest to be present for his children. Susan recalls how Mark attended Kate's high school open house a mere nine months after the scandal broke. Susan had been planning to go but ended up having an important business dinner to attend instead. The two had been "working very hard to keep the kids' lives on a normal track," says Susan, who could "tell from his voice that he knew the night was going to be difficult."

When Susan came home the night of the open house, friends called to tell her they had seen Mark: He was wearing a baseball cap pulled low over his face and didn't make eye contact with anyone. A former neighbor who had once been close to Mark reported grabbing him by the arm and pulling him in for a hug; she could "feel the relief in his embrace. He seemed happy to have a friendly face to make him feel comfortable—if only for a minute."

The next morning, Mark told Susan, "That was one of the hardest things I've ever had to do. To go into the school my children attend, where I once felt proud as could be of my name and family..." He trailed off. Then, using a nickname Bernie had invented for their daughter, he said, "I did it for Kitty—she's the best."

Later that year, when Susan met with Daniel's guidance counselor to talk about colleges, Mark stopped by the school again. He was in a better place by then, Susan says, and he wanted to lend Daniel direction and strength. Afterward, Susan took Mark to meet with the social worker who'd been helping their kids all year long. The social worker later told Susan that she could see how much pain Mark was in and that Daniel regularly expressed fears that his father would try to commit suicide again.

In August, Daniel left for his first semester of college at the University of Colorado at Boulder. Mark called Susan, "freaking out" because he wasn't sure he'd be able to pay the tuition.

"If you can't pay it, I'll liquidate some stocks to come up with the money," Susan soothed him. "Don't worry."

Mark, she says, was "horrified" that he wasn't going to be able to send his children to college.

"From now on, when your parents send the kids gifts, tell them it should be cash... to go in their college fund," he begged.

The landscape of Mark's life was very different from Andrew's, says Susan, something that she was painfully aware of. Mark was operating out of a "doomsday scenario" with a completely different picture of what was possible for him. She tried to help him look on the bright side, but since he had two children under the age of three in his household, his fears, Susan had to admit, weren't unfounded.

On Ruth's last visit to Bernie in prison, she delivered a blow they both knew was coming; it was something they'd discussed many times. Sitting across from Bernie on the preschool-size chairs that had been set up for visitors, surrounded by young families weeping and holding each other, she turned to her husband of fifty years.

"I have to give you up for them. I just have to, because..." She started to cry. "I have a life. I have to see the children. I have to think of myself."

She walked out of the prison gates and into the warm North Carolina air. It was September, and in New York the leaves were just starting to turn. New York seemed light-years away.

Ruth and Bernie were in contact later, when Bernie called to see if her decision was final.

"You know I'm having a hard time making this decision, but all the kids are upset and I need to get beyond this," Ruth said.

"I'm OK with it," Bernie said. "Whatever you decide."

He wasn't really OK with her decision, Ruth knew, but he had agreed to let her off the hook.

"He knew it was something I had to do. If he called I wasn't going to hang up on him, and if he e-mailed I could send him a curt reply, but if I had to make the break, it was easier to go cold turkey."

After that conversation, Bernie sent her "a few articles. Never a letter."

Ruth e-mailed Andrew and Mark to let them know she'd cut off contact with Bernie. "OK, I won't visit him anymore," she wrote. "Let's see how this works out."

"She acted as if none of the horrible things that happened had ever taken place," Andrew recalls, amazed. "I was struck by the fact that she'd cut off contact with him not because of what had happened, but only because it was getting in the way of having a relationship with me and Mark."

Ruth, who "truly believed that one thing had nothing to do with the other," waited for a response from her sons. Perhaps in their eyes the gesture she'd made wasn't enough. But it would have to be. It was the very best she could do.

Andrew's summer of 2010 was filled with nonstop work on Black Umbrella's first major event, a five-day primitive skills course set in the Adirondacks, taught by Tom Brown III. A core group of

Black Umbrella supporters, advisors, and friends learned fire making, shelter building, water purification, and primitive cooking. Andrew wanted to learn those survival skills as a way to deepen his experience and boost his credentials.

That fall, Catherine and Andrew held their second annual "Orphan's Thanksgiving." The year before, they'd invited a dozen people, a mix of old friends and those they'd met after the scandal broke. Andrew had prepared a traditional Thanksgiving feast, and they'd celebrated quietly with his daughters and their guests.

"That first year, there was a little bit of concern of 'Are people going to come?'" Catherine recalls. This time, they worried they'd overextended themselves: They'd more than doubled the previous year's guest list. Aside from Mark and Stephanie, who tended to maintain a radio silence during the holidays, multiple friends e-mailed and called, asking, "Are you doing Thanksgiving this year? Because I want to come."

Catherine looked at the two twenty-pound turkeys in front of her. Black Umbrella now required near-constant attention. She was managing the busy school and social calendars of three kids. And now it looked as if thirty people were coming to dinner. "How am I going to pull this off?" she fretted aloud.

Andrew circled her waist with his arms and pulled her close.

"Honey, we just do it. This is our tradition now."

Chapter Twenty-one

INTO DARKNESS

Susan and Mark were on the phone, discussing the logistics of Kate's upcoming swim meet, when Mark blurted out, "Susan, my wife is about to leave me. I can't deal with this right now."

"She was happy to stay when there was all that money," Susan said, succumbing to a flash of mean-spiritedness.

"I don't need that coming from you. OK?" Mark said, furious.

For Mark, the prospect of a second divorce was unthinkable. He'd done it once before and couldn't bear to live apart from his children again, especially without his immediate family to fall back on. The thought of a second divorce felt shameful to him; he didn't want to be a two-time failure. Then there was how it would be interpreted: In his opinion, having his wife walk away from their marriage while the whole world was pointing fingers at him would make him look guilty.

"I'm sorry. You're right. Please forgive me."

The next day, Susan sent Mark an e-mail, apologizing again for her offensive remark. Then she sent one to Stephanie, paraphrased here.

"I have had more than one husband now," she wrote, "and I

know what a good husband Mark is. I urge you to stay with him; you will never meet a man like him again."

Stephanie never responded.

The plans for Ruth's Christmas visit were in place, and Mark and Andrew had cleared the meeting with their lawyers. Ruth would stay with Susan; Mark and Andrew would meet with her then. Neither had seen her since the confession.

In preparation for a story the *Wall Street Journal* had commissioned on the two-year anniversary of their father's arrest, both brothers prepared statements for their PR team. Andrew's life was now devoted to family, work, friends, cycling, and managing his health. In late September, to celebrate their "anniversary of not getting married," Catherine and Andrew had ridden their bikes more than two hundred miles to her family's farm upstate. As Andrew sat in front of his computer, thinking about how much his life had changed, he wondered how to properly convey his misery over what had happened as well as his sense of hope that life could be good again. What would Mark write? he wondered. In the end, the combined statement read:

> Mark remains unalterably bitter about his father's deception and the injury his father has inflicted on his own family as well as thousands of others.
>
> Andrew was also deeply impacted by his father's deception and the harm it caused to his family. He now works for Black Umbrella, a security consulting firm that builds crisis preparedness plans for families. The firm was launched in February 2010 by his fiancée, Catherine Hooper.
>
> In his spare time, Andrew enjoys cycling, and rides 125 miles each week around Manhattan and its surrounding areas.

Andrew wasn't sure which one of them looked worse—the one who was "unalterably bitter," or the one who was trying to put something so terrible behind him.

On December 8, 2010, the day before the second anniversary of Bernie's confession, Irving Picard filed a lawsuit against Mark's and Andrew's children, seeking $354,000 in damages from their trusts. The *Wall Street Journal* ran an article about the lawsuit, naming Mark's and Andrew's minor children by their initials only. Eighteen-year-old Daniel did not receive the same treatment: They printed his full name.

It was a devastating blow to Mark, who became "completely unhinged" by the prospect of his young son's losing his anonymity just as he entered his first semester of college. In response, Mark called Susan "thirty times a day," asking, "Are you sure they're all right? Do they know about the article?"

"They're fine; they're fully armed," she kept reassuring him.

Mark, says Susan, was a wonderful father who talked to his children every day of their lives. The fact that he couldn't protect them from this ignominy sent him hurtling toward the abyss.

Abruptly, Mark changed his mind about seeing his mother. He called Andrew to tell him to call off the plan.

"The press is too hot. I can't deal with this. I'm not ready to see Mom," he said. Then he paused for a long time. "I have no pleasure in my life. The last thing I'm going to do is give her pleasure by letting her see me."

Andrew felt a familiar tick of alarm at the back of his neck. "That's awful. How can you say that? You have four beautiful children you love and who love you." Andrew paused. "Are things OK with Stephanie?"

"Yeah, things with her are good. I didn't mean it like that. I just don't want to see Mom."

After the two hung up, Andrew reflected on his brother's comments, feeling a spreading sense of unease.

"You have to call him back," Catherine urged when he relayed the conversation to her.

Andrew quickly redialed Mark's number.

"I can't stop thinking about how you said you have no pleasure in your life. That's a terrible thing to say. Do you really feel that way?"

"No, I don't. Things are actually really good: The business is picking up and things are finally on track with Stephanie. It has nothing to do with me. It's all Mom; I just don't want to see her. You don't need to worry about me. OK?"

"OK," Andrew said, chewing his lip. He hung up the phone.

On Thursday, December 9, with the deadline looming for Picard to file additional suits, and a copy of the lawsuit against his and his brother's children sitting on the table in front of him, Andrew called Mark.

"I'm not happy about these lawsuits," Andrew said. "But they're not as bad as they could have been."

Mark agreed.

"I think if Picard just filed these, there's a good chance he won't file any more suits. He only has until Saturday."

"You're probably right."

"This is an enormous load off my mind."

"Mine too."

They hung up and Andrew started to prepare lunch. As he scraped hummus onto a plate and chopped tomatoes, he felt all of the stress of that week drain out of him. Mark had seemed "completely normal" on the phone, in stark contrast to how he'd sounded the day before.

Andrew put a place mat on the table, poured himself a glass of filtered tap water, and sat down to eat, unaware that he'd just spoken to his brother for the very last time.

Susan heard from Mark that same night. Kate had just finished talking to him and had handed the phone to her mother.

"What are you doing tonight?" Susan asked.

"I'm not doing anything."

Aware that Stephanie had traveled to Disney World with her mother and Audrey, Susan said, "Oh, I don't want you to be alone this week. I'm planning to drive Kate into the city anyway. Let me drop her off with you."

"No, I'm fine. Me and Big Nick are going to have a fun night together."

"Are you sure? Because I can bring Kate in right now."

"Don't be silly."

They got off the phone. Susan, too, was comforted by how normal he sounded.

On the evening of Friday, December 10, Andrew opened his BlackBerry to find a typical e-mail from Mark, sent to him and their entire legal team, ranting about a new article he'd read online from the *Wall Street Journal*. Andrew clicked to read about Annette Bongiorno, one of Bernie's two main "back office" lieutenants, who had been living in Florida under house arrest since November:

> Federal prosecutors are ratcheting up pressure on one of Bernard L. Madoff's former "back office" employees to cooperate with their investigation as they have continued in recent months to scrutinize his brother and sons, according to people familiar with the situation.

The former longtime employee, 62-year-old Annette Bongiorno, was arrested last month and accused by prosecutors of fabricating account documents reflecting fraudulent trades and securities fraud, among other offenses. She faces up to 75 years in prison on the charges. Ms. Bongiorno, who spent several days in jail after her arrest, has been trying to post $5 million bail set by the judge so she can remain free pending trial....

It was the title that really upset Mark. "Madoff's Kin Eyed as Probe Grinds On," it read, making it seem as though Bongiorno was about to implicate the brothers in their father's crime.

"The headline was bad; it was scary," Andrew admits. "But when you read the article, it looked like they'd put the wrong headline with the story. Mark talked to Marty London and Marty Flumenbaum at great length about it, and both felt like they'd talked him down. They'd said, 'All they're doing is rehashing stuff they said a year ago. There's no reason to be concerned.'" When they'd gotten off the phone with Mark, according to the lawyers, he was no longer upset.

But by late Friday evening, Mark was once again in a rage. He'd just found out that Ruth was still planning to stay with Susan over Christmas, though Mark had canceled their meeting. He called Susan, apoplectic.

"My mother cannot come and stay at your house!" he yelled. "Let her stay at a hotel!"

Susan "just sat there" and let him scream at her. When he seemed to be slowing down, she said, "I understand. But my support of her does not mean I'm not supporting you. I love you. I would do anything for you. But your mother—"

"This is not OK with me!" he said, continuing to protest loudly.

"All right, all right, I'll talk to her."

Susan's husband, Rich, walked into the kitchen. One glance at her husband and she knew he'd had a bad day.

"Who's on the phone?" he mouthed, throwing his briefcase on the counter with a thud.

She covered the phone and whispered, "Mark, about his mom."

Rich rolled his eyes. "Can we give it a rest for tonight?"

Susan nodded and returned to her call. "Mark, let me call you back."

"OK, sorry. Go be with your husband," he said.

Susan didn't call him back that night, knowing he had a habit of getting anxious and worked up, then calming down a few hours later. I'll call him in the morning, she thought. That would buy her a few hours to decide whether or not she was going to ask Ruth to stay in a hotel. She turned to her husband to soothe him about his day. She, too, was unaware she'd just had her last conversation with Mark.

December 11, 2010, was a black anniversary for the Madoff family. Two years earlier on that day, Bernie had been arrested and their lives had spiraled into an unrelenting hell. They'd been eviscerated in the press. Followed around the clock by paparazzi. Lost access to one another.

Where Andrew had started to slowly rebuild his life, Mark had watched his unravel.

At 4:00 AM, with his two-year-old son, Nick, asleep in the nursery and his dog, Grouper, somewhere in the house, Mark sat down at his computer to compose several e-mails. Then he fashioned a noose out of a vacuum cleaner cord and tied it to a beam on his living room ceiling. When it snapped, he took Grouper's black leash and tied it to the same beam. The second time he attempted to end his life he was successful.

Several hours later, Stephanie received her husband's e-mail. Frightened and concerned, she called her stepfather, Marty London, and asked him to check on Mark and Nick. When Marty raced over to the apartment, he found his son-in-law's body hanging from a beam. Nick was asleep in his room, Grouper next to his crib.

That morning, at 7:00 AM, Susan was on the phone with Ruth, discussing the *Wall Street Journal* article that had so upset Mark.

"I don't think it's so bad," Susan said.

"I didn't get it yet. Could you e-mail it to me?"

"Sure."

Susan hung up the phone, sent Ruth the article, and went back to bed.

At 7:30 AM, her phone rang. Susan looked at the caller ID. It was one of the friends she'd spoken to daily about Mark.

"I don't know how to tell you this…," he began. "Mark is dead."

Susan wasn't sure she'd heard correctly. "What?"

"Mark is dead. He killed himself last night."

Half asleep, sure she was having a bad dream, Susan said, "Oh, my God. I have to call his mother." Without asking for further details, she hung up the phone.

In slow motion, she dialed Ruth. When her former mother-in-law answered the phone, Susan blurted out, "Ruth, Mark died. He killed himself last night."

"What? That's not right. That can't be right."

"I'm pretty sure that's right. I'm pretty sure that's what his friend just told me. All right. Wait a minute. Let me call him back. I'll call you back." She hung up.

Surely she'd heard incorrectly. There had been so much innuendo over the past two years, an avalanche of news stories, most of them false — why would this one be any more real than the last?

She called Mark's friend back.

"You said Mark died?"

"Yeah."

"What happened?" Susan asked. She was numb, uncomprehending.

"I don't have any of the details yet."

"OK, thanks." She hung up the phone.

Susan went downstairs into her kitchen, where she walked in a slow circle, meditating, trying to think. Upstairs, her fifteen-year-old daughter with Mark, Kate, was asleep in her bed. Susan's youngest daughter, five-year-old Annabelle, was also asleep. Daniel was likely asleep, too, in his freshman dorm room in Boulder, Colorado.

Almost sleepwalking, she floated up the stairs to her bedroom. Her husband lay on his side, sleeping peacefully.

"Rich, wake up," she whispered. "Wake up."

"What's up?" he said, rubbing his eyes.

"Mark's dead."

Rich bolted to an upright sitting position. *"What?"*

"Mark's dead."

Still in a trance, Susan walked back down the stairs, her husband following. The minute she set foot in the kitchen, tears cascaded from her eyes.

"I don't know what to do. I don't know what to do. I don't know what to do," she said, walking in circles, wringing her hands.

She had suggested dropping Kate at Mark's house on Thursday night. Why hadn't she done the same thing Friday night? Why hadn't she insisted?

Wildly, she looked around the room. "I'm going to call Wendy."

In times of crisis, she often called Wendy, who was a therapist;

she always seemed to know what to do. Susan dialed her friend, continuing to circle her kitchen.

"Have you told Daniel yet?" Wendy asked, after expressing her condolences.

"I don't know if I should tell him over the phone."

"You have to. Before he finds out from anyone else."

In shock, thinking only about her kids, Susan forgot to call Ruth, who was waiting by the phone in her own state of numb denial, choosing not to believe what she'd just heard.

Her hand shaking, Susan dialed her eighteen-year-old son. His phone rang and rang. She texted him: "Please call. It's important." He didn't respond. By then, it was 8:30 AM and television stations had already picked up the story.

"Please," she whispered, closing her eyes as she listened to his ringing phone. "Please, please pick up."

An e-mail arrived in her in-box from the mother of a girl in Daniel's dorm. "If there's anything I can do for your family, please let me know," she had written.

Susan immediately called her.

"Julie, I can't wake up Daniel. Can you please wake up Nina?"

Minutes later, Julie called her back. She, too, was unable to reach her child.

Susan called the Boulder Police. "I have an emergency; I need to get ahold of my son. He's there in the dorm."

The Boulder Police Department connected her to campus security, who said, "We're sending two police officers over to your son's dorm to wake him up."

"Please, please just give him the phone and stay with him while I talk to him."

"Of course."

She waited, her husband's arm encircling her. Then she heard someone fumble with the phone and her son's familiar voice, laced with fright.

"Mom, what's wrong?"

"Daniel, Daddy died last night. He took his own life." She squeezed her eyes together and lifted her face to the ceiling as she heard her son wail.

"Mom, I didn't call him back last night."

"Daniel, Daddy knew how much you loved him. You don't have to worry about that. Daddy was just in so much pain. Do you want us to come get you, or do you want to get on a plane?"

"Can Rich come get me?"

"Yes. I'll call you back in a little while."

Then Susan frantically dialed Daniel's friend Nina, who answered this time. "You can't leave him alone. OK?"

"I'm going to go take a shower. Will's with him right now. Then I'm going to go downstairs and we're going to make sure he's not alone."

"OK. OK. Thank you."

Susan went upstairs to wake up Kate, her feet heavy, as though she were walking through wet cement. Her beautiful fifteen-year-old daughter lay peacefully on her pillow, sleeping. Susan sat down on her bed.

"Kate, wake up," she said gently.

Her daughter stirred, blinking.

"Listen, Kate, Daddy died."

Eyes now open, Kate slowly shook her head. "No, Mom, you're kidding. You're kidding. No."

Susan shook her head as well, the tears starting to flow. "Honey, I'm not kidding. I wish I were."

"No! Mom, you're kidding! No! You're kidding!"

For ten minutes, Kate lay in bed, repeating the phrase, until finally she burst into tears, sobbing unceasingly.

Annabelle crept into the room and hovered at the edge of

Kate's bed, clutching a coloring book. "Kate, will you color with me?"

Kate's sobs subsided and she gathered her sister into her arms, taking a crayon and starting to fill in the lines.

The phone began to ring incessantly. By 9:30, the press was calling as often as friends were.

Nina called to report on Daniel: "Don't worry. He's sleeping. He hasn't been alone at all. We're all hanging out in his room."

Susan's best friend, Doris, called.

"It's true," Susan said. "I can't talk right now. I'll call you later."

A *Wall Street Journal* reporter called: "Would you like to give a statement on the death of Mark Madoff?"

Susan went online to buy a plane ticket for Rich. While searching for fares, she kept picking up the phone, deflecting reporters' questions. Soon, she realized that Rich wasn't going to be able to fly out and return to New York within twenty-four hours. Susan called Daniel again.

"Listen, honey, I can't get you back today unless you fly back alone. Can you manage that?"

"Yeah, I can."

The rest of the day, Susan says, was "spent very numbly." Her parents showed up. Her brother arrived. The kids' former nanny, Bridget, came over with Mark's younger son, Nick; she'd picked him up from Marty London. In the middle of it, Susan noticed that a call from Stephanie had arrived. She immediately called her back.

"Oh, Steph...," she began.

"I'm really trying not to lose it. I'm really trying not to lose it, Susan."

"I understand. Bridget is here with Nick and we're going to keep him for the day. She'll bring him to you when you get to Greenwich, OK?"

Everything felt "surreal," Susan says: The house was bustling with people, and Mark's adorable little boy, Nick, was running around. His unmistakable resemblance to the Mark she'd known from childhood photos tore at her heart.

Rich, normally "very macho and not prone to tears," kept breaking down as he watched Nick play with his daughter, Annabelle. "Nothing throws me," he said. "But I can't believe he left those children. I can't believe he left Daniel and Kate."

Andrew, too, was lying in bed when he got the call. Sophie had crept in at 7:00 AM with *Frog and Toad Together*; she and Catherine were reading aloud from the book. Andrew half dozed, contemplating a bike ride on what was shaping up to be a gorgeous winter morning, when his phone rang.

Andrew looked over and saw that the caller was Marty London. He whispered the name out loud. Both he and Catherine knew. Instantly. It had been Marty who'd called after Mark's first suicide attempt. He and Andrew rarely spoke.

Catherine grabbed Sophie and hustled her out of the room.

"Something awful has happened. Mark is dead. He hanged himself."

The words were exactly what he'd expected to hear, but he felt his entire being collapse like a fan. All the strife, anger, and hurt feelings were gone in an instant—replaced with a cavernous void of loss.

"Do you need me to come down there?" Andrew asked.

"No, no, no, no. Please don't. The scene down here is too awful to describe. I tried to get him down, but he used some kind of cable. You don't want to see this."

Andrew, becoming hysterical, allowed the phone to drop from his hand.

Catherine came back into the room, alone. She climbed onto the bed and held Andrew as he wailed.

Andrew's phone rang.

"It's Susan," he said to Catherine as he extracted himself from her embrace.

"Andy," Susan said. "I didn't call him back last night. We got into a fight about his mother."

"I think he did this to punish my father," he said.

"I feel so guilty..."

"Susan—I can't deal with this right now."

"All right, all right, I'll talk to you later."

Gathering himself, Andrew entered Anne's room to repeat the same agonizing ritual Susan had gone through that morning.

"Uncle Mark is dead. He killed himself."

After attending to his sobbing daughter, it was Andrew's turn to cry—as Anne volunteered to go to Roosevelt Island, where Emily was having a sleepover, to break the news to her younger sister and bring her home. Then Andrew went into the bathroom, ran the tap, splashed water on his face, and prepared to make the most difficult call of all.

All of the anger he'd felt over the past two years bubbled to the surface as he dialed his mother. He didn't blame her, but he felt she had played a role. She could have done more.

Ruth answered the phone. It had been a year and a half since he'd heard the sound of her voice, and even then it had just been for a moment. He had so much he wanted to say to her, so much he needed to get off his chest. But now was not the time. He was going to tell her the truth: the whole truth and nothing but the truth—whatever the consequences. So he did.

"Mom, it's true: Mark is dead. He hanged himself."

Ruth screamed.

Andrew waited until her screams subsided.

"You need to get on a plane and come to New York *now*," he said.

"How?"

"I don't know. Call me from the airport and I'll figure it out."

"But I need to get a wig..."

"You need to get up here *right now*. I don't want to hear anything from you other than 'I'm on my way,' OK? Get in your car and drive to the airport and come here. Now."

"OK, I'm coming."

He slammed down the phone, wondering when the news would hit the media. The question was answered immediately. The phone rang, displaying the caller ID of Catherine's pastor: their first sympathy call. "If there is anything we can do, anything at all," he said. "We're here for you."

Sinking into his office chair, Andrew covered his face with his hands. Mark, Marty London had told him, had sent e-mails to Flumenbaum and Stephanie. But he hadn't sent one to him. Mark couldn't face him, even in writing. The anger he'd felt at his brother during his previous suicide attempt was gone. This one wasn't a cry for help — Mark had been determined. With his beautiful son sleeping in the room next to him, he had hanged himself not once, but twice. The vacuum cleaner cord had snapped on the first attempt. That meant he had to walk around the apartment looking for something stronger until he found Grouper's leash and could finish what he'd started. What must that have been like for him? What was going through his mind? The pain he was feeling must have been unimaginable.

Ruth hung up the phone. Still shrieking and gasping for air, she dialed her sister, Joan. The rest of the day was a blur: Bob drove them to the airport; Ruth and Joan "sat on the plane like zombies" and were met in New York by Joan's daughter, Diane.

At her niece's home, where she'd lived in the months after Bernie went to prison, Ruth's phone lit up with calls and text messages from people she hadn't spoken to since the confession. The second anniversary of Bernie's arrest—what would now become the day of her older son's death—was also the deadline for the bankruptcy trustee to file clawback suits against victims. The many people who had been admonished by their lawyers not to speak to Ruth were now free to call without reprisal.

One text message read: "This shouldn't happen to anybody."

"Even me, you mean," Ruth responded, finishing her sentence for the woman, formerly one of her closest friends. After that, she canceled her text service. She didn't want to spend the money on incoming texts, nor did she want to hear from people who hadn't tried to reach her before.

Handwritten notes were sent to her lawyer. She didn't care. All she could think about was the phone call she'd been trying to find the courage to make, to beg Mark to see her in person. "Please," she'd been planning to say, "please, let's just try. I've got to talk to you face-to-face." He'd sent her an e-mail, calling off their meeting. She'd sent a few in return, trying to explain her position. It was hard for her to express herself via e-mail. She needed to see him. Finally, she'd backed off, figuring she'd get to New York and he'd change his mind.

Then he'd killed himself.

Ruth's children were her life—there was no one who knew her who wasn't aware of that. She'd just wanted to provide comfort when her son was in such deep suffering. He thought she'd abandoned him for Bernie. It wasn't true: She would never abandon her children—not for Bernie, nor anyone. She'd been there the whole time, if only they'd been able to see it.

On Sunday, the day after she arrived in New York, Ruth drove with Joan and Diane to Susan's house, where Ruth would stay for the remainder of her trip. Susan and her husband were "incredible" to Ruth, who distracted herself with the myriad children, relatives, and friends flowing through the house. And though she wouldn't allow herself to think of the circumstances that had made it possible, one of her greatest wishes was about to come true.

Andrew had scheduled a meeting with her.

Over those two terrible days, Andrew had been trying to plan Mark's funeral, with Stephanie and Marty London.

"We can't have a funeral," Marty had said. "It's going to be a media circus."

"Are you sure? Isn't there a way to deal with that?"

"Let's have something quiet—a memorial. We can hold a proper funeral at a later date."

Andrew didn't love that idea, he says, but understood: He didn't want a media circus, either. When Marty called and began reading names from a list, Andrew thought, at first, that he was reading a suggested guest list. Instead, it was a list of people Stephanie didn't want at the memorial; Ruth was at the top of the list.

"You can't do that," Andrew had insisted on the phone to Stephanie.

"I want you to come up here and talk to me face-to-face," Stephanie cried. "But you have to come alone."

"If Catherine isn't welcome in your home, and neither are all these people, then I'm not comfortable there, either."

Eventually, Stephanie relented and agreed to a less exclusive memorial, but she was adamant that Ruth not attend. The memorial was planned for Thursday night, at Stephanie and Mark's house in Greenwich. Andrew felt "a great sense of dread" leading up to the service.

First, though, he had to take care of something else he'd been dreading.

Andrew waited for Ruth downstairs at Susan's house, on the big sectional sofa that felt like an embrace. The people surrounding Ruth had cleared out of the way so she could speak to her son alone. She came down the stairs to meet him, shaking with anticipation. "I was terrified because I hadn't had any contact with Andy at all—none. And I knew he was furious with me."

When Andrew saw her for the first time in two years, he was taken aback by his mother's "startling" appearance. He barely recognized her. Ruth's glamorous blond bob had been replaced by a bad haircut with a reddish cast. She looked old, awful. Clearly having cried for days, she wore no makeup. Always slender, she had now shrunk to a stick under her loose, rumpled clothes.

Ruth crossed the room and fell into Andrew's arms. Her frail frame trembled with sobs as he tightened his arms around her. For five minutes, they stood wrapped in an embrace, Ruth's tears wetting the front of her son's button-down shirt. When they finally parted, they sat next to each other on the couch. They began the conversation with tentative small talk, catching each other up on their lives. Eventually, talk turned to how angry Andrew was with his mother and why.

"I don't understand why you're so mad at me," she kept saying.

"Because you've made horrible choices that have impacted me; they've impacted Mark, and they've impacted you more than anybody. You fail to see how your own choices are hurting you, and I can't bear to see this happening."

"But you kept trying to make me choose between you and Bernie, when I was so scared. I was never on my own before. I loved him. I was terrified. And you left me there. You never told me you would have taken me in."

"If you had left and shown up on my doorstep when this whole thing first happened, I would have taken you in."

"I couldn't have known that."

"You never asked. And to be honest, it's not what you really wanted, so please don't pretend you thought I wasn't going to take you in when the reality was that you didn't want to leave, OK?

There were a whole host of milestone moments throughout the course of this process where you could have made that choice and never did. What about when they revoked his house arrest and put him at the MCC? Or after the sentencing when they carted him off to Butner?"

Ruth started to cry again. "I was so lonely. There was no one there to advise me. When Nick was born in February, my lawyer called to tell me. Why would I think you two wanted to speak with me?"

"You were getting the same message from everybody. I know that because I had the same conversation with every one of your friends. I kept saying, 'I don't understand what she's doing. She needs to get out of that house.' And they would say, 'I know, I keep telling her that.' Susan Blumenfeld had that conversation with you. So did Joan and Diane. It was such easy advice to take: Just get away from him. People did not come out of the gate suspecting or hating you. Being shunned was all a function of that. It was all a function of your actions after the confession. Of the choices you made initially and have continued to make."

"I didn't think I *had* a choice. And when Mark—"

She broke down, sobbing, after uttering his name.

The only time Andrew had spoken this frankly with his mother before was when he'd told her about Debbie's affair. That conversation had been the first adult talk he'd ever had with his mother in his life. Now the roles were reversed: Andrew was the adult, Ruth the child.

They finished the conversation. Ruth disappeared up the stairs to nap. Andrew felt good, relieved. He'd said what he'd needed to say, gotten everything off his chest, and hadn't pulled any punches. Whether his mother had processed his words was unimportant. He didn't tell her he blamed her for his brother's death, because he didn't. A forty-six-year-old man doesn't take his life because he thinks his mommy doesn't love him. But she could have tried harder, that much was true.

There was a good chance, he felt, that he and his mother would be able to rebuild their relationship. It would take time, but Andrew no longer said the word *never*. Life, he knew, was fragile, unpredictable — even miraculous.

Anything was possible.

Chapter Twenty-two
_____

REMEMBERING MARK

As the day of the memorial approached, Andrew found himself growing more and more angry with Stephanie for, he felt, "failing to support Mark emotionally and taking a bad situation and making it worse." When Mark had most needed her support in the eyes of the world, she'd changed her last name and the kids' names to Morgan and visited a divorce lawyer. On the anniversary of the worst day of Mark's life, she was in Disney World. Now she was creating enormous drama around his death. Whenever Andrew called her, he heard "chaos" in the background.

Once, he heard her scream, "Get me a gun! Get me a gun so I can shoot myself!" Marty London had picked up the phone and apologized, saying that Stephanie was out of her mind with grief. One night, Andrew heard, she'd gone on a rampage, breaking dishes and glassware all over the house.

Grieving on his own with Catherine and the kids, he chose to stay far away in the days leading up to Mark's memorial: "I wasn't going to infect myself or my kids with that poisonous atmosphere."

*   *   *

That Thursday afternoon, Andrew drove to Greenwich, Connecticut, with Catherine, Anne, and Emily. Pulling up in front of the comfortable modern home surrounded by manicured grounds, Andrew saw dozens of cars lining the block. None belonged to paparazzi, who'd arrived early, gotten their shots, and left. He drew a deep breath, slipped his arms around his daughters, and walked in the door.

The first person he saw was Errol, the affable Jamaican driver who'd worked for them at the firm. Andrew was happy to see him again but surprised that he was among those invited, when the immediate family had to bargain for the right to be there.

As he moved farther into the house, he spotted David Blumenfeld with his parents, Susan and Eddie Blumenfeld; David Kaplan; and Steve Ball—Mark's closest friends. All victims of Bernie's fraud. Although they had stayed in touch, they were now more free to talk because of the passing of the deadline for the lawsuits. But this wasn't the reunion anyone had planned.

Ruth had spent the day alone, at Susan's house, watching TV. She wasn't anxious to go, she says, since many of Mark's friends were victims and she didn't want to create conflict with her presence.

"Being excluded mattered to me; not being at the memorial didn't," she says. She was in mourning. Mark was dead. Nothing was going to change that fact.

Two-year-old Nick ran through the living room, knocking the wind out of Andrew with his uncanny resemblance to Mark. Later, after studying him, Andrew would find that Nick resembled Stephanie, too, but on that day—the first time he'd seen Nick since shortly after his birth—all he could see was his brother as a two-year-old.

No one, from Ruth to Susan to Andrew to Catherine, questioned the depth of Mark's despair. But neither could any of them understand the most wrenching component of the entire dark episode: the presence of two-year-old Nick, left alone in the apartment with his father's hanging body.

"If anything, it just underscored how much pain he was in. He adored his children; absolutely adored them," said Andrew. Looking at that precious, curly-haired boy tearing through the den with *SpongeBob SquarePants* playing on the TV in the background, and at the figure of five-year-old Audrey, wearing her princess dress, Andrew could no longer keep it together. My brother did this to them, he thought, as he leaned against a wall and sobbed.

One by one, Mark's friends approached Andrew and hugged him. So did his parents' friends. Andrew found it "difficult to see men whom I'd known for so long fall apart. I'd never seen them cry before."

People congregated by a small side table that held, alongside his urn, a collection of framed photographs of Mark taken throughout various stages of his life. Even Mark's method of burial had created family conflict. Mark and Andrew's uncle Peter owned a large cemetery plot at a Jewish cemetery, where his son, Roger, was buried.

"We've got a place for him there," he'd said to Andrew.

"Peter, no. We went through this. He made his wishes crystal clear. He wanted to be cremated."

Peter called Stephanie to argue his point, and in return, Andrew called Shana.

"Please tell your father to back off," he'd said. "Mark is not going in that cemetery."

"I'll talk to my dad," Shana assured him.

Someone handed Andrew a drink. He took two sips and put it down.

"That was everyone else's solution—to medicate," he says. "Certainly, that wasn't going to be my solution." Debbie sat in a corner of the sofa, her face stained with tears. Stephanie drifted over; Andrew gave her a hug. It was a horrible day for everyone.

Susan Blumenfeld sat next to Catherine as everyone gathered for the readings. "Andrew would be in the same place without you."

"Thank you, Susan. But I don't agree."

Susan Elkin felt she'd been "hit over the head with a brick" on meeting Catherine, she was so far from the "manipulative gold-digger" she'd heard about. Both of them, in their own ways, had supported the two men experiencing this tragedy; it gave them an instant bond. Later, through Susan and her children, Catherine would learn about the Mark Madoff she had never met.

Eventually, the service began. Adam Stracher served as MC. Six people were scheduled to speak: Andrew; Stephanie's brother, Rob Mikesell; Daniel; Kate; Adam; and a more recent friend and neighbor of Mark's named Joe.

Andrew got up to speak first. He'd written brief remarks that were all he felt he could get through. At some point in the future, he hoped, he would be able to properly eulogize his brother. This occasion, he says, "wasn't it." Standing in front of the large windows at the front of the house, he cleared his throat and started to read.

> My brother was not a barrel of laughs. He was a very light drinker, and was more than a little bit uptight. He was a hypochondriac. I remember when he first told me that he had Hashimoto's and then celiac diseases. They sounded so serious, and he delivered the news using his deep voice and signature big sigh, but I could see he was excited. After years of groaning and holding his stomach, he finally had a diagnosis. And best of all, he could pop a Synthroid and eat gluten-free pizza and be cured.
>
> Mark's life had a lot of happy times. And many of us were there to share them with him. Playing ice hockey, street hockey, and stickball. Summers in Montauk, and a couple of years at camp where Mark got homesick because

he was such a mama's boy. A lifetime of taking beautiful pictures of Roslyn, Africa, Seychelles, and Nantucket.

And, of course, fishing. When Mark and I were young, eight or ten, our family took trips to the Bahamas, where we would take a fifteen-foot Boston Whaler many miles out into the open ocean to fish the Yellow Bar. It was a coral formation at the edge of the famous Tongue of the Ocean. Thirty feet deep on one side of the boat, six thousand on the other. We would throw a chum bucket over the side and then wait for the sharks, mackerel, tuna, dolphin, and billfish to arrive. We caught them all, and our passion for fishing was born. In the years to come we would travel the world together exploring remote locations and sharing experiences that I will treasure for the rest of my life.

Andrew choked back tears before finding the strength to continue.

Two marriages, four wonderful kids, and not nearly enough time. And I'm angry with him. The last two years have been very tough. What happened really changed Mark, and it was horrible to see him in so much pain. He wasn't the same as he had been before. Where he had been outgoing and social, he became introverted and scared. He let friendships fade, and rebuffed efforts to help him.

There's a lesson to be learned there, and I hope it's not lost on any of us. Love is the answer to every question. It's up to each of us to seek it out and then hold on to it with everything we've got. I loved Mark. All of us did. He was my best friend. And I'm not going to remember him as the "unalterably bitter" man he described himself as last week, but rather as the laughing little boy sitting next to me on the boat, on the chairlift, on the hockey bench, and on the trading desk. Standing with me under the chuppah for his wedding and then for mine. Watching him in the maternity ward while he held Daniel, Kate, Audrey, and then Nick.

As Mark's friends and family quietly sobbed, Andrew closed with a poem by Langston Hughes.

Rob, Joe, Adam, Daniel, and Kate spoke next, sharing touching words about Mark. Kate brought the room to laughter when she remarked that her father had never dropped her off at school in the morning without yelling out the car window, "Learn a lot!"

The service drew to a close.

Mark's memorial felt "completely inadequate as a tribute to the person I'd loved for my entire life," says Andrew. He'd been to many funerals: There were always more people, more tears, more laughter, more to say. Somehow this one had been too brief; too many people who'd loved Mark weren't there to say good-bye and honor his memory.

There was no such thing as closure. No such thing as peace. Perhaps that would come in time, but for now Andrew just felt an aching sadness and a deep sense of loss. His anger at his father had never been stronger. If he were given the opportunity to strangle him, he'd have done it without a moment's thought. Bernie had turned all their lives upside down, and now Mark was dead.

Exhausted and drained, Andrew said his good-byes and left.

Chapter Twenty-three

FINAL SHOWDOWN

Somewhere in South Florida, Ruth Madoff is attempting to rebuild her life. Soon, she will have to "bite the bullet" and start looking for an apartment; she knows she can't depend on the kindness of friends and family forever. She has long given up on the idea of living out her golden years in luxury; the only thing she cares about is a minimum level of comfort.

"It doesn't have to be glamorous; I just need somewhere to put my toothbrush," she says. "The rent thing freaks me out. But where I live is very important to me, because I'm there a lot of the time. I figure by ninety, I won't care."

The rest of her dreams have been scaled back, too: "There's very little I care about. Being able to subscribe to the *New York Times*. Being able to fly to New York on a cheap fare to visit my family. I suppose if my shoes wore out I'd need new ones, and it's hard to find a pair for twenty-five dollars. Luckily, in Florida you can wear flip-flops all the time. It took me about six months to decide to spend the money on a Cuisinart, which I really wanted. Then I found one for a hundred dollars, so I got that. I have no health insurance, so I'd be scared if I got a disability. Of course I have Medicare, but if I needed assisted living...I don't even want to think about that. Those kinds of emergency situations scare me."

For now, she's accepted the fact that she'll have to stay in Florida, living smack in the middle of a hotbed of these victims. "I need some kind of an anchor; I can't move to a place without knowing a single person. I'd like to get to Manhattan, but what am I going to do — go to a play or a museum and be afraid to be recognized? I wouldn't bother to live there if I couldn't do those things. But I'm not worldly enough to even pick another place."

And there's no place, she knows, that Bernie's crime hasn't touched. "Everyone I knew and loved was a victim: all of my close family, friends, and acquaintances. When I watched Bernie's sentencing on TV, I saw a young woman I knew and liked from the American Jewish Congress talking about how she had to go on food stamps. Even my gynecologist here in South Florida told me that his mother was a victim. I didn't know what to do: I froze and said, 'I'm so sorry.' I have a niece who had to move to Florida because she and her husband couldn't afford to live in New York anymore. She spent a year holed up in her house, studying for the Florida bar exam, and when she tried to get a job, no one would hire her because of her association with the Madoff name. It continues to haunt me when I see my sister and her husband, ages seventy-four and seventy-seven, working day and night driving taxis to make ends meet.

"When I think about how Bernie ruined the lives of some of my best friends and family members, it makes me sick. Several times, I confronted him about the people he'd hurt and he said, 'They'll all be fine.' He doesn't get it. He's in complete denial about how much people are suffering out there. And he was such good friends with so many of them. I can't comprehend it. People's lives were ruined—really ruined."

Her sister, Joan, tries to include her in any social activities she has planned. But Ruth is all too aware that even among her sister's friends there are people who are uncomfortable in her presence. So she rarely goes out, choosing instead to stay home, watching movies on Netflix, cooking, and reading books from the local library.

"I'm prevented from doing so many things I want to do—stupid things, like the one-on-one training at the Apple store," Ruth says. "I wanted to join a bridge class and realized I couldn't do it. I don't know who I can trust."

Once a week, Ruth sees a therapist—her first time on the couch—but she admits, "When I speak to her, I don't feel like exploring. I'm not going to sit in her office for ten years and get to be eighty. I don't see how that exploration is going to be productive. It's too painful to do that, and I can't afford to speak to her every day anyway. I need to feel better *right now.*"

As for whether she'd ever join a support group, she says, "I can't—someone might call the press."

Sitting outside on a small patio, smoking a cigarette, she looks out over the lawn and says, "I just can't imagine my life changing at all. How could I ever get past it?"

Ruth's sister has just finished her morning work shift. She sinks into a couch in her home and closes her eyes. At seventy-four years old, Joan is still sprightly and active, but certainly has reason to be tired. Since her brother-in-law confessed to his massive fraud, her life has changed dramatically. No longer able to relax into her retirement years, she and her seventy-seven-year-old husband, Bob, spend their days shuttling fares to and from the airport and lifting heavy luggage up and down flights of stairs. "The hours are very long, but you can sleep in between jobs, which is nice," Joan says. Despite the fact that she's going to have to work for the rest of her life, she manages a sunny outlook: "It's weird, but I'm much more satisfied doing this than being retired. I worked my whole life; when I retired, I felt like I was at loose ends. Now we can go out to dinner once in a while, which we hadn't done in two years."

Joan's first job was in magazine publishing, as a circulation manager for *Newsweek International.* Then she got a job at Cahners Publishing as vice president of circulation, retiring in 1993 when she moved to Florida with her husband.

Like so many other victims, Joan and her husband spent their retirement years living off the returns on their original investment. They had no savings outside of the money they'd invested with Bernie. The day he confessed and those returns stopped, they were left destitute.

"In the beginning, I was using one sheet of toilet paper and tearing paper towels into quarters," Joan recalls. "I would shake when I walked into the supermarket because I had no money to buy food. One of the things that got me through each day was saying to myself, just get through the next two minutes. Or, just get through the next five minutes. I had to break up the time just to keep my sanity. In addition, I would walk at night and realize that the moon and stars were still there. Then we started this business, which has been a lifesaver. We started using the two cars we had as taxis. When we made a little money, we bought a third, which we use as a backup in case one doesn't start in the morning.

"I'm not unhappy anymore," she continues. "I was scared and shocked when all of this happened, but time has a funny effect: You learn to live with certain things. When I had a lot of money, I was always worried about spending a dime. Now that I have nothing, I don't worry so much. I shop in cheap, cheap, cheap places— you can't believe how cheap. And I enjoy it."

Joan has no animosity toward her sister, whom she sees as a victim, too. Nor has she ever had a moment's hesitation about her innocence.

"I know the upbringing she had. I know her mother and father.

And there is no way she would ever be a part of anything like that," she insists. Ruth's personality, she says, is a lot like their mother's was—kind, social, and very giving, which accounts for Ruth's "confusion" about her husband.

"She feels that since he's a human being, she can't abandon him no matter what he did, the same way you wouldn't abandon your own child," Joan explains. Though she understands Ruth's position, as Andrew does, she feels a great deal of frustration about the fact that her sister has been unable to cut ties with Bernie.

"Recently, I have been thinking he couldn't have been a very good husband or father, keeping that kind of a secret. And he did all these awful things. So there must have been a wall between them, and she lived with it for so long, it must have felt natural to her."

Joan admits that even she, at first, had trouble sorting out the Bernie she thought she knew from the one who confessed to his monstrous crime. Like Ruth, in the beginning, she thought he must have gotten into trouble by mistake, and even defended him to her friends.

"I've known him since he was twelve years old," she says. "When you accept somebody in a certain way for so many years, then all of a sudden you see the other side, it's hard to absorb."

When Joan started to grasp the details of what had really happened, she understood: This had been no accident. Bernie must have spent all his waking hours thinking about how to execute his fraud.

"In retrospect, how can Ruth have thought he was a wonderful husband and father, when all of these things were happening?" Joan asks.

"I would love for her to divorce him," she continues. "I think it would give her some feeling of self. She is living day to day, and I don't know what she's going to do in the future. If she were forty, she could go back to school and become a teacher—but at this age,

I don't know. I think it would be hard for her to have dreams of her own."

Joan pauses for a moment, knitting her brows. "It actually pisses me off that he's in jail and I'm paying taxes to feed him, clothe him, and give him medical care for the rest of his life. He probably doesn't feel guilt. I think his only issue is that he misses Ruth. I think he's content where he is, which bothers me, because he left everybody else in the lurch. If it weren't for Ruth, he would be fine. And I don't think that's punishment enough."

Like everyone else in the extended Madoff clan, Joan has never shared her private feelings with Ruth. She wanted her sister to have one place in her life she could go where she didn't feel as if she were being judged, interrogated, or admonished. She wanted her friendship to serve as a haven, given that Ruth had gone through so much.

"Maybe I shouldn't feel this way, but for the past two and a half years, my sister has been so trampled upon, and had so much grief, I didn't want her to have any more pain coming from me. I didn't want to add to her burden."

About her own burden, Joan remains silent. Then her phone rings; it is her husband, Bob, stuck at the airport with a dead battery and a fare about to arrive. Apologizing, she leaps to her feet, grabs her purse, and hurries out the door.

Twice a week, Ruth delivers food to the elderly and infirm through Meals on Wheels. On her other free days, she volunteers at a school in a blue-collar neighborhood, helping out in the classroom.

"My therapist said, 'You must go forward and get out there.' She sort of forced me into it," Ruth says. "I use my maiden name on my badge, and it's been the best thing that's happened to me. My therapist was incredible—she saved me. I just adore those kids."

The training session for working at the school was hard for Ruth; she had to go to a luncheon where people asked one another questions like "Where are you from? Can you tell me about your life?"

"I don't even remember what I said, but I never came out to anybody," Ruth recalls. "I'm pretty sure people knew who I was. They'd have to be deaf, dumb, and blind not to."

Ruth is loath to offer any more details about her volunteer work, fearful that if people find out she's working at the school, parents will protest.

Walking into the school on her first day, she was stopped by a heavyset female guard at the front door. Ruth froze in fear.

"You look like you need a hug," the woman said, gathering Ruth to her ample chest.

It wasn't the first time someone surprised Ruth with kindness. Once, she was shopping at Costco and heard someone call her name. Stopping abruptly, she thought, Oh no, who is that?

She "almost died," when she spotted the man across the aisle, a "big-time" victim she doesn't want to name. Smiling, he approached and embraced her.

"I was stunned," she says. "He couldn't have been nicer."

Later, she attended the bar mitzvah of Bernie's sister Sondra's grandson. "I was embraced by everybody I was scared to see," she recalls. "Everyone was kissing and hugging me and offering condolences, and it was a very beautiful day for me. Afterward, I wrote to Sondra's daughter and told her how incredible they were to have included me. They wrote back, 'Enough is enough; we have to move forward.'"

But those isolated examples have not been sufficient to convince Ruth to come out of hiding. "I'm always ashamed if someone recognizes me because I know what they've read. I was stunned when I finally ended up talking to Andy again and found out about the kinds of things he's been doing. I've been living in a dark cave.

"I'm just slogging through and not facing up to anything," she continues. "I don't know that it will ever be any different than it feels now. And I don't think after losing a child things could ever get better. I don't see much of a future for me and don't care if I have one. The future is hard to think about, because I don't want one. It's too much."

Then, in typical Ruth fashion, she turns a heavy conversation around with a charming aside: "I've thought about different scenarios, but they're kind of pipe dreams, like a movie where somebody goes to Tuscany, buys a house, finds a fantastic Italian lover, eats pasta every day, and never gains an ounce."

In April, Ruth takes a rare trip to Los Angeles to spend time with Andrew, who is visiting the Abel factory for a meeting. The author of this book has offered to let her stay in the apartment she is subletting, a quirky two-bedroom in the heart of Hollywood filled with vintage finds, thrift-store paintings, and furniture with mismatched fabrics. Ruth is staying in a bedroom that overlooks a small pool, and the minute she unpacks, she steps joyfully out onto the balcony and breathes in the scent of eucalyptus from a nearby tree.

"I could live here—I love it!" she says. Though the modest apartment is a far cry from the luxury digs she's used to, it offers her something far more valuable than space and comfort: total privacy. In LA, the world's most hated woman goes virtually unrecognized—free to walk the streets with the same sense of leisure she felt when she was known only as a wife, mother, and philanthropist to the small group of people that made up her social circle.

Over the next five days, between visits with Andrew, Ruth spends her time hiking in Runyon Canyon, walking to Trader

Joe's to replenish her modest food supply, and smoking cigarettes on the balcony of her room. On a Friday afternoon, she visits the Getty Center, where, like the thousands of other visitors passing through the graceful Japanese garden, she marvels at the landscaping. Strolling through an outdoor courtyard, she spots a couple with their two teenage sons; the four have their arms looped around one another and walk in comfortable lockstep.

"Look at them; they're so beautiful," she says, her blue eyes fixed on the foursome. "That's what we used to be like."

Ruth, one is often reminded, continues to straddle two worlds: past and present, rich and poor, happiness and horror.

On her third day in Los Angeles, she meets with Andrew at the Hollywood apartment where she is staying. Since Mark's suicide, the two have reached a tenuous peace. "I still have some trepidation about picking up the phone and saying, 'Hi, Andy, how are you?'" Ruth admits. "I do it, but not as often as I would like." Andrew continues to hope his mother will break free of his father and come to her senses. Ruth is willing to do anything to restore her relationship with her son—short of fulfilling his wishes. Though she knows it is her husband's actions that led directly to Mark's suicide, she remains unable to get in touch with her anger at Bernie.

"I can never forgive him, and yet I'm not angry with him. I don't know why. It's a combination of being numb and it seeming fruitless. And some other psychological thing that I'm probably unaware of."

She doesn't "know anymore" if she still loves him. "I just really miss him," she says. "I'm lonely and he's the only one who will ever love me like that. It's hard to imagine ever being that close to anybody again, where you can say whatever you feel and they get it without explanation. It's like a death."

Ruth is all too aware that the public—and more important, her family—is never going to fully embrace her if she continues to share sentiments like this. "I'm stupidly honest sometimes," she admits. Asked whether she thinks she'll ever marry again, she laughs grimly and says, "I'm off men."

Andrew has come to the apartment where she is staying on his last day in Los Angeles for a final confrontation, one he's been wanting to have for the past two and a half years. His goal: to convince his mother to leave his father and start a new life.

In order to accomplish that objective, he is planning to open two cans of worms: One, he is going to confront her about Bernie's affairs—specifically, about the claims made by Sheryl Weinstein, his father's onetime mistress, in her scandalous tell-all, *Madoff's Other Secret*. Two, he plans to patiently explain to his mother exactly how his father's actions ruined her children's lives. Like Joan, Andrew has no desire to put his mother through any more pain, but this conversation, he feels, is for her own good—a way to push her through the process of identifying her anger.

Stretched across a faded sofa, his hands clasped behind his head, Andrew begins, "How come you don't feel betrayed by Dad the way everyone else does?"

"I don't know. I don't know. Of course I was betrayed. But I still felt bad for him. I don't know why, because I lost a lot more than money."

"Did you read that Sheryl Weinstein book?"

"No. I don't want to, either."

"Why?"

"Because it will be too painful. Why would I?"

"Because it's what happened."

"I don't want to read it. Just because I know it happened, do I have to read every gory detail?"

"Do you even know in broad strokes the nature of what took place?"

"A little bit."

"Because Dad told you?"

"No, he didn't tell me. He always denied everything I ever accused him of. I didn't believe him, but I certainly wasn't stunned. Fifty years is a very long time to be faithful to someone."

Andrew looks searchingly at his mother. "What is your impression of how long this affair lasted?"

"I don't know. Could you please not tell me?"

The two face off like this for the next hour, Andrew continually bringing his mother back to the painful present, while she tries to push it away.

"I just think that she had every reason to make the book as salacious as possible," Ruth keeps insisting every time Andrew mentions Weinstein's claim that Bernie traveled with his mistress whenever he wasn't with Ruth. "I didn't say she lied about any of the sex."

"You keep talking about the sex—I could care less about the sex," Andrew says. "That's the least important part to me."

"So what am I not seeing here?"

"You're angry at Sheryl Weinstein for writing a book, but you're not angry at him for doing what he did."

"I am angry at him. I never said I wasn't angry at him for having an affair. Did I say that? I was wild. That was more devastating to me than anything I've ever heard. I still feel horrible about it. It makes me sick to think about it. It's the most hurtful thing that ever happened to me."

Perched on the edge of her vintage-patterned armchair, Ruth stares at the glass doors that lead out to the patio. "I don't know why he didn't just let me go. What was the point? The kids were gone. He didn't have any reason to stay with me. I wouldn't have cared. I would have been glad."

Andrew pulls himself to a sitting position. "In a divorce, there's a forensic accounting. He would have had to produce financial statements. How would you guys have possibly come up with a financial settlement? Suppose you took two hundred million dollars in a divorce, or a billion dollars. Where was he going to get that money? He couldn't have written a check big enough to satisfy your anger."

"I guess that's true. Does that mean I don't feel bad that he's in jail for the rest of his life and that his son killed himself?"

"Because of *him*."

"I know. I should hate him more. Maybe that's denial. It probably is. But there's nothing I can do about it."

Andrew lights up with anger. "You're so wrong. You're so wrong," he insists. "What's getting in the way of you living the rest of your life successfully is your inability to see Bernie for who he is and move away from him. It's not enough to cut him off because not doing so would get in the way of having a relationship with me; you need to see him for what he is: a horrible person who is now rotting in prison—because that is what he deserves."

"I haven't gotten to that point yet," Ruth says. "Trust me, I'm trying to. I wish I could have him in front of me now. It would help me if Bernie was not in jail and I could leave him. If he weren't in prison and this book had come out, I would have been out of there in a heartbeat."

"But you could still confront him. You could still divorce him. You're going to stay married to him because he's in prison?"

"I wish I had that opportunity now. I wish he were here in front of me, so I could question him and accuse him and cry and sob and leave. But I haven't got that option."

"You absolutely do. The fact that he's in prison is completely irrelevant. First of all, it's not like he's dead. He's in prison. He'd be happy to talk to you."

"What's the point? If he told me the truth it wouldn't make it any better. He's in prison for the rest of his life. I regret not having the chance to confront him before all of this happened. I was an idiot not to go further with it."

Her jaw starts to work.

"I really think he loves me. I believe that. I don't know why." She turns to her son, her eyes pleading. "Do you?"

Andrew gives her a look infused with sympathy and restraint. "I don't doubt that, but I think his capacity to feel different emotions is messed up at a minimum." It's not about whether he loved her or not, he tells Ruth, it's that his actions were completely independent of his emotions, and that he served his needs with complete disregard for the impact they would have on his family. Even worse, he had no remorse. "He had no true compassion," Andrew continues. "No moral compass whatsoever."

"He seemed compassionate to me always. He was sensitive in so many ways," Ruth muses. Then she pauses. "But he will never convince me that he had to do what he did to you boys—never. I guess I never realized exactly what he had to do."

"That, to me, is everything," says Andrew, leaping forward. "All of my feelings about this are centered on the degree of effort he had to put in, in order to maintain the fraud. Anyone could imagine him managing people's money and somehow screwing it up, or being ashamed to face the music and saying 'I did a bad job and I can't bear to send people these statements telling them I lost their money, so I'm going to lie.' Then I could imagine him having a crisis of conscience and saying 'I can't believe I did that. Now what?' But he lied again and again and again, constantly bringing in new people. I picture Jerry O'Hara sitting in jail with two young kids at home. All of these people with young children who are going to spend the rest of their lives in jail. Families who trusted him with their life savings, thousands of victims who've lost everything. They got wrapped into this by the sheer force of his personality, and he destroyed them all."

"I agree with you."

"And what about what he did to me? I'm his son. We worked together forever. Do you think he's miserable every day that he and

I don't have a relationship? Does he miss me horribly? Is it painful for him to go on because I'm not by his side, supporting him and talking to him?"

"I do think he's miserable. How could he not be?"

"In the last few years, all he was doing was using me as a shield. If you saw a war criminal grab a child and hold the child in front of him while he was being shot at, you would call that person an incomprehensible monster. That's precisely what he did. He used me and Mark as a shield to protect himself. He did the same thing to all of us."

Ruth starts to cry. "I guess I just can't face it."

"What can't you face?"

"That he's a monster. That's why I feel I have to see him, to get my head around it."

"I don't blame you for wanting to do that. But I don't think you're going to get the satisfaction you're looking for. He's not going to see your side. He's incapable of it. Even if he said he could see your side, he's not capable of being sincere."

"I wouldn't care if he lied. But I don't think he would."

Andrew doesn't answer, his shoulders rising as he takes a deep breath.

"I don't know how to get rid of this angst I'm suffering," Ruth continues.

She pauses, considering. "Maybe I'll go to see him one more time and tell him we're done. I was stunned by a sixteen-year affair; that blew me away. Going to get laid every now and then I don't find quite as bad. I'd like to see him and tell him all the things that I'm feeling. I can break it off then."

"It is going to be much harder to confront him face-to-face than it is here. You are going to forget half of the things that we talked about. You're not going to have the words. It's going to be unsatisfying. He's going to dismiss it and deny it, and you're going to end up feeling frustrated."

"I feel a little embarrassed that the thing that stopped me from going to see Bernie was not a fifty-billion-dollar fraud but an affair that he didn't tell me about. After the terrible crime he committed, I wonder why I would care about an affair. But I do."

Again, the tears start to flow. "It's so shameful, I can't stand it." She closes her eyes for a moment. "If I had to do it over again, I would have abandoned Bernie early on because of the consequences for Mark and, less so, the consequences for me, which I didn't even think about at the time. It just never occurred to me that I would be hated by the world because I didn't walk out the door. I made the choice to leave Bernie, and I'm not even having a hard time living with that, except for the fact that it took me so long and caused Mark to die. I guess I've been in denial about a lot of stuff."

"Don't—don't—don't—don't—you don't need to carry that," Andrew insists. "You did not kill Mark."

"I don't think I did either, to tell you the truth. But I wish I'd had the chance to be a comfort to him. Nothing will ever change what happened to Mark. Nothing. But I know I can't continue this way. I really am in limbo."

Ruth does not visit Bernie again—nor does she break it off. In August 2011, it is widely reported that Ruth has decided to divorce Bernie; the report is false. Ruth remains in a state of uncertainty, unable to make the final move to sever ties with the man she has loved for most of her life. Despite her failure to act, her relationship with Andrew improves steadily. Though he remains mystified about his mother's choices, the passage of time has softened his stance. He can envision a relationship with his mother whether or not she divorces Bernie. For the first time in two and a half years, he is sanguine about the future and admits that, in many ways, his life is better now—because it's his own.

"At the end of the day, I lost my career, which I didn't like anyway. I lost money, but it's just money; I can make more. I have the love of my daughters and this wonderful woman. I wasn't planning on abandoning my father, or turning my back on him, or never speaking to him ever again for the rest of my life, but after understanding everything he did — no problem. I do not lie in bed awake at night thinking about him in prison and start weeping because it's so painful for me to think about. I think about him sitting in prison and it rolls off my back, because he deserves it. When I think about all the suffering that everybody else is experiencing, I feel horrible; I couldn't care less about the fact that he is suffering in jail."

Andrew admits there is a part of him that wishes he could get Bernie to explain his actions, but after listening online to the conversations his father had with *New York* magazine reporter Steve Fishman, he realizes there's no point. Bernie can't be honest with Andrew any more than he can be honest with himself.

"I don't feel a need to confront him point by point on all the things that he did to put me in this position, because I don't believe a word that he says. He's proven himself a liar, and he's proven that he can talk to me and be completely untruthful, so what he says is absolutely irrelevant. There's nothing that he can say that would give me a sense of satisfaction that I now have insight into why he did what he did or how he did what he did — that's totally unimportant to me."

What Andrew does want is to make a settlement with trustee Irving Picard, so he can get on with his life. He would also like a declaration by the U.S. Attorney's Office that he is no longer under suspicion. "And that's going to have to be enough," he says. "I'm not going to get more than that."

Once the trustee reaches terms with Andrew's lawyers, the process to have the settlement approved by the bankruptcy court can take months. So far, several settlements the bankruptcy court has approved have been challenged by victims' groups. So the trustee, says Andrew, doesn't want to keep making new settlements when he has no idea what the magic formula is to get them behind him.

"I can't say that I have sympathy for the trustee, but I certainly understand what he's up against and know it's not his fault that it's taking so long. So I take that into account when I set my own expectations."

The next step after that? To try to repair his shattered reputation.

"One of the reasons I've always felt uncomfortable about the prospect of going on TV and telling my story is that I don't know if I'm that sympathetic a character," Andrew admits. "At the end of the day, I lived a life of great wealth and privilege. I took home millions of dollars in salary over the course of my twenty-year career at the firm. And even though all those years were spent on the legitimate side of the firm, people have a hard time drawing a distinction between the two—and I get that. Mark and I were always very proud of who we were and what we were able to accomplish. We were in charge of a large trading operation that generated tens of millions of dollars in profits year after year, and supported over one hundred traders, support staff, and their families. We were elected to positions of leadership by our peers in the industry and received numerous honors for our years of service. All of that was wiped out in a flash when our father, the man we'd loved and admired for our entire lives, confessed that he was no more than a common thief. But our plight was no worse than that of the thousands of victims of our father's crimes. How many families' hopes and dreams were destroyed in that instant? How many retirees lost what they'd worked their whole lives to save? It's too terrible to think about. But I do, every day."

At the end of a story that can have no positive outcome, Andrew, incredibly, is able to find one.

"When I reflect back on the challenges I've faced in my life, the dissolution of my marriage and years of being emotionally dead, then contrast it with the three years I've spent with Catherine, I don't think about the confession, or the loss of my career and family. Those were certainly major events that helped shape who I am, but none of those were the big event. The big event was meeting her. Because everything I have, today, has come from that: my ability to be happy and experience joy and love, the strength of my family, the relationship with my daughters, the friends I have met—it all flows from her."

There are moments, of course, when Andrew wonders if he'll ever see his father again. Bernie has already lived ten years longer than either of his parents. Andrew knows that he could die at any moment: He could have a heart attack, or a stroke, or get killed in prison. "I have reconciled myself to that, to the extent that I can," he says.

No doubt, Andrew would have chosen a different path for his life. Instead, he will need to start from scratch. He accepts that. On a bright spring morning, Andrew buckles up his well-worn Sidi cycling shoes, wheels his Cannondale road bike out of his apartment, and heads across 73rd Street toward Central Park, as he has done every Saturday for the past three months. Today's ride—the graduation event for the New York Cycle Club's Special Interest Group program—will cover 106 miles. The club teaches advanced group riding skills to its participants, and today's ride is the culmination of months' worth of training. Beginning at the Loeb Boathouse, the group will ride north through Harlem and over the George Washington Bridge. Eighty-five participants began in the elite "classic" division that Andrew has joined; that number has been whittled down to forty-five. The group is expected to average at least twenty miles per hour over the course of the ride, and though Andrew knows it won't be easy, he is fitter than he has been since high school.

When Andrew reaches the boathouse, he finds he is among the first to arrive. He gets off his bike and does some last-minute stretching while a group leader explains the details of the day's route. Then he hops onto his seat and begins to pedal, breathing in the scent of the trees that line the bike path. His fellow riders— among them an architect, a banker, a designer, an environmental lawyer, and a musician—surround him, each starting slowly, conserving their energy. Andrew does the same.

With 105 miles to go, his journey has only just begun.

Epilogue

Writing this book has been an extraordinary experience. Like millions of people all over the world, I was fascinated by the Madoff story. So when the opportunity arose to talk to the elusive and previously silent family—to ask questions of those who could actually answer them—I jumped. Sitting down for the first time with Catherine, Andrew, and Ruth, I asked them to reveal every detail of what they'd been through— even things they knew, unequivocally, they did not want to share with the public. With the exception of Catherine, one of the most open people I've ever met, the family was tentative at first. But as they got to know and trust me, our conversations became increasingly—sometimes heartbreakingly—candid. Though the limelight was the last thing any of them wanted, they welcomed the opportunity to respond to years of false reports, innuendo, and outright lies. During the six months of interviews I conducted, I was therapist, reporter, witness, and interpreter. I watched each one of them grow stronger as they unburdened themselves and began to put the story behind them. I watched the rift between Andrew and his mother start to heal as they brought to the surface issues they'd never before discussed.

More than once during my conversations with Ruth, I was struck by the similarities between her and my own mother—in particular, the way in which my mother has steadfastly remained by my father's side, in spite of his repeated breaches of our family trust. But unlike Andrew, I no longer pray that my mother will see the light and leave my father; I know that she loves him and doesn't want to be left alone. Writing this book allowed me to put my own story into perspective. When Andrew made the comment that he "needed to make [his] mother see the truth," I was able to call upon my own experience and say, "But she might not ever see, and you can love her anyway." When Ruth insisted that Bernie was, in fact, "kind and sensitive in a million ways" and that it was hard for her to see him as a monster, I was able to recall, for her, the many wonderful memories I have of my own father and explain that his early kindnesses don't excuse his later behavior. Nor does his later behavior negate the early, good memories I have.

If there is one thing I learned from this experience, it is that no matter how deep you dig, there are no simple answers to life's hardest questions. How does a person trust again after being deceived, lied to, or cheated? Why do we continue to feel love for those in our lives who have committed unthinkable acts? We feel hurt only after we've allowed ourselves to love. We feel fear only after our faith in what is good has been shaken. We feel betrayed only after we have allowed ourselves to trust. Living with unanswerable questions is perhaps the biggest challenge for anyone who has ever experienced a betrayal: small, large, or, in this case, monumental.

In the end, it was the Madoffs who insisted that the most private, painful chapters in their saga—the ones they'd once thought better to lock away forever—needed to be included in this book. The public, they had grown to understand, would settle for nothing less than the whole truth. I thank the Madoff family for coming to that brave decision, and for entrusting their story to me.

My hope is that you have read this book with an open mind and heart. That you have come to know Catherine and Andrew as I have: She, a woman who stood by her fiancé while the entire world pilloried him. He, a man who defied every law of loyalty and family to do the right thing and turn in the father he loved to the authorities, and who then insisted on rebuilding his life, even as it crumbled around him.

My other wish is that the public will allow Ruth Madoff, who has lost her son, husband, worldly possessions, privacy, and dignity, to heal from her losses in peace.

Last, I am left with the specter of Bernie Madoff himself. After listening to his closest family members describe their relationships with him, I feel no nearer to understanding him than they do. Despite the black nature of Bernie's crime, when it comes to the human heart, nothing is black or white. Bernie remains to me—and to them—a mystery.

—Laurie Sandell

Acknowledgments

First, I must acknowledge my agent, Amanda Urban, whose support, editorial insight, and, at times, tough love have been invaluable to me. Over the years, she has never failed to guide me in the right direction. I respect and admire her immensely.

Andrew Madoff, Ruth Madoff, Susan Elkin, and Joan Roman contributed their most personal and painful experiences to this project. I have great respect for each one of them for having the strength and the courage to tell their stories. Catherine Hooper spent a multitude of hours sifting through photographs, sharing memories, and acting as a go-between. Without her, this book would not have happened.

I cannot think of a more supportive publisher than Little, Brown and Company. Not only do they care about books, they care about people. I owe a huge debt of gratitude to publisher Michael Pietsch for believing in this project from the beginning; to my editor, the fiercely smart, talented, and tireless Judy Clain; and to Nicole Dewey, Heather Fain, Mario Pulice, Mary Tondorf-Dick, Ben Allen, Holly Hartman, Deborah Jacobs, Pamela Marshall, Giraud Lorber, Anthony Goff, Scott Sherratt, Nathan Rostron, Liese Mayer, and Michelle Aielli.

I would like to acknowledge Diana Henriques, author of *The Wizard of Lies,* for her gripping account of the scandal. Her book helped me understand the financial intricacies of the story and served as an invaluable resource while writing my own book.

Blue Mountain Center provided me with a monthlong retreat to write the first draft of this book; without them, I never would have made my deadline. While I was there, Harriet Barlow kept me engaged in compelling conversations about secrets and lies, Ben Strader took heroic measures to keep my project under wraps, Alice Gordon was an unflagging cheerleader, Nica Horvitz and Sophie Kazis met every request, Alan Stafford and Laurie Murdock made sure I was fed and happy, and Sis Eldridge and Diane McCane left me in stitches every morning.

Thanks are due to Dan Slater for his expert financial fact-checking, and to Dale Hoffer, Michelle Humphrey, Tracy Costa, and Jean Bleich for their careful transcriptions, as well as their discretion.

The cafés I write in allow me to sit all day long, nursing one cup of coffee (or ten): In New York, I would like to thank Housing Works Bookstore Cafe and Smooch; in Los Angeles, 18th Street Coffee House. Hopefully no one will read this section of the acknowledgments page except for the wonderful people who work there.

I thanked my beloved group of friends in my first book, and I am deeply grateful to the same people here, but I am singling out Genevieve Field, who did a brilliant and exacting line edit of the manuscript; Michelle Fiordaliso, Merrill Markoe, and Alison Brower for their brainstorming abilities; Alexandra DeFurio for taking the most flattering photo of me in existence; Rob Tourtelot for my website; and my mother for her unwavering kindness and love. I also acknowledge Julie May, Melissa Stein, Karen Ramos, Melissa Gelernter, Abigail Pesta, Amy Spencer, Alex Lydon, Sean McGinly, Saïd Sayrafiezadeh, Amanda Stern, Paul Robertson, Ariel Foxman, Carole Radziwill, and Andy Kamman for their enthusiasm and support. I am lucky to have such special people in my life.